THE Peerage of IRELAND.

A COMPLETE VIEW
Of the several ORDERS of NOBILITY, their DESCENTS, MARRIAGES, ISSUE, and RELATIONS; their CREATIONS, ARMORIAL BEARINGS, CRESTS, SUPPORTERS, MOTTOS, CHIEF SEATS, and the High OFFICES they possess;

So methodized
As to display whatever is truly useful in this instructive and amusing Branch of Knowledge.

Together with
The ARMS of all the LORDS SPIRITUAL and TEMPORAL.

By Mr. KIMBER,
AUTHOR of the
PEERAGES of ENGLAND and SCOTLAND.

Corrected to Jan. 20, 1768.

LONDON,
Printed for H. WOODFALL, J. FULLER, G WOODFALL, R. BALDWIN, W. JOHNSTON, B. LAW, T. LONGMAN, T. LOWNDES, J. WILKIE, J. JOHNSON, W. BATHOE, Z. STUART, W. NICOLL, and E. JOHNSON. 1768.

HERITAGE BOOKS
2012

HERITAGE BOOKS
AN IMPRINT OF HERITAGE BOOKS, INC.

Books, CDs, and more—Worldwide

For our listing of thousands of titles see our website
at
www.HeritageBooks.com

A Facsimile Reprint
Published 2012 by
HERITAGE BOOKS, INC.
Publishing Division
100 Railroad Ave. #104
Westminster, Maryland 21157

Originally published by
E. Kimber, London, 1768

— Publisher's Notice
In reprints such as this, it is often not possible to remove blemishes from the original. We feel the contents of this book warrant its reissue despite these blemishes and hope you will agree and read it with pleasure.

International Standard Book Numbers
Paperbound: 978-0-7884-1767-2
Clothbound: 978-0-7884-9166-5

TO THE

RIGHT HONOURABLE

ROBERT Lord CLIVE,

Baron of PLASSEY,

Knight of the moſt Honourable
Order of the BATH,

This Compendious

PEERAGE of IRELAND,

Is, with all due Reverence, inſcribed,

By his LORDSHIP's

moſt obliged,

moſt obedient,

and moſt dutiful ſervant,

Jan. 18, 1767.

E. KIMBER.

ADVERTISEMENT.

THE Editor may, without vanity, pronounce this manual the beſt account of the PEERAGE of IRELAND, extant, as from the kind and generous communications of many Noble Peers, and their Friends, he has had better opportunities than perhaps were ever preſented before, of giving the Public the pedigrees of thoſe Peers, whoſe illuſtrious anceſtors have diſtinguiſhed themſelves by their behaviour in war and peace, equally with thoſe of any other country in Europe. What deficiencies may be obſerved by the Reader ſhould not be wholly aſcribed to the Editor, ſome Lords, perhaps, not thinking the ſatisfaction of the Public in this regard a matter of importance; but the Editor differs widely from their ſentiments, and, waving the uſual and natural incentives to their compliance, holds it incumbent upon every Nobleman to permit the information in queſtion, that the World may know by what great and eminent Virtues, or by what Public Services, their Families have merited the exalted privileges of Nobility.

ADVERTISEMENT.

Some errors, no doubt, have escaped even a sedulous attention; but to preclude all trifling attempts at criticism thereon, he affirms, that where one error is visible in this Compendium, he is able to fix ten, upon any Peerage-writer, from Dugdale to the present time. Whoever walks in this perplexing track, must be so sensible of the difficulties that occur in his way, that he will be very sparing in charging faults upon another, which, in travelling the same road, he would find himself unable to amend.

The Editor returns, with all that grateful respect and duty that inspires his breast, his most sincere and humble thanks to the many Noble Lords who have assisted him in the perfection of his design, and will ever preserve the truest sense of their favours.

PEERS OF IRELAND.

Peers of the Blood Royal.

E. of Connaught   E. of Dublin

Duke of Leinster

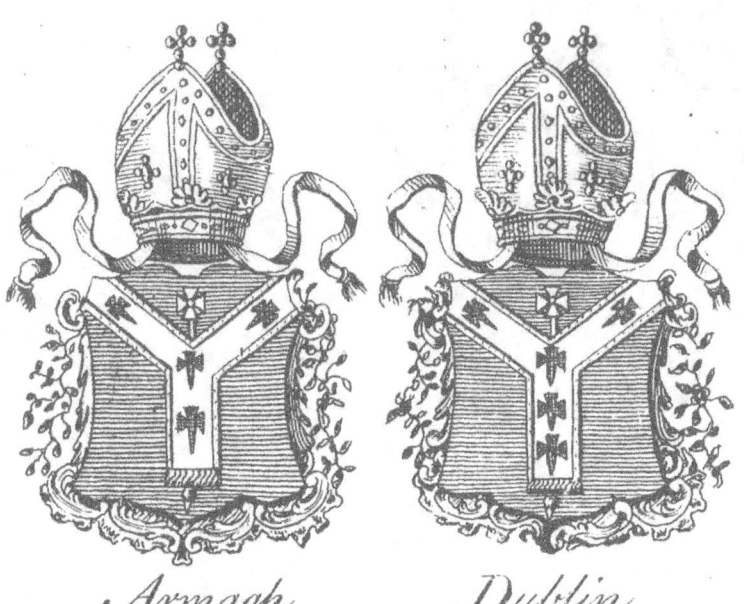

Armagh   Dublin

Cashel   Tuam

24

THE
Peerage of IRELAND.

DUKE.

DUKE of LEINSTER.

THE moſt high, puiſſant, and moſt noble Prince, JAMES FITZ-GERALD, Duke of Leinſter, Marquis and Earl of Kildare, Earl and Baron of Offaley, premier Marquis, Earl, and Baron of the kingdom of Ireland, and Viſcount Leinſter, of Taplow, in the kingdom of Great Britain; one of the Lords of his Majeſty's moſt honourable Privy-council, in Ireland, ſucceeded his father Robert, the nineteenth Earl of Kildare, on Feb. 20, 1743. His Lordſhip was born on May 29, 1722; created Viſcount Leinſter of Taplow in 1746; in 1761, Marquis of Kildare, and in 1766, Duke of Leinſter *(ut infra.)* On Feb. 7, 1746,7, he married Lady Emilia, ſecond ſurviving daughter of Charles, ſecond

B   Duke

Duke of Richmond, Lenox, and Aubigny, and by her Grace (who was born Oct. 6, 1731) has had issue, . George Earl of Offaley, who died unmarried on Sept. 26, 1765, in the nineteenth year of his age. 2. William, now Marquis of Kildare, born on March 3, 1748,9. 3. Lord Charles, born on July 30, 1761; 4. Lord ———, born in Jan. 1765. 5. Lady Caroline-Elizabeth-Mabel, born June 12, 1750, and died on April 13, 1754. 6. Lady Emilia-Mary, born March 15, 1752. 7. Lady Louisa, born June 19, 1760, and died Jan. 23, 1765. 8. Lady Harriot, born Oct. 9, 1762, and died Sept. 3, 1763; and 9. Lady ———, born in 1766.

Robert, the nineteenth Earl of Kildare, and father of the present Earl, succeeded John the eighteenth Earl, Nov. 9, 1707. He married, in March 1708, the Lady Mary Obrien, eldest daughter of William Earl of Inchiquin, and had issue four sons and eight daughters, viz.

1. William, Lord Offaley, born Jan. 24, 1714, and died in his infancy.

2. George, born October 11, 1720, also died in his infancy.

3. James, the present Duke of Leinster, &c.

4. Charles, born Dec. 16, 1724, died at the age of nine years.

5. Lady Mary, born Dec. 24, 1715.

6. Lady Elizabeth, born May 11, 1717.

7. Lady Henrietta, born June 11, 1719.

8. Lady Catharine, born Oct. 2, 1723.

9. Lady Anne, born Dec. 31, 1726.

10. Lady Frances, born Jan. 8, 1727; which six daughters all died young.

11. Lady

11. Lady Margaret, born July 2, 1729, was married March 1, 1747, to Wills, Earl of Hillsborough; which title see.

12. Lady Charlotte, born April 3, 1734, died Oct. 18, 1743.

John, the eighteenth Earl, was born in 1661, and married, first, Mary, eldest daughter of Henry Obrien, Lord Ibrackan, by whom he had a son, James, who died young; and secondly, in 1684, he married the Lady Elizabeth Jones, eldest daughter and coheir of Richard Earl of Ranelagh; but leaving no issue, and dying on Nov. 9, 1707, was succeeded by his first cousin, Robert, son of his uncle Robert, brother of his father Wentworth, the seventeenth Earl of Kildare. Which Robert Fitz-gerald, Esq; father of the late Earl of Kildare, preserved the city of Dublin from being plundered and burnt, after King James's defeat at the battle of the Boyne, 1690.

This noble Duke is descended from Otho, or Other, a rich and powerful Lord in the reign of Alfred the Great, descended from the Dukes of Tuscany; who passing from Florence into Normandy, and thence into England, there the family flourished, until Richard Strongbow, Earl of Pembroke, their kinsman, engaged them to partake in his expedition to Ireland, in which Maurice Fitzgerald embarked, and was one of the principal conquerors of that kingdom; for which he was rewarded with a great estate in lands in the province of Leinster, and particularly the barony of Offaley, and the castle of Wicklow; and died covered with honours, in the year 1177, 24 Hen. II.

Of this family there were several Barons of Offaley, before they were Earls of Kildare; and of it were the Earls of Desmond, March, and Macclesfield; the Lord Grandison, and Barons of Bromley; the Earls of Kerry; and some others have been Knights of the Garter. Gerald, the eldest son of Maurice, who died in 1177, was Lord Offaley, and Chief Justice of Ireland; his son and successor, Maurice, was Lord Chief Justice in 1219 and 1232, and built the castle of Sligo. Thomas, Lord Offaley, his son, was father of Thomas, who founded the abbey of Tralee; and, dying without issue, was succeeded by his brother Maurice, who left issue Gerald Fitz-Maurice, his heir, and Thomas, who was Chief Justice of Ireland. Gerald Fitz-Maurice had issue Maurice, who, in 1272, was Chief Justice of Ireland: but he dying without issue, we return to his uncle Thomas, who had two sons, John and Maurice, whereof

John was created Earl of Kildare, 10 Edward II. and on Aug. 27, 1329, Maurice his brother was created Earl of Desmond. To the former King Edward II. gave the town and castle of Kildare, together with the services of the freeholders and farmers; as also William Vesey's lands in Ireland, which were forfeited in 1291, when he was Lord Justice. He was succeeded by his son Thomas, the second Earl, who built Laughlin-bridge, and was Lord Justice of Ireland in 1320 and 1326.

Maurice, the fourth Earl, was, in the year 1347, leader in the army of King Edw. III. at the siege of Calais; and in 1360, 1371, and 1375,

1375, was Lord Juftice of Ireland; as was his fon Gerald, the fifth Earl, in 1405. Thomas, the feventh Earl, was, in 1454, 1456, 1460, and 1471, Lord Deputy of Ireland; as was his fon and fucceffor, Gerald, the eighth Earl, in the years 1478, 1479, 1483, 1485; and in 1490 was made Lord Lieutenant of Ireland, a Knight of the Garter, and prefented by King Henry VII. with a gold chain, which he wore as a mark of his royal favour. He was fucceeded by his fon and heir, Gerald, who, in 1513, was made Lord Juftice of Ireland, and the next year marched with his army into Leix, where he vanquifhed O'Moor, and the O'Rileys, who rebelled; and in 1515, being made Deputy of Ireland, he flew O'Toel, fent his head to the mayor of Dublin, and reduced the province of Ulfter: but being accufed of feizing the King's revenues, he was fent prifoner to London, and condemned thro' the malice of Cardinal Wolley; but the King pardoned him, and reftored him to his honours; and he was in 1524 again made Lord Deputy of Ireland: but great complaints having been made to the King againft his adminiftration, he was commanded to repair to London, which he accordingly did, leaving Thomas, his eldeft fon, about twenty-one years of age, Deputy in his ftead; but afterwards the faid young Lord, upon a falfe report that his father, then a prifoner in the Tower, was beheaded, defied the King's authority, and proclaimed open war: whereupon he, and five of his uncles, whom he had drawn in to take his part, were attainted; and, upon the King's fending an army, were all taken and put to death,

death, Feb. 2, 1535-6; the old Earl dying before them of grief, in the Tower of London, was buried there. Thomas the tenth Earl, who suffered with his uncles, was succeeded by his brother Gerald, who became the eleventh Earl, which honour remains to his posterity.

Creations.] Baron of Offaley, in the county of Kildare, originally by tenure; by creation, A. D. 1205, 7 John; Earl of the town of Kildare, May 14, 1316, 10 Edw. II. Marquis of Kildare and Earl of Offaley, Mar. 3, 1761, 1 Geo. III. Duke of Leinster, Nov. 16, 1766, 6 Geo. III. and Viscount Leinster of Taplow, in the county of Bucks, Feb. 21, 1746-7, 20 Geo. II.

Arms.] Pearl, a saltire, ruby.

Crest.] On a wreath, a monkey at gaze, proper, environed about the middle, and chained, topaz.

Supporters.] Two monkeys proper, environed and chained, as the crest.

Motto.] *Crom a Boo.*

Chief Seats.] Carton, in the county of Kildare; Dullardstown, in the same county; and Kildare-house, near Dublin.

EARLS.

EARL of CLANRICARDE.

THE right honourable Smyth De Burgh, Earl of Clanricarde, and Baron of Dunkellin, succeeded his father, Michael, the late Earl, Nov. 29, 1726, and changed his name to De Burgh, by act of Parliament. He married Hester, daughter of Sir Henry Vincent, of Stoke d'Aubernon, in the county of Surry, Bart. by whom he has had issue Henry, Lord Dunkellin, and John-Thomas.

Michael, the late and eleventh Earl of Clanricarde, was, in the tenth of Queen Anne, summoned to Parliament by the title of Lord Dunkellin, in the life-time of his father; he was one of the Privy-council to K. George I. and Sept. 19, 1714, married Anne, eldest of the two daughters and co-heirs of John Smyth, of Tydworth, Hants, Esq; Speaker of the English House of Commons at the Union; and afterwards Chancellor, Under-treasurer, and Teller of the Exchequer; widow of Hugh Parker, Esq; son of Sir Henry Parker, of Honington, in the county of Warwick, Bart. and mother of Sir Henry John Parker, Bart. by which Lady, who died Jan. 1, 1732-3, he had issue a son and two daughters, viz.

1. Smyth, now Earl of Clanricarde. 2. Lady

2. Lady Anne, married to Dennis Dally, Efq;

3. Lady Mary, who, in April 1741, married George Jennings, Efq; fon of Sir John Jennings, Knt.

In the year 1066, Serlo de Burgo, and John Monoculus, two brothers, the fons of Euftace, a Norman, accompanied William the Conqueror into England, where, in the county of York, the faid Serlo built the caftle of Knaresborough, and was fucceeded by John his brother: he married to his firft wife Beatrix, daughter and fole heir of Ivo de Vefey, a Norman, and by her had Euftace, Lord of Knaresborough, and Richard the Red, whofe fon, named Walter, had three fons, whereof Hubert was Earl of Kent, William was anceftor to the Earl of whom we are fpeaking, and Jeffrey was Bifhop of Ely.

William, the fecond fon, firnamed Aldhelm, was Steward of the Houfhold to King Henry II. of whom he obtained great part of the province of Connaught, which was governed by his family for a long time; and in the year 1177, the faid King made him one of the Governors of Ireland. He had a fon Richard, who was Lord of Connaught; as alfo, in 1227, Lord Juftice of Ireland. This Richard had two fons, Walter and William, of which, Walter marrying Maud, daughter and fole heir of Hugh de Lacy (the younger,) Earl of Ulfter, he, in her right, became Earl thereof. William, the fecond fon, being flain in 1270, left iffue Sir William Bourk, Knt. who died in 1324, and from him defcended, in a direct male

male line, Ulick de Bourk, or de Burgh, who by King Henry VIII. July 1, 1544, was created Baron of Dunkellin, in the county of Galway, and Earl of Clanricarde, in the same county.

Richard, the fourth Earl, was, in 1601, knighted in the field of battle, by Sir Charles Blount, Lord Mountjoy, Lord Deputy of Ireland, for his good services against the rebellious Earl of Tyrone, and the Spaniards; and on April 3, 1625, 22 James I. was created Baron Somerhill, and Viscount Tunbridge, in England; and on Aug. 23, 1628, 4 Charles I. was created Baron of Imanry, in the province of Connaught, and Viscount Galway, Irish honours, and Earl of St. Alban's in England. He married Frances, only daughter and heir of Sir Francis Walsingham, Knr. Secretary of State to Queen Elizabeth, (widow first of Sir Philip Sidney, and secondly of Robert Devereux, Earl of Essex,) by whom he had a daughter, Lady Honora, wife of John Powlet, Marquis of Winchester, and a son,

Ulick, the fifth Earl, who, in 1636, succeeded him in all his honours; and on Feb. 21, 21 Charles I. was created Marquis of Clanricarde. In 1649 he was appointed Lord Deputy of Ireland; and dying in 1657, left issue, by the Lady Anne, daughter of William Compton, Earl of Northampton, an only daughter, Margaret, wife of Lord Charles Mulkerry, eldest son of the Earl of Clancarty. Upon his death without issue male, the titles of Marquis of Clanricarde, Earl of St. Alban's, &c. became extinct; and Richard Bourk, son of Colonel William Bourk, succeeded as Earl of Clanricarde.

Creation.] *Ut supra.*
Arms.] Topaz, a cross ruby; in the dexter canton, a lion rampant, diamond.
Crest.] On a wreath, a cat-a-mountain sejant, guardant, proper, gorged with a plain collar, and chain gold.
Supporters.] Two cats guardant, collared and chained, as the crest.
Motto.] *Un Roy, une Foy, une Loy.*
Chief Seats.] At Portumny, Lough Reah, and Kilcoley, in the county of Galway.

EARL of CASTLEHAVEN.

An account of this noble family will be found in my Peerage of England, under the title of Lord AUDLEY.

EARL of CORKE and ORRERY.

An account of his Lordship's family, &c. will be found in my Peerage of England, under the title of Lord BOYLE.

EARL of ANTRIM.

Alexander Macdonnel, Earl of Antrim, and Viscount of Dunluce, was born on July 22, 1713, and succeeded his father Randal, the fourth Earl, October 19, 1721. On April 10, 1735, his Lordship married, first, Elizabeth, daughter of Matthew Pennefather, Esq; by whom he had one daughter, which died in its infancy. Her Ladyship deceasing in March, 1736-7, he married, secondly, on Jan. 2, 1739, Anne, eldest daughter and co-heir of Charles-Patrick Plunket, of Dillonstown, in the county of Louth, Esq; member for Bannagher, and by her, who died Jan. 15, 1755, he has issue two daughters, Ladies Rachel and Anne, and one son, William-Randal, Viscount Dunluce, born Nov. 4, 1749. His Lordship is a Privy-counsellor, and Governor of the county of Antrim. His Lordship married, thirdly, July 5, 1755, the relict of James Taylor, Esq;

Randal, the fourth Earl of Antrim, married Rachel, eldest daughter of Clotworthy, Lord Viscount Masareene, (who, secondly, married Robert-Hawkins Magill, of Gill-Hall, in the county of Downe, Esq;) by whom he had issue one son, the present Earl, and one daughter, Lady Helena.

This family is of Scotch extraction, and was seated in the north of Ireland near three hundred years since; thereof was Alexander Macdonnel, who, by the Earl of Sussex, then Lord Lieutenant, was presented with a gold hilted sword and silver spurs, for his services against the Scots. Sir Randal Mac-Sorley Macdonnel was created Baron of Antrim, Viscount Dunluce, and Earl of Antrim.

Randal, the second Earl, was, in the reign of Charles I. employed to procure forces in Ireland for his Majesty's service in Scotland, under the Marquis of Montrose; and, on Jan. 26, 1643-4, was created Marquis of Antrim. He was afterwards very serviceable to King Charles II but dying without issue, he was succeeded in the Earldom only, by Alexander his brother, father of the late Earl.

Creations.] Viscount Dunluce, in the county of Antrim, June 25, 1618, 16 James I. Earl of the same county, Dec. 12, 1620, 18 Jam. I.

Arms.] Quarterly, 1st Topaz, a lion rampant, ruby, for Macdonnel. 2d, Topaz, a dexter arm issuing from the sinister fess point, out of a cloud proper, holding a cross croslet fitchy, sapphire. 3d, Pearl, a ship with its sails furled up, diamond. 4th, Party per fess, sapphire and emerald; the under part wavey, a dolphin naiant, in fess, pearl.

Crest.] On a wreath, a dexter arm couped at the shoulder, attired topaz, turned down, pearl, the hand proper, holding a cross croslet as in the coat.

Supporters.] The dexter, a savage, or wild man, proper, wreathed about the temples and middle, emerald. The sinister, a falcon proper, with beak, legs, and bells, topaz.

Motto.] *Toujours prest.*

Chief Seats.] At Ballymagary, in the county of Antrim, burnt down by accident, April 9, 1750. At Glenairn, and at Ballycastle, in the same county.

EARL

EARL of WEST-MEATH.

Thomas Nugent, Earl of West-Meath, and Baron of Delvin, Lord Lieutenant and Custos Rotulorum of the county of West-Meath, a Lord of the Privy-council, succeeded his father, John, the late and fifth Earl, on July 3, 1754; and married Mary Durand, daughter and heir of Walter Durand Stapleton, Esq; by which Lady (who died in the West-Indies, in 1750,) he had issue one son, Richard, Lord Delvin, who deceased in 1761, without issue. His Lordship married, secondly, Catharine White, youngest daughter of Henry White, of Pitchfords-town, in the county of Kildare, Esq; and had issue by her, Thomas, who died in his infancy; George-Frederick, now Lord Delvin, born in Nov. 1760; Henry, born in Nov. 1762; and Lady Catharine, born in April 1766.

John, the late Earl, succeeded his brother Thomas, the fourth Earl of West-Meath, and married the Hon. Margaret Molza, daughter of Count Molza, of the dutchy of Modena, in Italy; by whom he had issue three sons, viz. Thomas the present Earl, Edward and Charles, and Lady Frances, his only daughter. He was a major-general in the French service, but resigned in the year 1740, and died at Nivills in Brabant, in the 83d year of his age.

Thomas, the fourth Earl of West-Meath, in April 1714, succeeded his brother Richard, the third Earl, and about the time of the Revolution was appointed Lieutenant Col. to the Earl of Tyrone's regiment in K. James's army; after which he had a regiment of foot, and then succeeded Colonel Parker in the command of a regiment of horse: for his services in which

stations

stations he was outlawed May 11, 1691; but being in the city of Limerick, when besieged by King William's forces, and one of the hostages exchanged for the observation of the articles of surrender, his outlawry was reversed, and he was restored to his honours and estate. In 1684, he married at the age of sixteen, Margaret only daughter of John Lord Bellew; and by her, who died in 1700, had two sons and nine daughters, whereof two survived him, which were, Lady Mary, married in 1705, to Francis Lord Athunry, and died at Galway in July 1725; and Lady Catharine, married to Andrew Nugent, of Dyfert, Esq; His Lordship died June 14, 1752.

In the reign of King Henry II. when the kingdom of Ireland became first subject to the English Crown, Sir Gilbert de Nugent, with his brethren and relations, accompanied Sir Hugh de Lacy in that expedition, to which Sir Hugh the King allotting the county of Meath to be holden of the Crown by Knight service, he gave to Sir Gilbert, in recompence of his services, his sister Rosa in marriage; and as a portion with her, the Barony of Delvin, to him and his heirs, to hold by the service of five Knights fees. Sir Richard, his second brother, succeeded as second Baron of Delvin, whose only daughter and heir became the wife of Johns, or Jones, who in her right possessed the Barony of Delvin; which honour and estate continued in his family, as some compute, for 120 years, until by the failure of heirs male, and the marriage of Catharine, daughter and heir of John Fitz-Johns, Baron of Delvin, to Sir William Nugent, of Balrath, the estate and title reverted to the family about the year 1327;

which

which Sir William was defcended of Chriftopher, third brother of Sir Gilbert, aforefaid. Sir Richard Nugent was the eighth Baron of Delvin. To him fucceeded his grandfon, Sir Richard Nugent, the ninth Baron, who was twice Lord Deputy of Ireland, and conducted the public affairs with great honour and integrity, till taken prifoner by O'Connor, in 1528. To him fucceeded his fon, Sir Chriftopher, 10th Baron, who was knighted in 1566, and made Captain of Siewht-William in the Annally, which place his father held for life; and he expreffed fuch forwardnefs and fidelity in the fervice of the Crown, that, in 1567, articles were made with his Lordfhip by the Queen, authorifing him to extirpate the O'Mores, fons of Ferraffe M'Roffe, and their followers. But notwithftanding this Commiffion and his fervice to the Crown, he was fent prifoner to London in 1580; and committed to the Tower, on fufpicion of holding correfpondence with the rebels of Leinfter: but his innocence being foon after fully proved, he was enlarged, and returned to Ireland; and fo acceptable were his fervices to the Queen, that, befides divers leafes of lands, in 1567, fhe ordered him a grant in fee-farm of fo many manors and forfeited lands in the counties of Cavan and Longford, as fhould amount to the Crown rent of 100l. a year. He died on Auguft 17, 1602, and Richard his eldeft fon fucceeded him as 11th Baron of Delvin, who was knighted in 1603, and had efpecial livery of his eftate in 1606; but in 1607 he was arrefted, and committed to the Caftle of Dublin for high treafon, being concerned in a confpiracy with the Earls of Tyrone and Tyrconnel, M'Guire, &c. to furprize

prize the Caftle of Dublin, cut off the Lord Deputy and Council, diffolve the State, and fet up a Government of their own. Having efcaped out of the Caftle, a proclamation was publifhed for apprehending him : but next year his Lordfhip furrendered himfelf, and made his fubmiffion to his Majefty, who thereupon took him into favour, and directed a pardon to be paffed for his life, lands, and goods; and ordered, that he fhould enjoy the full benefit of all his former warrants for granting lands to him by patent; and he fo effectually regained the King's favour, that he advanced him to the dignity of Earl of Weft-Meath, by patent, with the annual creation-fee of 20 l. payable from the Crown revenues arifing out of the county of Weft-Meath. In 1634, he fat in the Parliament, and was a leading man in the Houfe of Peers: but refufing to join with the Lords and Gentry of the Pale, in the Rebellion of 1641, a fevere courfe was threatened to be taken with him for his denial; whereupon, quitting his houfe, he was efcorted to Dublin by a party of horfe; but being attacked near Athboy by a thoufand rebels, he was obliged to yield: they feized his plate and money to the value of 100 l. ftripped his Countefs and her gentlewoman in a fhameful manner, maffacred his fervants, damaged his houfes and lands to the amount of 20,000 l. and he died of the wounds he received on that occafion.

He was fucceeded by his grandfon Richard, the fecond Earl of Weft-Meath, who was in 1650, General of the Irifh Forces raifed by the province of Leinfter againft the rebels ; and, in 1652, was excepted from pardon for life and eftate, by Cromwell's Act of Parliament for
fettling

settling of Ireland: but his Lordship, with others of the Irish party, entering into certain articles with the Commissioners of the Government, leave was given him to transport one thousand Irish foot into Spain; in 1653, he had an order to enjoy such of his estate as lay waste and undisposed of; and after his return from Flanders, where he was in the service of Spain with his regiment, the Government being credibly informed that the public peace was disturbed in England, the Lieutenant-General of the Army was required, in August 1659, to apprehend his Lordship, with other leading men in the county of Galway: but surviving all these troubles, he was considered after the Restoration as a person meriting, in an especial manner, his Majesty's grace and favour.

Creations.] Baron of Delvin, in the county of West-Meath, originally by tenure, temp. Hen. II. by frequent summons to Parliament in succeeding reigns; and Earl of the county of West-Meath, Sept. 4, 1621, 19 James I.

Arms.] Ermine, two bars, ruby.

Crest.] On a wreath, a cockatrice, rising proper, his tail nowed, his comb and wattles, ruby.

Supporters.] Two cockatrices as the crest, with wings displayed.

Motto.] Decrevi.

Chief Seat.] At Clowin, in the county of West-Meath.

EARL of DESMOND.

An account of this noble family will be found in my Peerage of England, under the title of Earl of DENBIGH.

EARL of MEATH.

Edward Brabazon, Earl of Meath, Lord Brabazon, Baron of Ardee, a Lord of the Privy-council, and Governor of the counties of Dublin and Wicklow, succeeded his brother Chaworth, the late and sixth Earl, and has issue by his wife, Martha, daughter of the Rev. Mr. Collins, of Nottingham, Anthony Lord Brabazon, representative in Parliament for the county of Dublin, and married to Miss Leslie, by whom his Lordship hath issue; and the hon. William Brabazon, Esq; member for Wicklow.

Chaworth, the late Earl, married Juliana, daughter of the late, and sister of the present Sir Thomas Prendergast, Bart. by which Lady, who deceased Dec. 12, 1758, he had no issue.

Chambre, the fifth Earl of Meath, succeeded his brother Edward in 1708. In 1675, he was appointed ranger of his Majesty's parks in Ireland; but was attainted by king James II's parliament, and had his estate sequestered. He commanded a regiment of foot at the battle of the Boyne, and was wounded at the attack of Limerick. In the first of George I. he was appointed one of the privy council, and marrying Juliana, only child of the Viscount Chaworth, had issue two sons and three daughters. viz.

1. Chaworth, the late Earl.
2. Edward, of Tarah, the present Earl.
3. Lady Juliana.
4. Lady Mary, who died unmarried in January, 1737.

5. Lady

5. Lady Catharine wife of Thomas Hallowes of Glapwell, in the county of Derby, Efq.

6. Lady Frances wife of the late Brigadier general, Henry Ponfonby, brother of Brabazon, Earl of Befborough.

This antient and noble family took their furname from the famous province of Brabant, from whence Jaques or James le Brabazon, commonly called the great Warrior, came to the aid of William Duke of Normandy, in his conqueft of England; and to the faid Jaques fucceeded John his fon, whofe refidence was at Bechworth, in Surry, temp. Hen. I. and II. where he was fucceeded by Adam his fon, who lived in the time of Henry II. From him, in a direct line, defcended Sir William Brabazon, who, in 1534, was made vice-treafurer of Ireland, fo continued till July, 1552; and was, in 1543, 1546, and 1549, one of the lords juftices of Ireland.

Sir Edward, his eldeft fon, was, in 1616, created Baron of Ardee, in the county of Louth, by King James I. and his eldeft fon Sir William, was created Earl of the county of Meath.

Creations.] Baron of Ardee, in the county of Louth, July 19, 1616, 14 James I. And Earl of Meath Apr. 16 1627, 3 Charles I.

Arms.] Ruby on a bend topaz, three martlets, diamond.

Creft.] On a wreath a mount proper, and thereon a falcon rifing topaz, belled of the fame.

Supporters,] Two wyverns topaz, collared and chained, of the fame, winged and membered, ruby.

Motto.]

Motto.] *Vota, vita mea.*
Chief Seat.] At Killrothery, in the county of Wicklow.

EARL of BARRYMORE.

RICHARD BARRY, Earl of BARRYMORE, Viscount Buttevant, Baron Barry, of Barry's-court, Olethan, and Ibawne, a captain in the ninth regiment of Dragoons was born in October 1745, succeeded his father, James, the fifth Earl, in December 1751, and on Apr. 16, 1767, married Lady Amelia Stanhope, third daughter of William, Earl of Harrington.

James the late and fifth Earl, succeeded his father James, Jan. 5, 1747-8; and, June 8, 1738, married Margaret youngest daughter of Paul Davis, Viscount Mount-Cashell, and sole heir to her brother Edward, Viscount Mount-Cashell, by whom he had issue, 1. James, born in 1738, and died in 1739; 2. James, who died an infant; 3. Richard, the present Earl; and the Ladies Anne, Catharine, and Margaret, all deceased.

James, the fourth Earl, was Colonel of a regiment of foot, was taken prisoner in 1708, at Campo Major, by the Spaniards; and, in 1710, was made Lieutenant-general of her Majesty's armies. In 1710 and 1714, he was chosen member in the British parliament for Stockbridge, and in 1714 for Wigan; which he continued to represent till 1747, when his son was chosen in his room. He married, first, Elizabeth, daughter of Charles Lord Clifford, and sister of Charles,

Earl of Cork, by whom he had a son, who died an infant; Lady Charlotte, who died in 1708; and Lady Anne, wife of James Maule, Esq; but died soon after her marriage. His second wife was Lady Elizabeth Savage, daughter and heir of Richard, Earl Rivers, by whom he had a daughter, Lady Penelope, wife of Major-general James Cholmondeley, brother of the Earl of Cholmondeley. In July 1716, he married, thirdly, Lady Anne Chichester, daughter of Arthur, Earl of Donegal; and by her, who died in 1754, had four sons and two daughters, viz.

1. James, the late Earl.
2. Lady Catharine, who died in 1738, unmarried.
3. Richard, chosen, in 1747, Member for Wigan, in the room of his father, and married, in May 1749, Jane, daughter of Arthur Hyde, of Castle-Hyde, in the county of Cork, Esq; which Lady died Oct. 19, 1751, without issue.
4. Arthur, who is unmarried.
5. John Smith Barry, of Marbury, in Cheshire, Esq; who, in April 1746, married Dorothy, eldest daughter and coheir of Hugh Smith, of Weald-Hall, in Essex, Esq; and has several children.
6. Lady Anne, wife of ——— Taylor, Esq; and died March 21, 1758.

This noble family, who have been renowned for their loyalty, and valour, are said by Camden to derive their name from the island of Barry, in the county of Glamorgan, in Wales; and from their riches and estates have been called by the people Barrymore, or the Great Barry.

William

William Barry, marrying Angareth, daughter of Nefta, and niece of the Prince of South Wales; by her had Robert, Philip anceftor of the Earl of Barrymore, Walter, and Gerald, which laft, well known by the name of Giraldus Cambrenfis, was fecretary to K. Henry II. and tutor to Earl John, (afterwards King,) that Prince's fon, whom he attended into Ireland, wrote a defcription of the country, as before he had done of England and Wales; and was made Bifhop of St. David's. Sir Robert, in the year 1170, went into Ireland, where he did great fervice for Dermot, King of Leinfter, againft Donald, King of Offory, was killed at Lifmore, about 1185, and Philip his brother marrying the fifter of Robert Fitz-Stephen, the faid Robert gave to William the fon of Philip three cantreds of land in the county of Cork.

Creations.] Baron Barry of Olethan and Ibawne, originally by tenure; Baron Barry of Barry's-Court, in the county of Cork, anno 1490, 6 Henry VII. Vifcount Buttevant temp. Ric. II. and in 1555, 3 Philip and Mary; and Earl of Barrymore all in the county of Cork, Feb. 28, 1627, 3 Charles I.

Arms.] Pearl, three bars gemels, ruby.

Creft.] On a wreath, a caftle, pearl, from the top whereof iffues a wolf's head, diamond.

Supporters.] Two wolves of the latter, their ducal collars and chains, topaz.

Motto.] *Boutez en avant,* i. e. *Pufh forward.*

Chief Seats.] At Caftle-Lions, in the county of Cork; at Wardley-Hall, in the county of Lancafter; and at Rock-Savage, in the county of Chefter.

EARL

EARL of DONEGAL.

Arthur Chichester, Earl of Donegal, Viscount Chichester, and Baron of Belfast, succeeded his uncle Arthur, the late and fourth Earl, in September 1757, being son of John, second son of Arthur, the third Earl, as will appear hereafter. His Lordship was born June 13, 1739, and on Nov. 16, 1762, married Lady Anne, daughter of James Duke of Hamilton (by Elizabeth, daughter and heirefs of Edward Spencer, of Rendlesham, in the county of Suffolk, Esq;) by whom he had two daughters, Lady Charlotte-Anne, born Sept. 3, 1763, and Lady Henrietta, born Jan. 16, 1765, both deceased; also Lady Elizabeth-Juliana, born March 24, 1767, now living.

Arthur, the third Earl of Donegal, succeeded his father Arthur; and, in 1705, was Major-general of the Spanish forces; and was killed, April 10, 1706, at the fort of Monjuick, after many glorious services, and buried at Barcelona. He married, first, Lady Barbara Boyle, youngest daughter of Roger, the first Earl of Orrery; by whom he had a son Charles, who died young; and his Lady dying Nov. 20, 1682, he married, secondly, the Lady Catharine Forbes, only daughter of Arthur, the first Earl of Granard; and by her, who died June 15, 1743, had issue two sons, and six daughters, viz.

1. Arthur, born March 28, 1695, who succeeded him as fourth Earl, and, in 1716, married Lady Lucy Ridgeway, one of the two daughters and coheirs of Robert, Earl of Londonderry;

donderry: but by her, who died July 16, 1732, he had no iſſue.

2. John, born in 1700, was, in 1725, member of parliament for Belfaſt; and, Sept. 13, 1726, married Elizabeth, eldeſt daughter of Sir Richard Newdigate, of Arbury, in the county of Warwick, Bart. ſiſter of the preſent Sir Roger, and died June 1, 1746; and his Lady in 1747; leaving two ſons, Arthur, the preſent Earl; John, member for Belfaſt; and a daughter.

3. Lady Catharine, born in 1687, was married in Sept. 1713, to Clotworthy, Lord Viſcount Maſareene.

4, 5, 6. Ladies Jane, Frances, and Henrietta, burnt in the houſe at Belfaſt, which took fire by accident.

7. Lady Mary, died unmarried.

8. Lady Anne, married, July 12, 1716, to James, Earl of Barrymore.

Of this family, which has been ſeated at Raleigh, in the county of Devon, for many generations, was John Chicheſter, Eſq; who, in the 34th, 45th, and 46th of Edward III. was member of parliament for Melcombe Regis, in the county of Dorſet; as alſo, in the 4th of Richard II. anno 1381. In the reign of Henry VIII. lived Edward Chicheſter, whoſe wife was Elizabeth, eldeſt daughter of John Bourchier, Lord Fitz-Warren, and Earl of Bath; from which match deſcended Sir John Chicheſter, Knt. who, in the firſt of Queen Mary, and fifth of Elizabeth, was member in the Engliſh parliament for the county of Devon: he had eight daughters and five ſons. Of the ſons, Sir Arthur, the ſecond, was, in 1604, Lord Deputy

Deputy of Ireland; and in 1612 was created Baron of Belfaſt, by James I. In 1616 he was made Lord High Treaſurer of Ireland; in 1622 ſent, by King James I. to the Palatinate, and from thence to the Emperor; and, at his return, was made one of his Majeſty's privy-council in England; but dying without iſſue, in 1625, he left his eſtate to his third brother, Sir Edward, who was created Lord Chicheſter, Baron of Belfaſt in the county of Antrim, Viſcount Chicheſter of Carrick-Fergus, in the ſame county, by Charles I. and his eldeſt ſon, Arthur, was created Earl of Donegal, by the ſame King.

Creations.] Baron Chicheſter of Belfaſt, and Viſcount Chicheſter of Carrick-Fergus, both in the county of Antrim, April 1, 1625, 1 Charles I. Earl of the county of Donegal, March 30, 1647, 23 Charles I.

Arms.] Quarterly, firſt and fourth checqué, topaz and ruby; a chief, vair; ſecond and third ſapphire, frettée, pearl.

Creſt.] On a wreath, a ſtork with wings expanded, head topaz, and in its beak a ſnake, pearl, all proper.

Supporters.] Two wolves ruby, each ducally gorged, and chained, topaz.

Motto.] *Invitum ſequitur honos*; or, *Honor ſequitur fugientem.*

Chief Seats.] At Belfaſt, in the county of Antrim; at Carrick-Fergus, in the ſame county; and at Bromfield, in Eſſex.

C   EARL

EARL of CAVAN.

Ford Lambart, Earl of Cavan, Viscount of Kilcourfie, and Lord Lambart, Baron of Cavan, was born in 1718, and succeeded his father Richard, the fourth Earl, on March 10, 1741. On March 24, 1741-2, his Lordship married Elizabeth, daughter of James Wall, of Dublin, Esq; who died in 1766, and left only a daughter, Lady Gertrude Lambart.

Richard, the late and fourth Earl, was an officer in King William's army in Spain, Portugal, and the West Indies; and one of his Majesty's Privy-council. He married at Barbadoes, Margaret, daughter of Captain Trant, brother of Sir Patrick Trant, by which Lady, who died in Aug. 1737, he had issue,

1. Gilbert, Lord Lambart, who died young.
2. Ford, the present Earl.
3. Lady Gertrude, wife of William, Earl of Kerry; and secondly, of James Tilson, Esq;
4. Lady Esther, of Warner Westenra, Esq; member for Maryborough.
5. Lady Castilina, who died unmarried.

Of this ancient family, which is of French extraction, was Radulph de Lambart, who came into England with William the Conqueror, and was father of Hugh, whose son Sir William married Gundred, daughter of William, Earl of Warren and Surry, and widow of Roger de Bellamont, Earl of Warwick, by whom he had a son Henry, Standard-bearer to Henry II. and thereby got lands in the north of England. From him descended Sir Oliver, who, in the reign of Queen Elizabeth, attending the Earl of

Essex

Essex-to-Cales, in Spain, was there knighted, by that Earl; and afterwards returning with him into Ireland, was, for his singular service in the North, against O'Neal, Earl of Tyrone, as well as against others of the Irish rebels, made Camp-master-general, and President of Connaught; and was created Lord Lambart, and Baron of Cavan, by King James I.

His son Charles, who succeeded, and was the second Baron, in 1641, when the rebellion broke out, raised a regiment of foot for his Majesty's service; on May 12, 1642, he was made Governor of the city of Dublin; and, the 12th of July following, Commander of his Majesty's forces within the city and suburbs, and was created Earl of Cavan, and Viscount Kilcourfie.

Creations.] Lord Lambart, Baron of Cavan, Feb. 17, 1617, 15 James I. Viscount Kilcourfie, in the King's county, and Earl of the county of Cavan, Apr. 1647, 22 Charles I.

Arms.] Ruby, three narcissus's pierced, pearl.

Crest.] On a wreath, a mount, emerald, and thereon a centaur party per pale, proper, his bow, ruby, and arrow, topaz.

Supporters.] Two men in armour to the waist, diamond, garnished, topaz, their trowsers, ruby, fringed of the second, their swords and knees, proper, each having a steel cap, adorned with six ostrich feathers, pearl and ruby.

Motto.] *Utquocunque paratus.*

Chief Seat.] At Lambarton, in Queen's-county.

EARL of INCHIQUIN.

WILLIAM OBRYEN, Earl and Baron of INCHIQUIN, and Baron of Burren, a Knight companion of the moſt honourable Order of the Bath, and a Lord of the Privy-council, ſucceeded his father, William, the third Earl, on Dec. 24, 1719; and, March 21, 1720, married Lady Anne Hamilton, eldeſt daughter and heir of George, Earl of Orkney (by Elizabeth, eldeſt daughter of Sir Edward Villiers, and ſiſter of his Lordſhip's mother,) and by her, who ſucceeded her father in his honours, Jan. 29, 1736, had iſſue four ſons and ſeven daughters.; William, George, Auguſtus, and Murrough, Lord Obryen, all deceaſed: Of the daughters are living Lady Mary, now Counteſs of Orkney, who married Murrough, eldeſt ſon of the Hon. James Obryen, and nephew of her father (ſee that title, in my Peerage of Scotland) and Lady Anne. The Counteſs died in Nov. 1757, and lies buried at Taplow, with nine of her children, where alſo her father and mother, the Earl and Counteſs of Orkney, were interred. His Lordſhip married, ſecondly, Mary, daughter of Stephen Moore, Viſcount Mount-Caſhell, but has by that Lady no iſſue.

William, the third Earl of Inchiquin, and father of the preſent Earl, ſerved in the army under King William III. both in Ireland and Flanders, and by him was made Governor of the royal fort and town of Kinſale. In Queen Anne's reign he commanded a regiment of foot, and was of the Privy-council to her and King George I. He married Mary, youngeſt daughter of Sir Edward Villiers, and ſiſter of

Edward,

Edward, firſt Earl of Jerſey, by whom he had three ſons and two daughters, viz.
1. William, the preſent Earl.
2. Charles, an officer in the royal navy, who died without iſſue.
3. James, an officer in the army, and late member of parliament for the town of Younghall, who married Miſs Mary Jephſon, by whom he has iſſue.
4. Lady Mary, wife of Robert the nineteenth Earl of Kildare.
5. Lady Henrietta, wife of Robert Sandford, of Caſtlereagh, in the county of Roſcommon, Eſq;

William, the ſecond Earl, and father of the late Earl, was by King Charles II. made Captain-General of his Forces in Africa, Governor and Vice-Admiral of Tangier, and of the adjacent parts; afterwards, by King William, he was made Governor of Jamaica, and Vice-Admiral of the Seas thereof, in which iſland he died in January, 1691-2.

This moſt antient and noble family of Obryen, who, with ſignal bravery, have repelled the invaſion of the Danes, and other foreign enemies, is lineally deſcended from Bryen Borainhbe, or Borau, who, in 1002, was proclaimed King of all Ireland, and was deſcended originally, in a direct male line, from Hiberius, eldeſt ſon of Mileſius of Spain; and the ſame King Bryen Borau marrying Cormflaith, daughter of Murrough M'Fluir, had Tiege Obryen, his heir, whoſe wife was More, the King of Leinſter's daughter, and by her had Thurlogh Obryen, who was Monarch of Ireland twelve years.

He married More, daughter to O'Heyne, and by her had Dermoid Obryen, who was King of Munster four years; and by Sarah, daughter of Teige M'Carty, had Thurlogh Obryen, who was King of Munster five years; and he marrying Nariat, daughter of O'Fogherta, had Daniel More Obryen, who was King of Cashel and Limerick thirty years; and from him, in a direct male line, descended Teige Obryen, whose son Thurlogh Obryen was Prince of Limerick and Thomond, whose eldest son Connor, was the last of twelve Princes of the Obryen family, after the landing of King Henry II. in Ireland, that reigned successively in Thomond, and were stiled either Kings of Limerick or Thomond, instead of being Sovereign Monarchs of all Ireland, as their ancestors deservedly were. Donogh, the eldest son of the said Connor, was the second Earl, and his son Connor the third Earl. His eldest son again was Donogh, the fourth Earl, who was President of Munster, one of the Privy Council; and being a person of great courage, conduct, loyalty, and worth, was much in favour both with Queen Elizabeth and King James I. From him descended Henry the eighth Earl of Thomond, who married the Lady Elizabeth Seymour, eldest daughter of Charles Duke of Somerset; and dying without issue, the title became extinct; but leaving his estate to Percy Wyndham, Esq; second son of Sir William Wyndham, Bart. he took the name of Obryen; and in 1756 was created Earl of Thomond, as will be seen in its proper place.

    Daniel Obryen, third son of Connor, third Earl of Thomond, was created Viscount Clare,

and

and Baron of Mayfearto, July 17, 1662. His son, the second Viscount, was outlawed for his service to King James II. and, being in the French service, was killed at the battle of Ramilies, in 1706; and his eldest son was late y in the French service, under the title of Viscount Clare. Murrough, the youngest brother of Connor the last King of Thomond, had a son Dermoid Obryen, who was the first Baron of Inchiquin, whose father Murrough, resigning his title and principality to Henry VIII. was by letters patent, July 1, 1544, created Earl of Thomond for life; and Baron of Inchiquin. Murrough Obryen, the sixth Baron of Inchiquin, taking early to arms, went into Italy, and served in the Spanish troops: but the Civil War breaking out in England, he returned thither, and being sent on the King's service, he commanded a body of troops under the Earl of Ormond, Lord-Lieutenant of Ireland, and fought many successful battles against the Irish: for, meeting Owen Roe O'Neill near Callin, in the county of Kilkenny, he defeated his army, and pursued him over the Shannon. The Lord Inchiquin afterwards marched against the Lord Muskerry, and routed him near Charleville: the same day, he attacked Lord Taaffe, and entirely routed his body of troops. Three days after, he fought Sir Oliver Stephenson, at Lascarrol, who was killed in the battle, and his army totally destroyed. Sir Alexander M'Donall, coming afterwards to the assistance of the Lord Muskerry, was met at a place called Knocknanoss, in the county of Cork, by the Lord Inchiquin, who entirely defeated his army, Sir

Alex-

Alexander losing his life in the battle; the Lord Inchiquin afterwards took Cashel, and other places that held out, and reduced Munster to obedience. Sir William St. Leger, Lord President of Munster, whose daughter the Lord Inchiquin had married, dying, the Earl of Portland was appointed to succeed him: but the Lord Inchiquin, thinking he had merited to succeed his father-in-law, refused to give up his garrisons or troops to the Earl of Portland; and some time afterwards, the King (remembering his past services, and how useful he had been to him) appointed him Lord President of Munster, by which means he had the command of all the troops, for which, in 1643, he was voted a traitor by the Parliament of England.

In 1649, he marched to the assistance of the King's friends north of Dublin; Drogheda surrendered to him. He afterwards took Dundalk, and other garrisons: but, in 1652, an Act passing in England for settling the affairs of Ireland, he and the Earl of Ormond were excepted from pardon; and Oliver Cromwell, bringing over a mighty force with him, obliged them to fly to France, where the Lord Inchiquin was made Lieutenant-General of the French King's army; and upon the conquest of Catalonia, he was appointed Viceroy thereof. From thence, being ordered to command the troops sent to assist the Portuguese, upon their revolt from Spain, he, with his eldest son, and all his family, were taken by an Algerine Corsair, which occasioned the sending of Count Schomberg in his place. Lord Inchiquin, having purchased his own and his son and family's liberty from the Algerines, returned into France;

France; and upon the Restoration of the Royal Family, he came into England with Charles II. and by him was created Earl of Inchiquin.

Creations.] Baron of Inchiquin, in the county of Clare, July 1, 1543, 35 Hen. VIII. Earl of the same place, and Baron of Burren, Oct. 21, 1654, 6 Charles II. the patent being dated at Cologne.

Arms.] Quarterly, 1st, ruby three lions passant, guardant in pale, party per pale, topaz and pearl. 2d, Pearl, three piles issuing from the chief, and meeting in point, ruby. 3d, Topaz, a pheon's head, sapphire. 4th, as the first.

Crest.] On a wreath, a naked arm issuing out of a cloud, both proper, brandishing a sword pearl, the pomel and hilt topaz.

Supporters.] Two lions guardant, party per fess, topaz, and pearl.

Motto.] *Vigueur de Dessus.*

Chief Seats.] At Rostellan, in the county of Cork; and at Cliefden and Taplow, in Buckinghamshire.

EARL of MOUNTRATH.

CHARLES-HENRY COOTE, Earl of MOUNTRATH, Viscount Coote, of Castle-Coote, Baron Coote, of Castle-Cuff, and Baronet, a Lord of the Privy Council, succeeded his father, Algernon, the sixth Earl, in August, 1743.

Algernon, the late and sixth Earl of Mountrath, succeeded his brother Henry, March 27, 1720; and, in 1721, married the Lady Diana Newport, youngest daughter of Richard, Earl of Bradford, by whom he had a son, the present Earl. He was one of the Privy-council, and Governor of Queen's county. In January 1723-4, he was chosen Member in the British Parliament for Castle-Rising, as he was in 1727; and in 1741, for Heydon.

This noble family is descended from Sir John Coote, a native of France, who married the daughter and heir of the Lord Boys of that kingdom, and had issue, Sir John, who settled in Devonshire. From him descended Sir Charles Coote, who settled at Castle-Cuffe in Queen's county, and served very young in the wars against the Earl of Tyrone. In 1620, he was sworn of the Privy Council, and was created a Baronet of Ireland: but was shot dead at Trim, in 1642, as he was forcing that place, in which he succeeded, though with the loss of his life. He married Dorothea, younger daughter and co-heir of Hugh Cuffe, of Cuffe's-wood, in the county of Corke, Esq; and had four sons: 1. Sir Charles; 2. Chidley, from whom is descended the family of Killester; 3. Sir Richard, ancestor to the Earl of Bellamont; 4. Thomas, who was Governor of Coleraine for the Parliament, after the reduction of the kingdom by Cromwell, and died without issue.

The eldest son, Sir Charles, the second Baronet, was Lord President of Connaught; and having a good interest in the army, was very instrumental in restoring King Charles II. for which services his Majesty was pleased to create him Baron and Viscount Coote, and Earl of Mountrath, in Queen's-county. He was the same year made Colonel of a regiment of horse, being before Colonel of a regiment of foot, and one of the Lords Justices, but died, Dec. 18th, the next year.

Creations.]

Creations.] Baronet, Ap. 2, 1621, 19 James I. Baron Coote, of Caftle-Cuffe, in the King's county; Vifcount Coote, of Caftle-Coote, in the county of Rofcommon, and Earl of Mountrath, in the Queen's county, Sept. 6, 1660, 12 Charles II.

Arms.] Quarterly, firft, pearl, a chevron, diamond, between three coots, proper. 2nd, Ruby, on a fefs topaz, between three horfes currant, pearl, as many heurts. 3d, Sapphire, ten billets, four, three, two, and one, on a chief topaz, on the latter a demi lion rampant, naiffant diamond. 4th, as the firft.

Creft.] On a wreath, a coot, proper.

Supporters.] Two wolves, diamond, ducally gorged, pearl.

Motto.] *Vincit veritas.*

Chief Seats.] Ruifh-hall, in the Queen's county; and Wood-hall, in Hertfordfhire.

EARL of DROGHEDA.

CHARLES MOORE, Earl of DROGHEDA, Vifcount Moore, and Lord Moore, Baron of Mellefont, a Lord of the Privy-council, Colonel of the eighteenth regiment of Dragoons, and Governor of Kinfale, fucceeded his father, Edward, the fifth Earl, and on Feb. 15, 1766, married Lady Anne Conway, eldeft daughter of Francis Earl of Hertford, by whom he has iffue a fon.

Edward, the late Earl, fucceeded his brother Henry, in 1727, and married Lady Sarah, daughter of Brabazon, Earl of Beflborough, by whom he had four fons and one daughter, viz.

1. Henry,

1. Henry, Lord Moore, who died at Thoulouse in France, in 1752.
2. Charles, Lord Moore, born June 29th, 1730, now Earl of Drogheda.
3. Ponsonby.
4. Edward-Loftus, born Dec. 29, 1736.
5. Lady Sarah, married in 1748 to William Pole, of Ballifin, in Queen's county, Esq;

And their mother dying in child-bed, Jan. 19, 1736-7, his Lordship married, Oct. 13, 1737, Bridget, daughter of the late William Southwell, Esq; Colonel of the Battle-axe Guards, and brother of Thomas Lord Southwell, by whom his Lordship had issue,

1. William, born Dec. 11, 1743, member in the present Parliament for Clogher.
2. Lady Mary-Lucy, born May 6, 1739.
3. Lady Alice, born in October, 1740.
4. Lady Lucy.

This noble family, which is of French extraction, came into England soon after the conquest and made the manor of Moore-court in Kent their residence, till marrying the heiress of the family of Benenden, in the same county, they made that their residence; and John Moore of Benenden marrying Margaret, daughter and heir of John Brent, Esq; widow of John Dering of Surrenden, had six sons; Owen, the eldest; George, the third; and Nicholas, the fifth, had no issue. Sir Thomas, the fourth, was ancestor of Lord Tullamore. The second son was Sir Edward Moore, Knt. so made in the field, a person of great courage, and conduct, and for his many and eminent services, both at home and abroad, Queen Elizabeth, after the expulsion of the
Monks,

Monks, gave him the abbey of Mellefont, where his pofterity have remained ever fince. He married Margery, daughter of William Brabazon, fourth fon of John Brabazon, of Eaftwell in the county of Leicefter, Efq; anceftor of the Earl of Meath, by whom he had Garret, or Gerald Moore, who ferved under the Earl of Effex and Lord Mountjoy, in the war with Tyrone and the Spaniards; and for his great fervices to the crown, King James I. was pleafed to create him Lord Moore, Baron of Mellefont, and Vifcount Moore of Drogheda.

His fon Charles, who was fecond Vifcount, was one of the privy council to King Charles I. and after performing fignal fervices, he loft his life fighting for his king and country, Auguft 15th. 1643, at Portlefter in Meath, by a cannon fhot, as he was upon an eminence giving directions for an affault.

Henry his fon, who fucceeded him, as well in his employments as in his honours and eftate, was colonel of a troop of horfe, and governor of the counties of Meath, Louth, &c. and, was created Earl of Drogheda.

Creations.] Lord Moore, Baron of Mellefont, in the county of Louth, July 20, 1616, 14 James I. Vifcount Moore, Feb. 7, 1621, 19 James I. and Earl of Drogheda, June 14, 1641, 13 Charles II.

Arms.] Sapphire on a chief indented, topaz; three mullets pierced, ruby.

Creft.] In a ducal coronet topaz, a Moor's head proper, wreathed about the temples, pearl and fappire.

Supporters.] Two greyhounds, pearl.

Motto.]

[38]

Motto.] *Fortis cadere, cedere non potest.*
Chief Seat.] At Monafter-Evan in the county of Kildare.

EARL of WATERFORD and WEXFORD.

An account of this noble family will be found in my English Peerage, under the title of Earl of SHREWSBURY.

EARL of GRANARD.

GEORGE FORBES, Earl and Viscount of GRANARD, Baron of Clanehugh, and Baronet, a Lieutenant-general, and Colonel of the 29th regiment of Foot, succeeded his father, George, the third Earl, in August, 1765, and married Mary, daughter of Arthur Davis, of Carrickfergus, Esq; by whom he has issue a son, ———, Lord Forbes, married to a sister of the present Earl of Berkeley.

George, the late Earl, was a Privy-counsellor, and Senior Admiral of the Royal Navy, succeeded his father, Arthur, the second Earl, August 24, 1737, married Mary, eldest daughter of William, the first Viscount Mountjoy, and relict of Phineas Preston, of Ardsallagh, in the county of Meath, Esq; and by her, who died Oct. 4, 1758, had issue two sons, and one daughter, viz.

1. George, the present Earl.
2. John, Admiral of the Blue, late a Lord Commissioner of the Admiralty, and member in the present Parliament for Mullingar.
3. Lady Mary.

His

His Lordship, in March 1724, was chosen a member in the British parliament for Queenborough; and in 1741 for the boroughs of Air, &c. In April 1733, he was appointed Minister plenipotentiary to the Czarina. In May 1734, he was made Rear-admiral of the White; in December following, Rear-admiral of the Red; in November 1735, Governor of Barbadoes; and in July 1738, being then Vice-admiral of the Blue, he was appointed Commander in chief of a squadron for the West-Indies.

Arthur, the second Earl of Granard, was of the privy council to William and Mary, and married Mary, eldest daughter of Sir George Rawdon of Moyra, in the county of Downe, Bart. ancestor of the present Earl of Moyra, by whom he had three sons and two daughters, viz.

1. Arthur, Lord Forbes, killed in a duel in Flanders, unmarried.
2. Edward, Lord Forbes, an officer in the army, killed at the battle of Hockstet in 1704, unmarried.
3. George, the late Earl.
4. Lady Jane, wife of Major Josias Champagne, of Portarlington.
5. Lady Dorothy, who died unmarried.

The descent of this noble family is from that of the Lord Forbes in Scotland; for James, the first Lord Forbes, had, by Egidia his wife, daughter of William Earl Marishal, two sons; William, his heir, from whom descended the present Lord Forbes, (see that title in my Peerage of Scotland;) and Patrick, the second, from whom descended Sir Arthur Forbes,

Forbes, Knight, and Baronet of Nova Scotia; whose son and heir, Sir Arthur, in the reign of Charles I. was a man of great interest in the Province of Ulster, and an Officer of horse in his Majesty's army. In 1660 he was appointed one of the Commissioners for settling the affairs of Ireland; and, in 1671, being Marshal-general of the army, was then appointed one of the Lords Justices, as he was in 1675; and, in 1684, being appointed Lieutenant-general, &c. he was created Earl of Granard.

Creations.] Baronet of Nova Scotia, Sept. 26, 1628, 3 Ch. I. Baron of Clanehugh, and Viscount of Granard, in the county of Longford, Nov. 22, 1675, 27 Charles II. and Earl of Granard, Dec. 30, 1684, 36 Charles II.

Arms.] Sapphire, three bears heads, couped, pearl, muzzled, ruby.

Crest.] On a wreath, a bear passant, pearl, guttée de sang, and muzzled, ruby.

Supporters.] On the dexter side, an unicorn erminois (yellow powdered with black:) on the sinister, a dragon ermine, his wings expanded.

Motto.] *Fax mentis incendium gloriæ.*

Chief Seats.] Newtown-Castle-Forbes, in the county of Longford; and at Symon's-court, in the county of Dublin.

EARL FITZ-WILLIAM.

See this noble family, under the same title, in my Peerage of England.

EARL of KERRY.

FRANCIS-THOMAS FITZ-MAURICE, Earl of KERRY, Vifcount Clanmaurice, baron of Kerry and Lixnaw, was born on Sept. 9, 1740, and fucceeded his father, William, the fecond Earl, on April 4, 1747.

William, the late Earl, born in 1694, fucceeded his father Thomas; and, June 29, 1738, married Lady Gertrude Lambart, eldeft daughter of Richard Earl of Cavan, by which Lady, who married, fecondly, July 7, 1750, James Tilfon, of Pallice, in King's county, Efq; he had one fon, the prefent Lord; and one daughter, Lady Anne Margaretta, born Oct. 6, 1741.

Thomas the firft Earl, and father of the late Earl, was the twenty firft Lord Kerry, who married Anne, daughter of Sir William Petty, Knt. and fifter of Henry Earl of Shelburne, by whom he had had five fons and three daughters, viz.

1 William, the late Earl.
2. Thomas;
3. James, who both died young.
4. Thomas, who died unmarried.
5. John, created Earl of Shelburne, (fee that title.)
6. Lady Elizabeth Anne, wife of Sir Maurice Crofbie of Ardfert, Knt.
7. Lady Arabella, wife of Arthur Denny, of Tralee, Efq.
8. Lady Charlotte, wife of John Colthurft, of Ardrum, in the county of Cork, Efq.

This

This very antient and noble family is a branch of the family of Kildare, who are originally defcended from the great Duke of Tufcany, and of which was Otho, a noble Baron of Italy, whofe fon Walter, attending the Norman conqueror into England, was made conftable of the caftle of Windfor; and by Gladys, daughter of Rywal ap Conyn, had three fons; of whom Gerald, the eldeft, married Nefta, daughter of Rees Gruffyd, or Griffith, Prince of South Wales, and had Maurice and William. Maurice was anceftor of the family of Kildare, and William had a fon Odo, who inherited the caftle of Carew: from him defcended Reymond, who had a principal hand in the reduction of Ireland to the fubjection of Henry II. and Dermoid Mac-Carty, King of Cork, fought his aid againft his fon Cormac O'Lehanagh, which he undertook, and delivered the King from his rebellious fon, for which that Prince rewarded him with a large track of land in the county of Kerry, where he fettled his fon Maurice, who gave his name to the county, which he called Clan-Maurice; and is enjoyed by the prefent Earl of Kerry, who is Vifcount Clan-Maurice. This Maurice married Bafilia, fifter of Richard Strongbow, Earl of Pembroke, whom he fucceeded as chief governor of the kingdom; and had Maurice his heir, who, by Joanna, daughter to Miles Fitz-Henry, chief governor of Ireland, had a fon and heir, Thomas, who affumed the name of Fitz-Maurice, and was the firft Lord of Kerry.

Creations.] Baron, originally by tenure, and by patent from Richard II. Vifcount Clan-Maurice

Maurice in the county of Kerry, and Earl of that county, June 17, 1722, 9 Geo. I.

Arms.] Pearl, a Saltire ruby, and chief ermine.

Crest.] On a wreath, a centaur, party per fess, proper and pearl, with his bow and arrow of the former.

Supporters.] On the dexter a lion ruby; on the sinister, a griffin topaz.

Motto.] *Virtute non verbis.*

Chief Seat.] At Lixnaw, in the county of Kerry.

EARL of DARNLEY.

See this noble family, in my Peerage of England, under the title of Lord CLIFTON.

EARL TYLNEY.

JOHN-CHILD TYLNEY, Earl TYLNEY of Castlemain, Viscount Castlemain, Baron of Newtown, and Baronet; Ranger and Keeper of Epping-forest, member in Parliament for the borough of Malmesbury, and Fellow of the Royal Society, succeeded his father, Richard, the first Earl, in March, 1749.

This noble Lord is descended from the ancient family of Child, of Northwick, Pencook, Pool-court, and Shrowley, all in Worcestershire, where we meet with some of this name in the years 1320, 1349, 1350, and 1353: But the prime ancestors of this family were originally Lords of Arcal-Pawe, thence called Child's-Arcal, in the county of Salop.

Josiah Child, being an East-India merchant, and some time Governor of that Company, was

was created a Baronet; and by his firſt wife, Anne, daughter of Edward Boate, of Portſmouth, had two ſons, Joſiah and Richard, who both died in their infancy, and a daughter, Elizabeth, wife of John Howland, of Stretham, in the county of Surry, Eſq; by whom ſhe had a daughter of her name, wife of Wriotheſley, Duke of Bedford, mother of the late and preſent Dukes. By his ſecond wife, Mary, daughter of William Atwood, of Hackney, in Middleſex, Eſq; he had a ſon Joſiah, who ſucceeded him, and two daughters, Rebecca and Mary. Rebecca was wife of Charles Somerſet, Marquis of Worceſter, by whom ſhe had Henry, the ſecond Duke of Beaufort, father of the late and preſent Dukes, and after him married John Lord Granville, of Potheridge. Mary, the ſecond daughter, was wife of Edward Bullock, of Foulkborn-hall, in the county of Eſſex, Eſq; Sir Joſiah, their father, marrying to his third wiſe Emma, youngeſt of the daughters and co-heirs of Sir Henry Bernard, of Stoke, in the county of Salop, by her had two ſons, Bernard, who died unmarried, and Richard.

Joſiah, the ſecond Baronet, dying Jan. 20, 1704, without iſſue, his only ſurviving brother, Richard, ſucceeded, whom his Majeſty was pleaſed to create Baron of Newton, Viſcount Caſtlemain, and Earl Tylney. He married Dorothy, only daughter and heir of John Glynne, of Henley-Park, in Surry, Eſq; by Dorothy, daughter of Francis Tylney, of Rotherwick, in the county of Southampton, Eſq; by which Lady, (who died in Feb. 1743-4, to whom

whom a large eftate defcending, his eldeft fon was by Act of Parliament to affume the name of Tylney,) he had iffue,

1. Richard, who died of the fmall-pox in 1734.
2. John, the prefent Earl.
3. Jofiah, who married, in 1754, Henrietta, only daughter of Robert Knight, Lord Luxborough, now Earl of Catherlogh.
4. Lady Emma, married, in June 1735, to Sir Robert Long, Bart. Knight of the Shire for Wilts, deceafed.
5. Lady Dorothy.

Creations.] Baronet, July 18, 1678, 30 Cha. II. Baron of Newton, in the county of Donegal, and Vifcount Caftlemain, in the county of Kerry, Apr. 17, 1718, 5 Geo. I. Earl Tylney, of Caftlemain, Jan. 11, 1731, 5 Geo. II.

Arms.] Quarterly, firft and fourth, ruby, a chevron ermine between three eaglets clofe, pearl; fecond and third, pearl, on a bend fapphire, three efcallop fhells of the field.

Creft.] On a wreath, an eagle with wings expanded pearl, enveloped around the neck with a fnake, whofe tail is waved over his back, all proper.

Supporters.] Two eagles reguardant pearl, each enveloped with a fnake, as the creft.

Motto.] *Imitari quam invideri.*

Chief Seat.] At Wanftead-houfe, in the county of Effex.

EARL of EGMONT.

An account of this noble family will be found in my Peerage of England, under the title Lord LOVEL and HOLLAND. I shall just subjoin a
Note. The several branches of this family have the universal privilege of bearing Supporters to their Arms, as is evident from the ensuing authority, copied from the original entry, in the Office of Arms, London:

"This is to certify all whom it may concern, that it appears from the antient seals of this family, and from the ancient paintings in the glass windows of the house of Weston, in the county of Somerset, that the family of Perceval, of the line of Weston, of which the Earl of Egmont is the chief, have borne and used for Supporters to their Arms, two Eagles, sable, as depicted and blazoned in a book marked 3d D. 14. p. 182, and 186. in the Office of Arms, London, from the time of K. Edward I. Witness our hands, as waiters of the month, this 16th day of April, and in the thirteenth year of the reign of George II, King of Great Britain, France, and Ireland, Annoque Dom. 1740.
   CHARLES GREENE, Lancaster.
   RICHARD MAWSON, Portcullis."

EARL of BESBOROUGH.

For an account of this noble family, see my Peerage of England, under the title of Lord PONSONBY.

EARL VERNEY.

RALPH VERNEY, Earl VERNEY, Viscount of Fermanagh, Baron Verney, of Belturbet, and Baronet, succeeded his father Ralph, the first Earl, on Oct. 4, 1752, and on Sept. 11, 1740, married Mary, daughter of Henry Herring, Esq; Merchant of London, then a Director of the Bank. His Lordship is Member in the present British Parliament for the town of Caermarthen, a Lord of the Privy Council, and Fellow of the Royal Society.

Ralph, the late Earl, succeeded his father John, second Viscount Verney, June 23, 1717; and, was created Earl Verney. He married Catharine, daughter and co-heir of Henry Paschal, of Baddow-hall, in the county of Essex, Esq; and by her, who died Nov. 28, 1748, had two sons and two daughters, viz.

1. John, who married, in July 1736, the daughter of Josiah Nicholson, of Clapham, Esq; but dying in June 1737, left her with child of a daughter, of which she was delivered Oct. 23; and in 1741, took to her second husband Richard Calvert, of London, Esq; brother of Sir William Calvert, Knight and Alderman.

2. Ralph, the present Earl.

3. Lady Elizabeth, wife of Bennet the present Earl of Harborough.

4. Lady Catharine, who died in 1750, unmarried.

Of this antient family, which have been long seated in the county of Bucks, was Sir Ralph Verney, Knt. whose son John Verney stands one of the most eminent in the catalogue of of Gentry taken for the said county in 1433. He married Margaret, daughter and heir of Sir Robert Whittingham, of Penley, in the county of Hertford, Knt. Sheriff of London in 1419; and, being by that marriage possessed of the said estate at Penley, was therein succeeded by Sir Ralph, their son, who, in 1466, was Lord Mayor of London.

From him descended Sir Edmund Verney, of Middle-Claydon, in the county of Bucks, who was by King Charles I. made Knight Marshal of his Houshold, and lost his life with great courage and honour, fighting for that Prince, at the battle of Edgehill, in the county of Warwick, Oct. 23, 1642. His son and heir, Sir Ralph, was, by Charles II. created a Baronet, and was succeeded by his son John; who, by Queen Anne, was created Baron Verney, of Belturbet, in the county of Cavan, and Viscount of the county of Fermanagh.

Creations.] Baronet, March 16, 1661, 14 Charles II. Baron Verney, of Belturbet, in the county of Cavan, and Viscount of the county of Fermanagh, June 16, 1703, 2 Anne; Earl Verney, in the province of Leinster, Feb. 7, 1742, 16 George II.

Arms.] Sapphire on a cross pearl, five mullets, ruby.

Crest.] On a wreath, a phœnix in flames, beholding a ray of the sun, all proper.

Supporters.] Two tigers pearl, each gorged with a ducal coronet, sapphire, chained topaz.

Motto.] *Ung tout seul.*

Chief Seats.] At Middle-Claydon and Bidlesden, in the county of Bucks.

EARL of PANMURE.

See an account of this noble family in my Peerage of Scotland, p. 200.

EARL of BLESSINTON.

WILLIAM STEWART, Earl of BLESSINTON, Viscount of Montjoy, Baron of Ramalton, and Baronet; a Lord of the Privy-council, and Governor of the county of Tyrone; succeeded his father, William, the second Viscount Montjoy, Jan. 10, 1726, and on Jan. 10, 1733, married Eleanor, daughter and heir of Robert Fitzgerald, Esq; (Prime Serjeant at Law from 1717 to 1734,) by whom he had issue two sons, William, Viscount Montjoy, born March 13, 1734, and Lionel-Robert, born on April 12, 1736, both deceased. In 1745 his Lordship was created Earl of Blessinton.

William the late, and second Viscount Montjoy, was Colonel of a regiment of foot, successively Brigadier-general, Major-general, and Lieutenant-general; afterwards was, by his late Majesty, made Colonel of a regiment of Dragoons, a Privy-counsellor, Master of the Ordnance, and one of the Keepers of the Great Seal. He married Anne, younger daughter, and at length heir, of Murrough Boyle, Viscount Blessinton; by which Lady, who afterwards married John Farquarson, Esq; and died Oct. 27, 1741, he had issue five sons and four daughters, who all died young, except Mary, wife

wife of James Lord Tyrawley, and the present Earl of Bleſſinton.

The firſt of the family of Stewart that came into Ireland was Sir William Stewart, Knt. a younger brother of the Earl of Galloway, in Scotland, who, in 1623, was created a Baronet by King James I. He was ſucceeded by his ſon Sir Alexander, who, Sept. 3, 1653, was killed at the battle of Dunbar, in Scotland. He married Catharine, daughter of Sir Robert Newcomen, Bart. by whom he had iſſue an only ſon,

Sir William, who was born ſix weeks after his father's death, and was created Baron of Ramalton, in the county of Donegal, and Viſcount of Montjoy, a fort in the county of Tyrone, by King Charles II. by whom, at the ſame time, he was made Maſter of the Ordnance, and Colonel of a regiment of Foot: in 1686 he went into Hungary, and, at the ſiege of Buda, was twice dangerouſly wounded; and after his return into Ireland he was ſent into France, by the Duke of Tyrconnel, where he was clapped into the Baſtile, and there remained a priſoner till the year 1692, when he was releaſed, and went to wait upon King William in Flanders, where, on Aug. 24, he was killed at the battle of Steenkirk. He married Mary, eldeſt daughter of Richard, Lord Coloony, by whom he had ſix ſons and two daughters, that ſurvived their infancy,

1. William, the late Viſcount.
2. Alexander, Captain of Foot.
3. Richard, who died unmarried in Aug. 1728.
4. Arthur, a Captain in the Army, who died in July, 1723.
5. Charles,

5. Charles, who, being bred to the sea service, loft his arm in 1697, in an engagement with the French, being then but sixteen years old. In 1715, he was chosen Knight for the county of Tyrone. In 1720, he was appointed Commander in chief of a squadron of ships to cruize against the Sallee rovers, and also Plenipotentiary to treat of a peace with the Emperor of Morocco. He was afterwards advanced to be Vice-admiral of the White, in April 1736; ain February following, was elected Member in the British Parliament for Portsmouth, and died unmarried, Febr. 5, 1740-1.

6. James, Major to the train of Artillery, succeeded his brother Richard as Representative for the county of Tyrone, and died in 1747.

7. Mary, married first to Phineas Preston, of Ardsallagh, in Meath, Esq; and, secondly, to George, late Earl of Granard, and died Oct. 4, 1758.

8. Catharine, married to Arthur Davys, of Carrick-fergus, Esq; in the county of Antrim, by whom she had a daughter, married to George Lord Forbes, now Earl of Granard.

Creations.] Baronet, May 2, 1623, 21 Jam. I. Baron of Ramalton, in the county of Donegal, and Viscount of Montjoy, in the county of Tyrone, March 19, 1682, 35 Charles II. Earl of Blessinton, in the county of Wicklow, Dec. 7, 1745, 19 Geo. II.

Arms.] Ruby, a fess checque pearl and sapphire, between three lions rampant, topaz.

D 2 *Crest.*]

Crest.] On a wreath, a dexter arm, couped below the elbow, and erect, holding a heart, all proper.

Supporters.] On the dexter, a man armed cap a pie, garnished topaz, having on his cap three feathers, two pearl, the other ruby. On the sinister, a Queen in her royal vestments, ruby, girded topaz, and over all a mantle purpure, doubled ermine, her feet bare, hair disheveled, and ducally crowned, topaz.

Motto.] *Nil desperandum.*

Chief Seats.] At Newton-Stewart, in the county of Tyrone; and at Blessinton, in the county of Wicklow.

EARL of TYRONE.

GEORGE DE LA POER BERESFORD, Earl and Viscount of TYRONE, Baron Beresford, and Baronet, a Lord of the Privy-council, was born Jan. 8, 1735-6, and succeeded his father, Marcus, the first Earl, in April 1763.

Marcus, the late Earl, was born in July, 1694, succeeded Sir Tristram Beresford, his father, as Baronet, on June 16, 1701, and was created a Baron, Viscount, and Earl. He married, in 1717, the Lady Catharine Poer, daughter and heir of James, Earl of Tyrone, by whom he had issue seven sons and eight daughters, viz.

1. James; 2. Marcus; 3. Marcus; who all died infants.

4. George de la Poer, the present Earl.

5. John, born March 14, 1737-8, who married Anne-Constantia Ligonday, whose father was a French General, taken at the battle of Blen-

Blenheim with M. Tallard, who being brought prisoner to England, married the Countess dowager of Huntingdon, by whom he had a daughter, mother of the above Lady.

6. William-Hamilton, born May 8, 1739, and died the next year.

7. William, born in 1743, who married Elizabeth, second daughter of John Fitz-gibbon, Esq; Member for the borough of Newcastle.

8. Lady Anne, wife of William Annesley, of Clough, in the county of Downe, Esq; now Viscount Glerawley.

9. Lady Jane, wife of Edward Cary, of Dungarvan, Esq;

10. Lady Elizabeth, died young.

11. Lady Catharine, wife of Thomas Christmas, Esq; and secondly, of Theophilus Jones, Esq; and died March 28, 1760.

12. Lady Sophia, who died in Sept. 1740.

13. Lady Aramintha, wife of George-Paul Monck, Esq; Member for Coleraine.

14. Lady Frances-Maria, wife of Henry Flood, Esq; Member for Callan.

15. Lady Elizabeth, wife of Thomas Cobbe, Esq; Member for Swords.

Sir Tristram Beresford, the third Baronet, was attainted, May 7, 1689, by King James's Parliament, for maintaining the religion and liberties of his country against that Prince. He married Nichola-Sophia, youngest daughter and co-heir of Hugh Hamilton, Baron Glerawley, and had issue one son, the late Earl of Tyrone.

The family of Beresford, which were originally of Beresford, in the county of Stafford, have flourished for many centuries in that county, as well as in the counties of Derby, Nottingham, Kent, Lincoln, and the city of London. Thomas Beresford, of Newton-Grange, in Derbyshire, served in the French wars in the reign of King Henry the sixth, and is reported to have muftered a troop of horfe, of his fons and their fervants.

Triftram Beresford, the third fon of Michael, fon of his feventh fon Humphry, fettled at Coleraine, in the county of Londonderry, whofe fon Triftram, for his faithful fervices, was created a Baronet by King Charles II.

Creations.] Baronet, May 5, 1665, 17 Cha. II. Baron Beresford, of Beresford, in the county of Cavan, and Vifcount of the county of Tyrone, Nov. 4, 1720, 7 George I. Earl of the fame county, July 18, 1746, 20 Geo. II.

Arms.] Pearl, crufuly fitchy, three fleurs de lys, and a border ingrailed, diamond.

Creft.] On a wreath, a dragon's head erafed, fapphire, with a fpear broken through his neck, topaz, the point, pearl, thruft through his upper jaw.

Supporters.] Two angels proper, in filver veftments, with golden hair and wings, each holding in his exterior hand a fword erect, of the firft.

Motto.] *Tandem fit furculus arbor* ; or, *Nihil nifi cruce*, the motto of his mother's family.

Chief Seat.] At Curraghmore, in the county of Waterford.

EARL.

EARL of CARRICK.

SOMERSET-HAMILTON BUTLER, Earl of CARRICK, Viscount Ikerrin, and Baron Butler of Lismullen, a Lord of the Privy-council, was born on September 6, 1718, succeeded his brother, James, the seventh Viscount Ikerrin, who died at eight years of age, Oct. 20, 1721, and was advanced to the dignity of Earl of Carrick, by King George II. On May 18, 1745, his Lordship married Juliana, eldest daughter of Henry Boyle, afterwards created Earl of Shannon, by whom he has issue Henry-Thomas, Viscount Ikerrin, born May 19, 1746; James, born Aug. 5, 1747; Lady Margaret, born Jan. 23, 1748-9; Pierce, and Lady Henrietta, twins, born Aug. 15, 1750.

Thomas, the sixth Viscount Ikerrin, married Margaret, eldest of the two daughters and co-heirs of James Hamilton, of Bangor, in the county of Downe, Esq; by which Lady, who died in May 1743, he had two sons:

1. James, the late Viscount, who succeeded his father, March 7, 1719-20.
2. Somerset-Hamilton, the present Earl of Carrick.

This noble family is descended from John Butler, second son of Sir Edmund Butler, who was some time Earl of Carrick, and brother of James, the first Earl of Ormond; which John was of Clonamilchon, in the county of Tipperary, and died in 1330. From him descended Sir James, whose son, Sir Pierce Butler, was created Baron Lismullen, in the county of Tipperary, and Viscount Ikerrin.

D 4 *Creations.*]

Creations.] Baron Butler, of Lifmullen, in the county of Tipperary, May 5, 1607. 5 Jam. I. Vifcount Ikerrin, in the fame county, May 12, 1629, 5 Charles I. Earl of Carrick, June 10, 1748, 22 Geo. II.

Arms.] Firft and fourth, topaz, a chief indented, fapphire; fecond and third, ruby, a crefcent for difference.

Creft.] In a ducal coronet topaz, a plume of five oftrich feathers, and thence a falcon rifing, all pearl.

Supporters.] On the dexter fide, a falcon with wings expanded, pearl, beaked and membered, topaz: On the finifter, a male griffin as the dexter, his beak, rays, plain collar, and chain, topaz; each charged on the breaft with a crefcent.

Motto.] *Soyez ferme.*

Chief Seat.] At Ballylinch, in the county of Kilkenny.

EARL of MALTON.

An account of this noble family will be found in my Peerage of England, under the title of Marquis of ROCKINGHAM.

EARL of HILLSBOROUGH.

An account of this noble family, is given in my Peerage of England, under the title of Lord HARWICH.

EARL of UPPER-OSSORY.

John Fitz-Patrick, Earl of Upper-Ossory, and Baron of Gowran, in the county of Kilkenny, Knight of the fhire for the county of Bedford, was born in May, 1745, and fucceeded his father, John, the firſt Earl, in 1758.

John, the late Earl, fucceeded his father Richard, as Lord Gowran, June 9, 1727, was created Earl of Upper Offory; and in July 1744, married the Lady Evelyn, youngeſt daughter of John, Earl Gower; by which Lady, who remarried in Feb. 1759, with Richard Vernon, Eſq; Member of Parliament for the town of Bedford; he had iſſue,

1. John, the preſent Earl.
2. Richard, born Jan. 24, 1748-9.
3. ————, born May 5, 1755.
4. Lady Mary, wife of the Hon. Stephen Fox, eldeſt ſon and heir of Henry, Lord Holland.

This moſt antient and noble family is defcended from Heremon, the firſt Monarch of the Mileſian race in Ireland; and after they had aſſumed the firname of Fitz-Patrick, they were for many ages Kings of Offory, in the Province of Leinſter; from whom, in a direct male line, defcended

Bernard Fitz-Patrick, who was, by K. Henry the eighth, created Baron of Upper-Offory. His ſon and ſucceſſor, Barnaby Fitz-Patrick, was companion and favourite to King Edward the ſixth, as may appear by many kind letters ſtill extant, written by that young Monarch to the ſaid Sir Barnaby, in 1551, whilſt he ſerved as a volunteer in France, under Henry II. against the Emperor; after his return, he behaved with great bravery against Sir Thomas Wyat, and was knighted in 1558.

Florence, the brother of Sir Barnaby, was the third Baron; he had four sons; Thady, the fourth Baron, father of Bryan the fifth Baron, father of Bryan the sixth Baron, whose son Bryan, the seventh Baron, was out-lawed in 1691; and, in Nov. 1731, the title was resolved to be extinct.

John, the second son of Florence, was the father of Florence, who was the father of John, who married Elizabeth, sister of James, the first Duke of Ormond; and had two sons; 1. Edward, who was a Brigadier-general, but drowned in his passage from England to Ireland, Nov. 10, 1696, unmarried. 2. Richard; and a daughter, Arabella, married to Sir Thomas Wiseman, of East-Grinstead, in Sussex, Bart.

Richard, the second son, was created Lord Gowran, and, in his younger days, signalized himself by his valour and conduct in the Royal Navy, where he had a command; and, in 1718, married Anne, one of the two daughters and co-heirs of Sir John Robinson, of Farningwood, in the county of Northampton, Bart. by which Lady, who died Nov. 14, 1744, he had two sons,

1. John, the late Lord.
2. Richard, who married Anne, daughter of Mr. Usher, of London, by whom he has issue.

Creations.] Baron of Gowran, in the county of Kilkenny, April 27, 1715, 1 George I. Earl of of Upper-Offory, in the Queen's county, Oct. 5, 1751, 25 Geo. II.

Arms.] Diamond, a faltire pearl, on a chief sapphire, three fleurs de lys, topaz.

Crest] On a wreath, a dragon emerald, surmounted of a lion passant, diamond.

Supporters.] Two lions of the latter, their ducal crowns, plain collars, and chains, topaz.

Motto.] *Fortis sub forte fatiscet.*

Chief Seats.] At Tentore, in Queen's county; at Farningwood, in the county of Northampton; and Ampthill, in the county of Bedford.

EARL of SHELBURNE.

An account of this noble family may be seen in my Peerage of England, under the title of Lord WYCOMBE.

EARL of SHANNON.

RICHARD BOYLE, Earl of SHANNON, Viscount Bandon, and Baron of Castle-Martyr, a Lord of the Privy-council, Master-general of the Ordnance, LL. D. succeeded his father, Henry, the first Earl, in January, 1765, and the same year married Miss Ponsonby, eldest daughter of the Right Hon. John Ponsonby, Speaker of the House of Commons, in Ireland, by whom he has had one son, who died in his infancy.

Henry, the late Earl, married, first, Catharine, daughter of Chidley Coote, of Killester, Esq; by whom he had no issue; and she dying,

March 5, 1725, he married, secondly, in September 1726, the Lady Henrietta Boyle, youngest daughter of Charles, Earl of Cork; and by her, who died Dec. 13, 1746, had issue six sons and three daughters, whereof the eldest son died young; the other sons and daughters were,

1. Richard, the present Earl, born Jan. 30, 1727.
2. Henry Boyle Walsingham, an Officer in the Army.
3. William, who died April 30, 1740.
4. Charles, born in May, 1734.
5. Robert, born in March, 1736, now a Captain in the Navy, and Member for Fowey, in Cornwall, in the present British Parliament, and for the borough of Dungarvan, in that of Ireland.
6. Juliana, married, May 18, 1745, to Somerset-Hamilton, Earl of Carrick.
7. Mary, born in Aug. 1731, died April 11, 1740.
8. Jane, baptized Sept. 22, 1737, and died April 23, 1748.

His Lordship, in October 1715, was chosen Knight of the Shire for the county of Cork, which he represented till he was advanced to the Peerage: he was, April 13, 1733, sworn of his Majesty's Privy-council; and, on Oct. 5. following, was chosen Speaker of the House of Commons, which high office he discharged till he was made a Peer: on Nov. 19, the same year, he was appointed Chancellor of the Exchequer, which he resigned Nov. 6, 1735, for Commissioner of the Revenues; which resigning in March 1739, he reassumed, April 11, following,

following, his place of Chancellor of the Exchequer. On May 20, 1734, he was sworn one of the Lords Juftices of Ireland; a poft which he ever after filled, in the abfence of the Lord Lieutenant, till his death. On Mar. 20, 1756, he was created a Baron, Vifcount, and Earl.

This noble Lord is immediately defcended from the Earl of Orrery's family; for Roger, the firft Earl of Orrery, by Lady Margaret, daughter of Theophilus Howard, Earl of Suffolk, had two fons, Roger and Henry; the former fucceeded him; and the latter, being a Lieutenant-colonel, died in 1691, leaving iffue by the Lady Mary, daughter of Murrough Obryen, the firft Earl of Inchiquin, who afterwards married Admiral Dilkes, four fons and two daughters, viz.

1. Roger, who died in 1705, unmarried.
2. Henry, the late Earl of Shannon.
3. Charles, a Captain in the Army.
4. William, Captain in the Army, married to Mary Beaufoy, only daughter and heir of Sir Samuel Garth, M. D. by whom he had iffue, Henry, Captain of a troop of horfe; Robert; Beaufoy, wife of John Wilder, of Nunhide, Berks, Efq; Elizabeth, of Mr. Grave, of Serjeants-inn, London; and Henrietta, of Mr. Nicholas.
5. Elizabeth, married, in 1707, to Brettridge Baddham, of Rockfield, in the county of Cork, Efq;
6. Margaret, to Jofeph Dean, of the county of Meath, Efq; and died in 1717.

Creations.] Baron of Caftle-martyr, Vifcount Bandon, in the county of Cork, and Earl

Earl of Shannon, March 20, 1756, 30 George II.

Arms, Crest, Supporters, &c.] The same as the Earl of Cork and Orrery.

Chief Seat.] At Castle-martyr, in the county of Cork.

EARL of MASSAREENE.

CLOTWORTHY SKEFFINGTON, Earl and Viscount MASSAREENE, Baron of Lough-Neagh, and Baronet, succeeded his father Clotworthy, the third Viscount Massareene, on Feb. 11, 1738-9, was created an Earl, and on March 10, 1738, married Anne, eldest daughter of the Rev. Dr. Daniel, Dean of Downe, and by her Ladyship (who died March 24, 1740) having no issue, on Nov. 5, 1741, he married, secondly, Elizabeth, only daughter of Henry Eyre, of the county of Derby, Esq; by whom he has issue five sons and two daughters; Clotworthy, Viscount Massareene, born on Jan. 28, 1742; Henry; William-John; Chidly; Alexander; Ladies Elizabeth and Catharine.

Clotworthy, the third and late Viscount, married the Lady Catharine Chichester, eldest daughter of Arthur, Earl of Donegal; and by her, who died in July 1749, had five sons and two daughters, viz.

1. Clotworthy, the present Earl of Massareene.

2. Arthur, Knight of the Shire for the county of Antrim, and an Officer in the Army, died April 8, 1747, without issue.

3. John, Rector of Clonmarney, in the diocese of Derry.

4. Hun-

[63]

4. Hungerford, Member in the prefent Parliament for the town of Antrim.

5. Hugh, Knight of the Shire for the county of Antrim, and an Officer of Horfe.

6. Catharine, wife of Arthur-Mohun, Vifcount Doneraile, and died April 3, 1751.

7. Rachael, unmarried.

This antient and noble family derive their name from the village of Skeffington, in the county of Leicefter, of which place Simon Skeffington was Lord in the reign of Edward I. from him defcended Sir William Skeffington, Knt. made fo by King Henry VII. in whofe reign he was three times Sheriff of the counties of Leicefter and Warwick; in the twenty-fecond of Henry VIII. he was Mafter of the Ordnance in England, and Deputy of Ireland, when he vanquifhed the Tools and Bournes. From this Sir William defcended

Sir William Skeffington, of Fifherwick, in the county of Stafford, who was created a Baronet.

Sir John Skeffington, the fifth Baronet, was, in 1660, appointed one of the Commiffioners for fettling the affairs of Ireland. He married Mary, daughter and heir of Sir John Clotworthy, Vifcount Maffareene, and thereby became Baron of Lough-Neagh, and Vifcount Maffareene, both in the county of Antrim; the faid honours being fo limitted in reverfion, after the death of Sir John Clotworthy, without iffue male, who was fo created, Nov. 21, 1660.

Creations.] Baronet, May 8, 1627, 3 Charles I. Baron of Lough-Neagh, and Vifcount Maffareene, Nov. 21, 1660, 12 Charles II. and Earl of Maffareene, all in the county of Antrim, July 3, 1756; 30 George II.

Arms.]

Arms.] Pearl, three bulls heads erased, diamond, armed, topaz; a chevron ermine between three chaplets, topaz.

Crest.] On a wreath, a mermaid with her comb and mirror, all proper.

Supporters.] Two stags, diamond, attired and unguled topaz, each gorged with a chaplet of white roses, barbed, and seeded, proper.

Motto.] Par angusta ad augusta.

Chief Seats.] At the Castle of Antrim, in that county; and at Fisherwick, near Litchfield, in the county of Stafford.

EARL of LANESBOROUGH.

HUMPHRY BUTLER, Earl and Viscount of Lanesborough, and Baron of Newtown-Butler; Governor of the county of Cavan, and a Lord of the Privy Council, succeeded his father Brinsley, second Lord Newtown-Butler, and first Viscount Lanesborough, on March 6, 1735, and in May, 1726, married Mary, daughter and heir of Richard Berry, of Warden's-Town, in the county of West-meath, Esq; by whom he had issue one son, Brinsley, Lord Newtown, born March 4, 1728, Member for the county of Cavan, and Joint Clerk of the Pipe with his uncle; also a daughter, Anne, who died unmarried.

Brinsley, the late Viscount, succeeded his brother Theophilus, as Baron of Newtown-Butler, March 11, 1723-4; and was created Viscount Lanesborough, in the county of Longford. In the reign of Queen Anne, he was sworn Gentleman Usher of the Black Rod, July 9, 1711, and was Colonel of the Foot-guards

armed

armed with battle axes, who are to attend the Lord Lieutenant. He was Member of Parliament for the boroughs of Kells and Belturbet, from the firſt of Queen Anne till he became a Peer. In May 1726, he was ſworn one of the Privy Council to King George I. as he was to King George II. His Lordſhip was at the expence of gilding the iron balcony of St. Paul's Cathedral, in London.

He married Catharine, daughter and co-heir of Nevil Pooley, of Dublin, Eſq; by whom he had twenty-three children. Thoſe who ſurvived were,

1. Humphry, the preſent Earl of Laneſborough.

2. Thomas, who is Member of Parliament for Belturbet, ſucceeded his uncle as Adjutant General of the Army; and, in May 1744, was appointed one of the General Governors of the county of Limerick. He married Mary, eldeſt daughter and co-heir of Duncan Cummins, of Dublin, Eſq; and had one daughter, Mary.

3. Robert, who ſucceeded the preſent Earl as Captain of the Battle-axe-guards, in Dec. 1726; and alſo ſucceeded him as Member of Parliament for Belturbet. He married, Aug. 30, 1753, Anne, daughter of Dr. Robert Howard, late Biſhop of Elphin.

4. John, who was appointed Joint Clerk of the Pipe, June 7, 1735; and is Member of Parliament for Newcaſtle, in the county of Dublin.

5. Judith, married, April 23, 1724, to Balthazar-John Cramer, of Ballyfoile, in the county of Kilkenny, Eſq; and died May 13, 1749, leaving iſſue.

This noble family is deſcended from John Butler,

Butler, of the county of Huntington, Esq; living in the reign of Edward III. from whom descended Sir Stephen Butler, who settled at Belturbet, in Ireland, in the reign of King James I. being an Undertaker in the province of Ulster; whose son Francis bore arms in the service of King Charles I. and was Member of Parliament for Belturbet after the Restoration; but becoming obnoxious to King James II. he was involved in the Act of Attainder in 1689, and had his estate sequestered.

He was succeeded by his eldest son Theophilus, who, in 1704, was Member of Parliament for the county of Cavan. He was also Clerk of the Pells, and one of the Privy Council to King George I. by whom he was created Baron of Newtown-Butler, in the county of Fermanagh; and dying without issue, was succeeded by his brother, the late Viscount.

Creations.] Baron of Newtown-Butler, in the county of Fermanagh, Oct. 21, 1715, 2 George I. Viscount of Lanesborough, in the county of Longford, Aug. 12, 1728, 2 George II. Earl of Lanesborough, July 3, 1756, 30 George II.

Arms.] Pearl, three covered cups in bend, between two bendlets ingrailed, diamond.

Crest.] On a wreath, a demi-cockatrice couped, emerald, with wings erect; pearl, the comb, beak, wattles, and ducal collar, gold.

Supporters.] On the dexter, a cockatrice, emerald, furnished as the crest. On the sinister, a wyvern emerald, with a plain collar and chain topaz.

Motto.] *Liberte tout entiere.*

Chief Seat.] Newtown-Butler, in the county of Fermanagh.

EARL

EARL of CLANBRASSIL.

JAMES HAMILTON, Earl of CLANBRASSIL, Viscount Limerick, and Baron of Claneboy, Chief Remembrancer of the Court of Exchequer, and a Lord of the Privy Council, succeeded his father, James, the first Viscount Limerick, in 1752, and was created Earl of Clanbrassil.

James, the late Viscount, was raised to the Peerage by Geo. I. From 1732, his Lordship sat in the British Parliament as Representative for Wendover, Taviftock, Morpeth, &c. to the time of his death; and on March 21, 1733, he was appointed one of the Common Council of the province of Georgia. In 1742, he was Chairman of the Secret Committee, to enquire into the conduct of Robert Earl of Orford, for ten years, the Report of which Committee was printed. He was also a Privy Counsellor, and Governor of the county of Louth.

On Oct. 15, 1728, he married the Lady Henrietta Bentinck, third daughter of William, first Earl of Portland, by whom he had four sons and five daughters, viz.

1. James, the present Earl of Clanbrassil, born Aug. 13, 1729.

2, 3, and 4. Sons, died young.

5. Ann, wife of Robert Jocelyn, Esq; son of Robert Lord Newport, then Lord Chancellor of Ireland, Dec. 11, 1752.

6. Lady Caroline.

7, 8, and 9, three daughters, who died young.

Sir John Hamilton, of Kedſaw, had three ſons; 1. Sir James, anceſtor to the Duke of Hamilton. 2. David. 3. Thomas, from which laſt deſcended Hans Hamilton, of Dunlop, in Scotland, Eſq; who had ſix ſons, who left Scotland in the time of King James I. and ſettling in Ireland, Sir James was, by that King, created Viſcount Claneboy, and his ſon James, who ſucceeded him, Earl of Clanbraſſil, whoſe ſon Henry, the ſecond Earl, dying, on Jan. 12, 1675, without iſſue, the titles became extinct.

James Hamilton, of Tullimore, Eſq; had four ſons; James, the eldeſt, had two ſons, James and Jocelyn; which laſt died unmarried; and a daughter, Chriſtian, married to James Hamilton, of Carrisfort, Eſq. James, the eldeſt, was a great aſſertor of the liberty of his country in 1689, for which he was attainted by King James's Parliament, and had his eſtate ſequeſtered: but the Revolution being happily effected, he was elected Member of Parliament for Bangor. In 1693, he was ſent over from Ireland with the Earl of Bellamont, to proſecute Thomas Lord Coningſby, and Sir Charles Porter, and preſented articles of impeachment againſt them to the Houſe of Commons. In 1699, he was one of the Commiſſioners appointed to enquire into the forfeited eſtates in Ireland; and marrying Ann, youngeſt daughter of John Mordaunt, Baron of Ryegate, Viſcount Avalon, and ſiſter of Charles Earl of Peterborough and Monmouth, by her he had two ſons and three daughters, viz.

1. James, the late Viſcount Limerick.
2. Jocelyn, killed in a duel, unmarried.
3. Sophia,

3. Sophia, married to Frederick Hamilton, Esq; eldest son of Gustavus, Viscount Boyne, and was mother of Gustavus, the late Viscount.

4. Cary-Eleanora, who died unmarried, in 1725.

5. Elizabeth, married to Thomas Fortescue, of Randalstown, in the county of Louth, Esq;

Creations.] Baron of Claneboy, in the county of Downe, and Viscount of the city of Limerick, May 13, 1719, 5 Geo. I. Earl of Clanbrassil, in the county of Armagh, Nov. 13, 1756, 29 Geo. II.

Arms.] Ruby, three cinquefoils pearl, on a chief topaz a lion passant, guardant, of the first, holding in his dexter paw a cheval-trap, sapphire.

Crest.] On a wreath, a demi antelope, pearl, horned topaz, supporting a heart, proper.

Supporters.] On the dexter side a lion ruby, gorged with a double tressure, flory and counter-flory, with fleurs de lys topaz. On the sinister, an antelope pearl, horned of the second, and gorged with the like tressure, ruby.

Motto.] *Qualis ab incepto.*

Chief Seats.] Dundalk, in the county of Louth; Tullimore, in the county of Downe; and Egham, in the county of Surry.

EARL of BELVEDERE.

Robert Rochfort, Earl of Belvedere, Viscount and Baron of Bellfield, Muster-master General of the forces in Ireland, and a Lord of the Privy Council, was born March 26, 1708, and was created Earl of Belvedere, Viscount and Baron of Bellfield. On Dec. 16, 1731, his Lordship

Lordship married, first, Elizabeth, eldest daughter of Richard Tenison, of Thomastown, in the county of Lowth, Esq; Commissioner of the Revenue, who died June 5, 1732, without issue; and his Lordship married, secondly, on Aug. 7, 1736, Mary, eldest daughter of Richard Viscount Molesworth, by whom he has issue three sons and one daughter, viz.

1. George, Viscount Bellfield, Member for the county of West-meath, born Oct. 12, 1738.
2. Richard, born Dec. 2, 1739.
3. Robert, Member for Philipstown, born in 1743.
4. Lady Jane, born on Oct. 30, 1737.

This antient family of Rochford, formerly stiled in their writings, *De Rupe forti*, were settled in Ireland in 1243; and in 1302, Sir Maurice Rochfort was Lord Justice of Ireland. In 1309, lived Sir Milo de Rochfort, whose second son Sir William had a son Edmund, who was father of Sir John, whose son John was seated at Kilbryde, in the county of Meath.

His son and successor Thomas, had two sons, Robert his heir, and Roger Lord of Kelladown. From the said Robert descended Robert Rochfort, who, June 6, 1695, was made Attorney-General to King William; and at the meeting of the Parliament the same year, was chosen Speaker of the House of Commons. In 1707, he was appointed Chief Baron of the Exchequer, in which post he continued till her Majesty's death: he had two sons, George his heir; and John, chosen Member of Parliament for the manor of Mullengar.

George was appointed Chief Chamberlain to the Court of Exchequer, which he held till his

his death, July 8, 1730. He represented the county of West-meath in Parliament, and was of the Privy-council. In 1704 he married the Lady Elizabeth Moore, youngest daughter of Henry, Earl of Drogheda, by whom he had issue five sons and six daughters, viz.

1. Robert, Earl of Belvedere.
2. Arthur, Member of Parliament for West-meath, who left issue.
3. George, Barrister at Law, who had three daughters.
4. John, who died young.
5. William, who had three sons, and four daughters.
6. Mary, married to Sir Henry Tuite, of Sonagh, in the county of West-meath, Bart.
7. Hannah; and 8. Elizabeth, who both died young.
9. Alice, married to Thomas Loftus, Esq; Member of Parliament for Clomines, and died July 13, 1748.
10. Thomasine, married to Gustavus Lambart, Esq; Member of Parliament for Kilbeggan.
11. Anne, married to Henry Lyons, Esq; Representative in Parliament for King's county.

Creations.] Baron of Bellfield, in the county of West-meath, March 16, 1737, 11 Geo. II. Viscount of the same place, Oct. 5, 1751, 25 Geo. II. Earl of Belvedere, in the county of West-meath, Nov. 13, 1756, 30 Geo. II.

Arms.] Sapphire, a lion rampant pearl, armed and langued, ruby.

Crest.] On a wreath, a robin-red-breast, proper.

Supporters.] Two stags proper, gorged with ducal coronets and chains reflexing over their backs, topaz.
Motto.] *Candor dat viribus alas.*
Chief Seat.] At Gaulstown, in the county of West-meath.

EARL of THOMOND.

The descent of this noble Lord will be seen in my English Peerage, under the title of Earl of EGREMONT; and under the title of Earl of INCHIQUIN, it is recited, that Henry, the last Earl of Thomond, left his estate to his nephew, Percy Wyndham, Esq; upon his taking the arms and firname of Obryen.

On Nov. 29, 1756, his Lordship was created Baron of Ibrackan, and Earl of Thomond. He is a Lord of the Privy-council, Lord Lieutenant, and Custos Rotulorum of the county of Somerset, and Member in the present Parliament for Minehead, in that county. His Lordship is a bachelor.

Titles.] Percy-Wyndham Obryen, Earl of Thomond, and Lord Ibrackan.
Creations.] *Ut supra.*
Arms.] Ruby, three lions passant-guardant, in pale, party per pale, topaz and pearl.
Crest.] On a wreath, a naked dexter arm, issuing from a cloud, brandishing a sword, all proper.
Supporters.] Two lions guardant, party per fess, topaz and pearl.
Motto.] *Vigueur du dessus.*
Chief Seat.] Shotgrove, in the county of Essex.

[73]

EARL of WANDESFORD.

John Wandesford, Earl and Baron of Wandesford, Viscount Castlecomer, and Baronet, succeeded his father George, the fourth Viscount Castlecomer, on June 25, 1751, and was created Earl of Wandesford. On Aug. 11, 1750, his Lordship married Agnes-Elizabeth, daughter and heir of John Southwell, of Enniscouch, in the county of Limerick, Esq; by whom he has issue John, Viscount Castlecomer, born April 23, 1753; and Lady ———, born in June, 1754.

George, the late and fourth Viscount Castlecomer, married Susanna, daughter of the Rev. Mr. Griffith, of the county of Cork; by which Lady, who died June 27, 1756, he had seven children, of whom three only survived him, viz.

1. John, the present Earl of Wandesford.
2. Susanna, married, Aug. 12, 1750, to Thomas Newenham, of Coolmore, in the county of Cork, Esq; who, in Oct. 1751, was chosen Representative for the city of Cork.
3. Elizabeth.

Of this family, which hath been long seated at Kirklington, in the county of York, was Geoffrey Wandesford, of Alnwick, who had a son Geoffrey, whose son, John Wandesford, of Westwick and Kirklington, dying in 1395, left three sons; from John, the eldest of which sons, descended, in a direct male line, Christopher, who, on May 17, 1633, was made Master of the Rolls in Ireland, a

E Privy-

Privy-counsellor, and one of the Lords Justices; also, in 1639 and 40, Lord Deputy, in which laſt year he died.

His eldeſt ſon, George, ſucceeded him, and ſuffered greatly in the rebellion of 1641. He died without iſſue, and was ſucceeded by his brother,

Sir Chriſtopher, who was created a Baronet, and, in 1681, was Member of Parliament for Rippon.

Chriſtopher, his eldeſt ſon, ſucceeded him, and was the ſecond Baronet. In 1704 he was choſen Member of Parliament for the borough of Kennis, alias Iriſh-town, was one of the Privy-council in Ireland, and was created Baron Wandesford, and Viſcount Caſtlecomer, in the county of Kilkenny.

Creations.] Baronet, Aug. 5, 1643, 14 Cha. II. Baron Wandesford and Viſcount Caſtlecomer, in the county of Kilkenny, March 15, 1706, 6 Anne; Earl of Wandesford, Aug. 5, 1758, 31 George II.

Arms.] Topaz, a lion rampant, ſapphire.

Creſt.] On a wreath, a church proper, ſlated ſapphire.

Supporters.] On the dexter ſide, a lion double queüe, ſapphire; on the ſiniſter, a griffon, topaz.

Motto.] *Tout pour l'Egliſe.*

Chief Seat.] At Kirklington, in the North-riding of Yorkſhire.

BIRMINGHAM, COUNTESS of BRANDON.

This noble Lady was eldeſt daughter of James Agar, of Gowran, Eſq; by Mary his wife, daughter of Sir Henry Wemyſs, and was relict, firſt, of Theobald, Viſcount Mayo, and, ſecondly, of Francis, late Lord Athenry, (ſee Earl of Louth,) but without iſſue by either. On Aug. 4, 1758, her Ladyſhip was created Counteſs of Brandon, in the county of Kilkenny, with remainder to the heirs male of her body; but her Ladyſhip has no iſſue.

Titles.] Ellis Birmingham, Counteſs of Brandon.

EARL of LOUTH.

THOMAS BIRMINGHAM, Earl of LOUTH, Baron of Athenry, premier Baron of Ireland, a Lord of the Privy-council, ſucceeded his father, Francis, the late and twenty-firſt Lord Athenry, March 4, 1749-50, and was created Earl of Louth in the year 1759. His Lordſhip married, firſt, Jane, eldeſt daughter of Sir John Bingham, of Caſtlebar, Bart. and ſhe deceaſing Sept. 11, 1746, he married, ſecondly, Jan. 10, 1750, Margaretta, youngeſt daughter and coheir of Peter Daly, Eſq; Counſellor at Law, by whom he has had iſſue two ſons, who died in their infancy, a daughter ſtillborn, and four daughters now living, viz. Ladies Elizabeth-Mary, Louiſa-Catharine, Mary, and Mathilda-Dorothea-Margaretta.

Francis,

Francis, the late Baron of Athenry, born in 1692, succeeded his father Edward in May 1709; and conforming to the established church, the next month, took his seat in parliament in 1713. He married in 1716, to his first wife, the Lady Mary Nugent, eldest daughter of Thomas, the fourth Earl of Westmeath, by whom he had issue three sons and four daughters, viz.

1. Thomas, the present Earl of Louth.
2. John, Captain of a sloop of war, killed in fight, with a French privateer in 1745.
3. Edward, Lieutenant of a company of foot, who died in 1743.
4. Bridget, the first wife of James O'Daly, of Carrownekelly, in the county of Galway, Esq; and died Feb. 2, 1733, without issue.
5. Margaret, married in Dec. 1741, to Gregory Byrne, of Byrnes-Grove, in the county of Kilkenny, Esq; without issue.
6. Mary, married, in Oct. 1748, to Edmond Costello, Esq; Counsellor at Law, and had two sons and a daughter.
7. Catharine, married, July 1, 1750, to Patrick Wemys, of Danesfort, Esq; Knight of the shire for the county of Kilkenny.

His Lordship married, 2dly, Aug. 17, 1745, Ellis, eldest daughter of James Agar, of Gowran, Esq; widow of Theobald, Viscount Mayo, by which Lady, who, in Aug. 1758, was created Countess of Brandon, he had no issue. (See the foregoing title.)

Edward, the twentieth Lord, married first the Lady Mary Burke, youngest daughter of Richard the sixth Earl of Clanrickard, and widow of Sir John Burke, of Derrymaclaghtny, and by her had two daughters, who died young.

He

He married, secondly, Bridget, eldest daughter of Colonel John Brown, of West-Port, in the county of Mayo, and had three sons, Francis, the late Lord, John, and Richard, who both died young; and two daughters, Bridget, married to George Brown, of the Neal, in Mayo, Esq; and Maud, who died an infant.

Francis, the nineteenth Lord, and grandfather of the late Lord, took up arms for King Charles I. whose right he maintained in Ireland till the battle of Worcester, when King Charles II. desired him to submit to the prevailing powers, who excepted him from life and estate: however, he survived those troubles.

Of this antient and noble family, which are of English extraction, and took their name from the town of Birmingham, in the county of Warwick, was Peter de Birmingham, who was Steward to Gervase Paganell, Baron of Sudley, of whom he held no less than nine Knights fees, of which he was enfeoffed in the reign of Henry I. and William, son of the said Peter, was possessed of the town of Birmingham, in the reign of Henry II. which continued in that family till the reign of Hen. VIII. About the year 1170, Robert de Birmingham attending Richard Strongbow, Earl of Pembroke, in his expedition into Ireland, he had large possessions given him by that Earl; and from him descended Peter, who was summoned to Parliament in the reign of Henry III. In that reign the Irish, in general, rebelled, when eleven thousand of them were slain in Connaught, by the Bourks and Birminghams. Peter, the third Lord, was, in 1299, summoned to attend Edward I. as a Baron of the realm by tenure, with his horse and arms, in his array for war against the Scots; and his second son, John de Birmingham, was Commander in chief of the English forces in Ireland, employed against Edward Bruce, brother to the King of Scots, who was crowned King of a great part of Ireland: but the said Sir John Birmingham routed him at Dundalk, took him prisoner, cut off his head, and sent it to King Edward, who, for his valour, created him Lord Athenry, and Earl of Louth, which last title expired with him.

Creations.] Baron, originally by Tenure, temp. Hen. II. and since by continued Writs of Summons to Parliament; Earl of Louth, April 23, 1759, 33 George II.

Arms.] Party per pale, indented, topaz and ruby.

Crest.] On a wreath, an antelope's head, couped, pearl, attired, topaz.

Supporters.] Two antelopes, pearl, their horns, plain collars, chains, and hoofs, topaz.

Motto.] None.

Chief Seat.] Turlovaughan, in the county of Galway.

EARL of FIFE.

JAMES DUFF, Earl of FIFE, Viscount Macduff, and Baron Braco, of Kilbride, in the county of Cavan, Member in the British Parliament for the shire of Banff, succeeded his father, William, the late and first Earl, in 1766, and married Lady Dorothea Sinclair, only daughter of Alexander, the ninth Earl of Caithness, by Lady Margaret Primrose, his wife, daughter of Archibald, Earl of Roseberry.

There

There are several considerable families in Scotland who claim their descent from the great and antient Macduffs, Thanes and Earls of Fife, of which this family is one; and the rise and descent of that illustrious house is fully set forth in all books of the history of families in Scotland. Mr. Lodge, in his Peerage of Ireland, gives it as the opinion of Scots writers, that the family of Duff derive their origin from Macduff, Thane of Fife. And it is beyond doubt, that Duncan, the eleventh Earl of Fife, who was killed at the battle of Falkirk, anno 1248, had a younger son Malcolm, who married a daughter of Duncan, Thane of Calder, by whom he got a considerable estate in the counties of Aberdeen and Banff, where he settled, and was progenitor of the Duffs.

The family of Fife are descended of the Strathbolgies, Earls of Athole, who for several generations lived in the north parts of Scotland. They were distinguished by the appellation of Strathbolgie, from the place of their residence, and were undoubtedly descended of David, son of Duncan, the sixth Earl of Fife, as is fully set forth in the books of Heraldry in Scotland, under the title of the Earl of Athole.

David de Strathbolgie, the eleventh Earl of Athole (the fifth generation from Duncan, Earl of Fife) married Jean, eldest daughter and coheir of John Cumin, Lord of Badenoch, by whom he got a considerable accession to his estate in the North, and by her had several sons. He was killed at the battle of Kilblane, anno 1335, and was succeeded by his eldest son,

David

Davide de Strathbolgie, twelfth Earl of Athole, who turned an enemy to his country, joined the English, and adhered to their interest ever after, for which he was forfeited, and died in England without male succession, in October 1375.

The younger brothers of this last Earl set led in the north of Scotland, and after their brother's forfeiture, were obliged to quit the appellation of Strathbolgie, and assumed that of Duff, to denote their descent from the great and antient Macduffs, Earls of Fife, of which there are many proofs in the histories of Scots writers, particularly in Sir Robert Douglass's late History of the Peerage of that kingdom, well authenticated.

Along with the great estate of Strathbolgie, now called Huntly, this family had the lands and estate of Muldavit and Baldavie, in Banffshire. They lie contiguous to the great estate of the family of Athole, of old called Strathbolgie, and were long their property; for Muldavit, Craighead, &c. were given off to a younger son of the Earl of Athole before the forfeiture, afterwards calling themselves Duffs. And soon after,

1. David Duff, of whom the Earl of Fife is lineally descended, was proprietor of the lands and Barony of Muldavit and Baldavie, in the county of Banff, and were designed by that title in the reign of King Robert II. of Scots, which is confirmed to them by a Charter under the Great Seal of that Prince, to and in favour of David Duff, and Mary Chalmers, his spouse, of the lands of Muldavit and Baldavie, dated February 3, 1404. By the above Charter,

ter, which is upon record, and the principal in the cuſtody of the family, it appears that the progenitors of them were poſſeſſed of a great eſtate, holden of the Crown in the reign of King Robert III. And beſides thoſe of Muldavit and Baldavie, they were proprietors of the lands of Craighead, Auchingre, Darbreich, Findachlyfield, and others; and this Barony of Muldavit continued to be one of the chief titles of their family till they ſold the eſtate, in the beginning of the reign of King Charles I. All which is inſtructed by inconteſtible documents upon record. David de Muldavit had a ſon and ſucceſſor,

II. John Duff, of Muldavit and Craighead, who flouriſhed in the reign of James I. of Scots.

III. John Duff, of Muldavit and Craighead, obtains a Charter under the Great Seal, from King James II. upon his father's reſignation.

IV. John Duff ſucceeded him, who, after his father's death, got his eſtate confirmed to him by James III. April 13, 1482.

V. Andrew Duff, his ſon, ſucceeded his father anno 1500. He obtained from James IV. a Charter of confirmation of the lands of Muldavit, Craighead, and others. 1504. He married Helen, grandchild of John Hay, Lord of the Foreſt Aboyne, Enzie, and Tullybovel, afterwards built an iſle in the church of Cullen, called to this day the Duff's iſle, and mortified certain lands to the ſupport of it. This Andrew Duff, of Muldavit left two ſons, Sir George, his heir; and John, who died unmarried.

VI. Sir George Duff, who was bred to the church, and got conſiderable benefices. He acquired alſo the lands of Caſtlefield, and others, as appears by a Charter under the Great Seal, dated July 10, 1515, in the public records. Sir George Duff died 1519, and was succeeded by his eldest son,

VII. John Duff, of Muldavit, Craighead, and Castlefield, and who, by a Precept from the Chancery in Scotland, was enfeoft in those lands, as heir to his father, on May 16, 1520. He left two sons; 1. George, afterwards Sir George; 2. John, who succeeded Sir George.

VIII. Sir George Duff, of Muldavit, never married, but he resigned the estate in favour of his brother,

IX. John Duff, of Muldavit, brother of Sir George Duff, who upon his, Sir George's, resignation, obtained a Charter under the Great Seal, from Mary, Queen of Scots, of the lands of Muldavit, and others, dated 26 November, 1550. This John died anno 1580, and was succeeded by

X. John Duff, of Muldavit and Craighead, who got a Charter under the Great Seal, upon his father's resignation, July 10, 1575, upon the lands of Muldavit, Craighead, and others. He made a resignation of those lands into the King's hands in favour of himself, upon which he got a Charter under the Great Seal, 24 February, 1610, who, with consent of Mrs. Agnes Gordon, a daughter of the family of Abergaldie, and John Duff, their eldest son, sold the estate to Hay, of Rannas, in the year 1626, and died 1627, leaving, by the said Mrs Agnes Gordon, a son,

XI. The said John Duff, of Muldavit, who got a Precept from the Chancery of Scotland, proceeding upon a retour of his service as heir to his father, 9 Nov. 1627.

XII.

XII. John Duff, his only son, designed in the publick archives, *Mercatori Burg &c. Burgi de Aberdeen*; and had the lands of Boighall. He died in the reign of King Charles II. and left,

XIII. Adam Duff, de Cluniebeg, who was fined in great sums, 1646, by the Covenanters in Scotland, on account of his loyalty and attachment to the interest of the Royal Family. He married Beatrix, daughter of Gordon of Cairnborrow, and had children; 1. Alexander, his heir; 2. John, ancestor of the Duffs of Cursendac; 3. William, progenitor of the Duffs of Cummin and Crombie; 4. ———, died abroad; 5. ———; 6. ——— died unmarried. Adam Duff, of Cluniebeg, died in April 1674, and was succeeded by his eldest son,

XIV. Alexander Duff, of Keithmore, whose armorial bearing is recorded in the Herald Office anno 1676, according to the Lord Lyon's Certificate, which is in these words: " I tes- " tify and make known, that the Coat armour " appertaining and belonging to Alexander " Duff, of Keithmore, lineally descended of " the family of Muldavit and Craighead, and " approven of and confirmed by me, Sir " Charles Erskine, of Cambo, Baronet, Lord " Lyon King at Arms, to him, is of this date " matriculated in my public Register." He married Helen, daughter of Alexander Grant, of Allachie, brother of Archibald Grant, of Bellintomb, ancestor of Sir Archibald Grant, of Monymusk, Bart. by whom he had three sons, and three daughters: 1. Alexander, his heir, afterwards of Braco; 2. William de Dipple, afterwards of Braco, the Earl of Fife's grandfather; 3. Patrick Duff, of Craigstown.

xv. Alexander Duff, of Braco, who was a Commissioner in Parliament, married Margaret, daughter of Sir William Gordon, of Lesmore, Baronet, by whom he had a son, and three daughters.

xvi. William Duff, of Braco, who married Mrs. Duff, Lady Braco, by whom he had one daughter, married to Patrick Duff, of Premna, Esq; Commissary of Aberdeen. He dying without male issue; the representation devolved upon his uncle, William Duff, of Dipple, before mentioned. Which

William Duff, of Dipple, second son of Alexander, of Keithmore, heir male, succeeded; he married Helen Gordon, daughter of Sir George Gordon, of Edinglassie, by whom he had William, afterwards Lord Braco, and Earl of Fife, and four daughters.

William, Lord Braco, was chosen a Commissioner to the British Parliament for the county of Banff, anno 1727, and, like a true Patriot, always adhered to the interest of his country; but afterwards preferring a private to a public life, declined being elected to the next Parliament. He was created a Peer of Ireland by the title of Lord Braco, of Kilbride, by patent, to the heirs male of his body, dated July 28, 1735. He was created Earl of Fife, Viscount Macduff, by patent, 26 April, 1759, of the said kingdom. He married, first, Lady Janet Ogilvie, daughter of James, Earl of Findlater and Seafield, by whom he had no children. He married, secondly, Jean, daughter of Sir James Grant, of Grant, Bart. by whom he had issue seven sons and seven daughters.

1. William, who died unmarried, aged twenty-seven years.

2. James,

2. James, now Earl of Fife.
3. The Hon. Alexander Duff, Esq; Advocate.
4. Patrick, who died young.
5. The Hon. George Duff, Esq; married to Miss Dalziel, a daughter of General Dalziel.
6. The Hon. Ludovick Duff, Esq; a Captain in the eighth regiment, married to Miss Davis, daughter of —— Davis, Esq;
7. The Hon. Arthur Duff, Advocate.
1. Daughter, Lady Anne, married to Alexander Duff, of Halton, Esq;
2. Lady Janet, married, first, to Sir William Gordon, of Park, Baronet; secondly, to George Hay, Esq; of Montblainy.
3. Lady Jean, married to Keith Urquhart, Esq; of Meldrum, Advocate, his Majesty's Sheriff of Banffshire.
4. Lady Helen, married to Robert Duff, Esq; of Cultore, a Captain of the Royal Navy.
5. Lady Sophia Henrietta, unmarried.
6. Lady Catharine, died unmarried.
7. Lady Margaret, married to James Brodie, of Brodie, Esq;

He died anno 1763, and was succeeded by his eldest son surviving, James, now Earl of Fife.

A ms.] Quarterly, first and fourth, or, a lion rampant, gules, armed and langued, azure, for Viscount Macduff, and Earl of Fife. Second and third, Vert, a fess dancette, ermine, betwixt a hart's head cabossed in chief, and two e'calops in base, or, for Duff of Braco, as representing Duff, of Muldavit, commonly called Craighead. Above the shield his Crown, over the same an helmet befitting his quality, mantled gules, doubled ermine; and on a wreath of his colours is set for CREST, A demi lion, gules, holding in the dexter hand a broad sword,

sword erected in pale, proper, hilted and pomelled, or ; SUPPORTED by two savages, standing upon a copartment below, wreathed about the head and middle with laurel, holding branches of trees in their hands. all proper. In an escroll above the Crest this MOTTO, *Deus juvit*; and on the copartment below, *Virtute et opera*.

Chief Seats.] Duff-house, in the county of Banff; Balreny-castle, and Rothiemay, in the same county; Mar-Lodge, in Aberdeenshire; and Innes, in the county of Murray; Whitehall, London.

EARL of MORNINGTON.

GARRET COLLEY-WESLEY, Earl and Baron of MORNINGTON, and Viscount Wesley, M. D. Professor of Music in Trinity-college, Dublin, was born July 19. 1735, and succeeded his father Richard, the first Lord Mornington, in 758. He was created Earl of Mornington, and Viscount Wesley, in 1760. His Lordship married ———, daughter of the Right hon. Arthur Hill, a Commissioner of the Revenue, in Feb. 1759.

This noble family derives its origin from the county of Rutland, whence they removed to Ireland in the reign of Henry VIII. when, in the twenty-ninth of that reign, Walter Colley was Solicitor-general of Ireland. Sir Henry, his son, who was of Castle Carbery, had a commission in the army of Queen Elizabeth, and served in Parliament for the borough of Thomastown. He was father of Henry, whose son Sir Henry was succeeded by his son Sir Dudley, who, in the first Parliament after the Restoration, was Member for Philipstown. He married

ried Anne, daughter of Sir Henry Warren, of Grangebegg, in the county of Kildare, Efq; by whom he had eight fons and feven daughters, of whom Elizabeth married Garret Wefley, of Dangan, in the county of Meath, Efq; whofe fon Garret, leaving no iffue, devifed his real eftate to Richard Colley, Efq; and his heirs male, provided they ufe the furname and arms of Wefley. The faid Dudley married to his fecond wife Elizabeth, widow of Henry Ballard, of Dublin, Efq; daughter of George Sankey, of Balenrath, in King's county, Efq; by whom he had three daughters, and was fucceeded by his eldeft fon,

Henry, of Caftle-Carbery, who married Mary, only daughter of Sir William Ufher, of Dublin, Knt. and died in 1700, having had five fons and fix daughters; of the daughters, Anne, the eldeft, married William Pole, of Balyfin, in Queen's county, Efq; Of the fons, William, Blayney, and George, died young. Henry, the fourth, was Member of Parliament for Strabane, and married the Lady Mary Hamilton, daughter of James, Earl of Abercorn, and had a fon, Henry, who died young, and three daughters, of whom Mary, the youngeft, was married, in Oct. 1747, to Arthur Pomeroy, Efq;

Richard, the youngeft, who took the furname of Wefley, as heir to his firft coufin before mentioned, was fecond Chamberlain in the court of Exchequer in 1713, was Sheriff of the county of Meath in 1734, and reprefented the borough of Trim in Parliament, till he was created a Peer, by King George II. He married, Dec. 23, 1719, Elizabeth, eldeft daughter of John Sale, Efq; Member for the borough of Carysfort; and by her, who died in June 1738,

had

had three fons and four daughters. Thofe who lived to maturity were Garret, the prefent Earl of Mornington, Elizabeth, married, April 9, 1743, to Chichefter Fortefcue, of Dromifken, in the county of Louth, Efq; and died in Oct. 1752; and Frances, married, Aug. 5, 1750, to William Francis Crofbie, of Ballyheigh, in the county of Kerry, Efq;

Creations] Baron Mornington, in the county of Meath, July 9, 1746, 20 Geo. II. Vifcount and Earl, Aug. 25, 1760, 34 Geo. II.

Arms.] Quarterly, 1ft and 4th, ruby, a crofs, pearl, between four faltires of plates, for Wefley; 2d and 3d, topaz, a lion rampant, ruby, gorged with a ducal coronet, proper, for Colley.

Creft.] On a wreath, an armed arm in pale, couped below the elbow; the hand proper, the wrift encircled with a ducal coronet, topaz, holding a fpear in bend, with the banner of St. George appendant.

Supporters.] Two game cocks, ginger, trimmed, proper.

Motto.] *Unica Virtus neceffaria.*

Chief Seat.] Dangan, in the county of Meath.

EARL of LUDLOW.

PETER LUDLOW, Earl of LUDLOW, Vifcount Prefton, and Baron Ludlow, of Ardfalla, in the county of Meath, was created a Baron, Nov. 18, 1755; Vifcount and Earl, Aug. 26, 1760; and in June 1753, married Lady Frances, eldeft daughter of Thomas Lumley Saunderfon, Earl of Scarborough, by whom he has iffue two fons, and a daughter.

Titles.] As above.
Creations.] As above.

Arms.]

Arms.]
Crest.]
Supporters.]
Motto.]
Chief Seat.]

EARL of TYRCONNEL.

GEORGE CARPENTER, Earl of TYRCONNEL, Viscount Carlingford, and Baron Carpenter, of Killaghy, in the county of Kilkenny, was born June 30, 1750, and succeeded his father, George the late and first Earl, in 1764. His Lordship is in his minority.

George, the late Earl, was Member in the British Parliament for Taunton, in Somersetshire, born Aug. 26, 1723, succeeded his father George, the second Lord Carpenter, July 12, 1749; and in March, 1747-8, married Frances, daughter and heir of Sir Robert Clifton, Bart. by the Lady Frances Coote, only child of Nanfan, Earl of Bellamont, and had issue Frances, born April 1, 1749, who died in May, 1750; George, born June 30, 1750; a daughter, born March 20, 1752; a daughter, born Aug. 15, 1753; and a son, born Jan. 3, 1757.

George, the second Baron Carpenter, succeeded his father George, the first Lord, Feb. 10, 1731; was Member of Parliament for Weobly, in Herefordshire, and Lieutenant-colonel in the first troop of horse-guards. He married Elizabeth, only daughter of David Petty, an eminent citizen of London, by whom he had the late Earl, and one daughter, Alicia Maria, born Dec. 4, 1729, married to Charles, Earl of Egremont, and since to Count Bruhl, a Saxon Nobleman.

This

This ancient and noble family is of great antiquity in the county of Hereford, and have been lords of the manor of Home, in the parish of Delwyn, near Weobly, for above three hundred years. George, the first Lord Carpenter, was the third son of Mr. Warncomb Carpenter, who was the sixth and youngest son of Thomas Carpenter, of the Home, Esq; This Thomas, dying in 1653, was succeeded in the manor of the Home, by his eldest son Richard, whose grandson Thomas, being the last of the eldest branch of the family, dying without issue in 1732, left the said manor of the Home to the said Lord Carpenter, who, from a private gentleman in the third troop of horse guards, rose gradually to the post of Lieutenant-colonel of horse, and then purchased the regiment, which he commanded till his death. He served in all the wars of Ireland and Flanders, the war of Spain, with great honour and reputation; and distinguished himself by his extraordinary courage, conduct, and humanity. He commanded the rear, and brought off the last retreat, at the battle of Almanza. At the battle of Almenara he was wounded, and received the compliments of Charles then King of Spain, and late Emperor of Germany, for his conduct in the engagement. He was again desperately wounded in defending the breach at Brihuega in Spain. In 1715, he obliged the rebels to surrender at Preston; and being chosen that year Member of Parliament for Whitchurch, in Hampshire, was appointed Envoy extraordinary and Plenipotentiary to the Court of Vienna. In 1716 he was made Governor of Minorca

Minorca and Port Mahon; Colonel of a regiment of dragoons, and General and Commander in chief of all his Majesty's forces in North Britain; and in 1722 was elected Member of Parliament for the city of Westminster. He married Alice, daughter of the Lord Charlemount, by whom he left issue only one son, the second Lord.

Creations.] Baron, May 29, 1719, 5 Geo. I. Viscount and Earl, May 28, 1761. 1 Geo. III.

Arms.] Pally of six, pearl and ruby, on a chevron, sapphire, three cross croslets, topaz.

Crest.] On a wreath, a globe in a frame, all topaz.

Supporters.] Two horses, party per fess, embattled, pearl and ruby.

Motto.] *Per acuta belli.*

Chief Seats.] The Home, in the county of Hereford; at Ashton Underhill, in the county of Gloucester; and at Longwood, in the county of Southampton.

EARL of MOIRA.

JOHN RAWDON, Earl of MOIRA, Baron Rawdon, of Moira, in the county of Downe, and Baronet, Fellow of the Royal Society, and LL.D. was born in 1720, and succeeded his father, Sir John Rawdon, the third Baronet, Feb. 20. 1723. In 1750 he was created Baron Rawdon, and in 1761 Earl of Moira. On Nov. 10, 1741, he married Lady Helena, youngest daughter of John, late Earl of Egmont, and by her, who died June 11, 1746, had two daughters; Catharine, born Jan. 1, 1742; and Helena, born May 27, 1744. He

married,

married, secondly, Dec. 23, 1746, Anne, sister of Wills, Earl of Hillsborough, who dying Aug. 1, 1751, without issue, his Lordship married, thirdly, on Feb. 26, 1752, Lady Elizabeth, eldest daughter of Theophilus, Earl of Huntingdon, by whom he has issue three sons and three daughters; Lady Anne, born May 16, 1753; Francis, Lord Rawdon, born Dec. 7, 1754; John-Theophilus, born Nov. 19, 1756; Lady Selina-Frances, born April 9, 1759; George, born Jan. 9, 1761; and Lady Sophia, born March 1, 1765.

This noble family is of great antiquity, as appears by the title-deed of their estate, granted by William the Conqueror, part of which estate, with the mansion-house, Lord Rawdon still enjoys. The following lines are taken from the original Deed, mentioned in Weaver's Funeral Monuments.

I William Kyng, the thurd yere of my reign,
Give to the Paulyn Roydon, *Hope* & *Hopetowne*,
Wyth all the bounds, both up and downe,
From heven to yerthe, from yerthe to hel,
For the and thyn, ther to dwel,
As truely as this Kyng right in myn:
For a crossebowe and an arrow
When I sal come to hunt on Yarrow.
And in token that this thing is sooth,
I bit the whyz wax with my tooth,
Before Meg, Mawd, and Margery,
And my thurd son Henry.

The lands were situated near Leeds, in Yorkshire; and he took his name from the town of Rawdon, where is the mansion-house of the family. The said Paulyn de Roydon was succeeded

ceeded by his son Thor, the father of Serlo, whose son Adam lived in the reign of Richard I. and was father of Michael, who died in the reign of Henry III. From him descended, in a direct male line, John, living in the first year of Henry VIII. and leaving two sons, John, living at Rawdon-hall the 8th Henry VIII. and Ralph, whose son Ralph had three sons, Laurence, Alderman of York; Robert, a citizen of London; and Sir Marmaduke, who was Colonel for King Charles I. Governor of Basing in Hampshire, and of Farringdon in Berkshire, which last he defended against General Fairfax, till his death, April 28, 1646. In 1627, he served in Parliament for Aldborough in Suffolk; in 1639 was chosen Alderman of London, but fined for the same, and in 1645 was made High-sheriff of the county of Hertford: he left ten sons and six daughters.

John, elder brother of Ralph, grandfather of Sir Marmaduke, succeeded at Rawdon-hall, whose son Michael succeeded him, and was succeeded by his son George, whose eldest son, Francis, was father of Sir George Rawdon, Member of Parliament for Belfast in 1639. He was shot in the right hand; and had two horses shot under him at Lisburn in the service of K. Charles I. Upon the Restoration, he had the command of a troop of horse, and was made Governor of Carrickfergus, and created a Baronet, May 20, 1665, by Charles II. He died in 1684, and was succeeded by his son Sir Arthur, the second Baronet, who was Captain of a troop of horse, and, at the time of the Revolution, had the command of a regiment of dragoons within the county of
Downe,

Downe, which county he reprefented in Parliament. He died Oct. 17, 1695, and by Helena, daughter and heir to Sir James Graham, third fon of William, Earl of Menteith, in Scotland, left two fons, and two daughters, viz.
1. John, who fucceeded him.
2. Edward, who died young.
3. Dorothy, who died young.
4. Ifabella, married to Sir Richard Levinge, of Parwich, in Derbyfhire, and of High-park, in the county of Weftmeath, Bart. and died in 1731, leaving no iffue by him, who died in 1747.

John, the only furviving fon, and the third Baronet, reprefented the county of Downe in Parliament; and, in 1716, married Dorothy, fecond daughter of Sir Richard Levinge, Knt. and Bart. and dying Feb. 2, 1723-4, had iffue by her, (who married, fecondly, with Dr. Charles Cobbe, late Archbifhop of Dublin, and died Sept. 2, 1733,) four fons, viz.
1. George, born in Feb. 1717, who died an infant.
2. Sir John, now Earl of Moira.
3. Richard, born in Oct. 1721, and died an infant.
4. Arthur Rawdon, of Rathmullyan, Efq; who was Sheriff of the county of Meath, in 1746; and married Arabella, daughter and heir of —— Chefhire, of Hallwood, in the county of Chefter, Efq; but died without iffue.

Creations.] Baronet, May 20, 1665, 17 Cha. II. Baron, April 9, 1750, 23 George II. Earl, Dec. 15, 1761, 1 George III.

Arms.] Pearl, a fefs between three pheons, diamond.

Creft.]

Crest.] In a mural coronet, pearl, a pheon, diamond, with laurel issuing thereout, proper.

Supporters.] Two foresters, with black hunting caps, their stockings pearl, each having a sheaf of arrows slung across his shoulder; and his exterior hand resting on a bow, all proper.

Motto.] *Nisi Dominus frustra.*

Chief Seats.] Moira, and Ballynahinch, in the county of Downe; Bramhall, in the county of Meath; and Rawdon-hall, in the county of York.

EARL of ARRAN.

ARTHUR GORE, Earl of ARRAN, Viscount Sudley, of Castle-Gore, in the county of Mayo, Baron Saunders, of Deeps, in the county of Wexford, and Baronet, a Lord of the Privy-council, was created a Baron and Viscount as above, Aug. 1, 1758, and Earl of Arran, in the county of Galway, Mar. 27, 1762, 2 Geo. III.

Arms.] Ruby, a fess, between three cross croslets, fitchée, topaz.

Crest]

Supporters.] Two horses, argent.

Motto.] *In hoc signo vinces.*

Chief Seat.]

EARL of COURTOWN.

JAMES STOPFORD, Earl and Baron of COURTOWN, in the county of Wexford, and Viscount Stopford, of the same county, was created a Baron on Aug. 22, 1758, and an Earl and Viscount, as above, March 27, 1762.

Arms.]

Crest.]

Sup-

Supporters.]
Motto] *Patriæ infelici fidelis.*
Chief Seat.]

EARL of MILLTOWN.

Joseph Leeson, Earl of Milltown, Viscount Rufsborough, of Ruffelftown, and Baron Rufsborough, of Rufsborough, in the county of Wicklow, was born March 11, 1711, and in January, 1729, married Cecilia, eldeft daughter of Francis Leigh, of Rathangan, in the county of Kildare, Efq; and by her (who died Nov. 29, 1737,) had iffue, Jofeph, Vifcount Rufsborough, born in December, 1729; Lady Mary, born in Nov. 1734, and married, in February 1764, to John Bourke, fon of John Bourke, Efq; Member of Parliament for Palmerftown, in the county of Kildare; Brice-Leefon, born in December 1735, and married, in Aug. 1765, to Mifs Maria Graydon.

His Lordfhip married, fecondly, in October 1738, Anne, daughter of Nathanael Prefton, of Swainftown, in the county of Meath, Efq; and by her Ladyfhip, who died Jan. 12, 1767, had iffue one daughter, Lady Anne, born in May, 1750.

This noble Lord is defcended from the antient family of Leefon, long feated at Whitfield, in Northamptonfhire.

Creations.] Baron, *ut fupra*, April 27, 1756, 29 Geo. II. Vifcount, Aug. 26, 1760, 33 Geo. II. Earl of Milltown, Ap. 30, 1763, 3 Geo. III.

Arms.] Ruby, a chief, pearl, on the lower part the rays of the fun iffuing from thence, proper.

Creft]

Creſt.] A demi-lion, rampant, with the ſun in his paws.
Supporters.] On the dexter an hunter, on the ſiniſter an hound.
Motto.] *Clarior e tenebris.*
Chief Seats.] Ruſborough, in the county of Wicklow; Bormount, in the county of Wexford. Town-houſe, Stephen's-green, Dublin.

EARL of FARNHAM.

ROBERT MAXWELL, Earl of FARNHAM, and Viſcount and Baron Farnham, of Farnham, in the county of Cavan, was created a Baron April 26, 1756, a Viſcount Aug. 26, 1760, and an Earl April 30, 1763. His Lordſhip is a Member of the Privy-council, and Repreſentative in the Britiſh Parliament for the borough of Taunton, in Somerſetſhire. His Lordſhip married ———, Counteſs Dowager of Stafford.
Arms.]
Creſt.]
Supporters.]
Motto.] *Je ſuis pret.*
Chief Seats.] Horſley, Surry; and near Bury, Suffolk.

EARL of CATHERLOUGH.

ROBERT KNIGHT, Earl of CATHERLOUGH, Viſcount Barrells, and Lord Luxborough, of Shannon, Member in the Britiſh Parliament for Great Grimsby, in Lincolnſhire, and Recorder of that town, was born Dec. 17, 1702, and married, in 1727, Henrietta, daughter of

F   Henry,

Henry, Viscount St. John, and sister of Henry, Viscount Bolingbroke, by whom he has issue one son, Henry, Viscount Barrells, who, on June 21, 1750, married Frances, daughter of Thomas Heath, of Stanstead, in Essex, Esq; and one daughter, Henrietta, wife of the Hon. Josiah Child, brother of the Earl Tylney. His Lordship married, secondly, May 18, 1756, Lady Lequesne, relict of Sir John Lequesne, Knt. Alderman of London.

This noble Lord is descended from Nicholas Knight, of Beoley, in the county of Worcester, who was seated there in 1484, and died in the year 1520. His son Robert Knight, purchased the manor of Barrells, in the parish of Wotten-Waven, in the county of Warwick, in 1554, and died in the year 1558. He was succeeded by his son William, who was father of Nicholas, whose son William was born in 1594, and died in 1651, leaving also two sons, John and Robert; the latter whereof left two sons, Thomas and Robert, which Robert was born Nov. 30, 1675, and died in 1744. He married first Martha, eldest daughter and co-heir of Jeremiah Powell, of Edenhope, in the county of Salop, Esq; Director of the Bank, and by her, who died in 1718, had issue one son and two daughters, viz.

1. Robert, now Earl of Catherlough.
2. Catharine, married to John Page, of Chichester, Esq; Representative in Parliament for the city of Chichester.
3. Margaret, married to Morgan Vane, Esq; second son of the late Lord Barnard.

He married, secondly, in 1731, Anne, eldest daughter of William Robinson, of Rookby-Park, in the county of York, Esq; sister of Sir Thomas

Thomas Robinson, Bart. by whom he had a son William, born in 1732.

Creations.] Baron Luxborough, of Shannon, Aug. 8, 1746, 20 Geo. II. Viscount Barrells, and Earl of Catherlough, April 30, 1763, .3 George III.

Arms.] Pearl, three bendlets, ruby, in a canton, sapphire, a spur with the rowel downwards strapped, topaz.

Crest.] A spur, topaz, between two wings, ruby.

Supporters.] The dexter, a lion reguardant, topaz; the sinister a wild boar, diamond, gorged with a ducal coronet, and chain, topaz.

Motto.] *Te digna sequere.*

Chief Seats.] Barrells, in the county of Warwick; Luxborough, in the county of Essex.

EARL of CHARLEMOUNT.

JAMES CAULFIELD, Earl and Viscount CHARLEMOUNT, and Baron Caulfield, of the county of Armagh, Governor of that county, was born Aug. 22, 1728, and succeeded his father, James, the late, and third Viscount Charlemount, April 21, 1734. In the year 1763 his Lordship was created Earl of Charlemount.

James, the late and third Viscount, married Elizabeth, daughter of Francis Bernard, of Castle-Mahone, in the county of Cork, Esq; one of the Justices of the Court of Common-Pleas, by which Lady, who married, 2dly, Thomas Adderly, of Innishannon, in the county of Cork, Esq; and died May 30, 1743, he had two sons; James, the present Earl, and Francis; and a daughter, Alice.

F 2   William,

William, the second, and father of the late Viscount, upon the abdication of James II. took up arms in defence of his religion and his country; and served during the wars in Ireland; as did also his two younger brothers: whereupon King William promoted him to be Colonel of a regiment of foot; and made him Governor of the counties of Tyrone and Armagh; as also Custos rotulorum of the aforesaid counties, and Governor of the fort of Charlemount; and for his good services at Barcelona in Spain, Queen Anne, in 1705, first made him a Brigadier, and afterwards a Major-general, Commissioner of the Great Seal, and a member of the Privy-council. He married Anne, only daughter of Dr. James Margetson, Archbishop of Armagh, and Primate of all Ireland, by whom he, who died July 22, 1726, after enjoying the Peerage for sixty years, had seven sons and five daughters, viz.

1. William, who died an infant.
2. James, the late Viscount.
3. Toby, who died an infant.
4. Thomas, born in March 1683, served under his father as captain in Spain, and was afterwards Governor of Annapolis Royal, where he died in the service of King George I.
5. Charles, Rector of Donoghenrie, in the diocese of Armagh.
6. John, Member of Parliament for Charlemount, and one of the Clerks in the Lord Privy-seal's office.
7. Henry Charles, who married Mary, daughter of Bryan Gunning, of Holywell, in the county of Roscommon, Esq;

8. Anne,

8. Anne, married to John Davies, of Carrickfergus, in the county of Antrim, Esq;

9. Sarah, married Feb. 28, 1716, to Oliver Anketel, of Anketel's-grove, in the county of Monaghan, and died in 1742.

10. Mary, born in Oct. 1690, married to John Mocre, of Drumbanagher, in the county of Armagh, Esq;

11. Alicia, who died an infant.

12. Letitia, born in July 1599, married to John Cook, of Dublin, Esq;

Sir Toby Caulfield, of the county of Oxford, Knt. in 1598 was sent into Ireland by Queen Elizabeth, under the Earl of Essex, Lord Lieutenant; and for his great services against the grand traitor and rebel, Con O'Neil, Earl of Tyrone, her Majesty was pleased to grant him part of the said Earl's estate, with other lands in the province of Ulster. After King James's accession, he was honoured with Knighthood, and made Governor of Charlemount, &c. He was afterwards made Master of the Ordnance; and, Dec. 22, 1620, 18 James I. created a Baron, with limitation to his nephew; and dying a bachelor, Aug. 17, 1627, was succeeded by his nephew,

William, son of his brother, Doctor James Caulfield, who was, by the said King, confirmed in the Offices held by the former Lord, and was succeeded by Toby, his eldest son, who was basely murdered by Sir Phelim O'Neil, in the Irish rebellion of 1641, and was succeeded by his brother,

Robert, who, having enjoyed his honours but a few months, died, and William, his next brother, was the fifth Lord; and was of the

Privy-council to King Charles II. Captain of a troop of horse, and Governor of Charlemount; on July 17, 1665, was created Viscount by the said Prince; and was succeeded by his second son, William, the second Viscount.

Creations.] Baron, Dec. 22, 1620, 18 James I. Viscount July 17, 1665, 17 Charles II. Earl Oct. 29, 1763, 3 Geo. III.

Arms.] Barruly of ten pieces, pearl and ruby; on a canton of the second, a lion passant, guardant, topaz.

Crest.] On a wreath, a dragon's head, erased, ruby, collared gemmels, pearl.

Supporters.] Two dragons, ruby, gorged, as the crest.

Motto.] *Deo duce ferro comitante.*

Chief Seat.] Castle-Caulfield, in the county of Tyrone.

EARL MEXBOROUGH.

JOHN SAVILLE, Earl MEXBOROUGH, of Lifford, in the county of Donegal, Viscount Pollington, of Ferns, and Baron Pollington, of Longford in the county of Longford, Knight of the most honorable Order of the Bath, and Member in the British Parliament for the Borough of Shoreham, in Sussex, was created a Baron, on Sept. 8, 1753, and a Viscount and Earl, Dec. 27, 1765. In 1760, he married Sarah, youngest daughter of Francis-Blake-Delaval, of Seaton-Delaval, in Northumberland, Esq; by whom he has two sons, John, Viscount Pollington, born April 8, 1761, and Henry, born Sept. 17, 1763.

This

This noble Lord is descended from an antient family in Yorkshire; of whom were the Savilles, Earls of Sussex, which title is now extinct; and George Savile, Marquis of Hallifax, whose son William, having no male issue, that title also became extinct. Of this family was also Sir Henry Savile, who, in 1619, founded two Lectures, one in Geometry, the other in Astronomy, with salaries to the Professors, thence called Savilian Professors. Also Sir George Savile, of Rufford, in Nottinghamshire, (whose ancestor, Sir George, was created a Baronet in 1611) is the nineteenth in lineal descent from Sir John Savile, of Savile-hall, Knt. Also Sir Henry Savile, of Methley, in the county of York, knighted at the Coronation of King James I. and by the same King created a Baronet; but his issue male failing, that title likewise became extinct.

Creations.] *Ut supra.*
Arms] Pearl, on a bend diamond, three owls of the field.
Cr. st.] On a wreath, an owl, as in the arms.
Supporters.] Two lions, collared and chained.
Motto.] *Be fast.*
Chief Seat.] Methley-hall, in the county of York *.

---

* At Methley-park, in the county of York, on sumptuous marble monuments of great elegance, erected to the memories of Sir John Savile, Sir Henry Savile, and Charles Savile, Esquire, and Aletheia his wife, the late father and mother of the present Earl, are the following Inscriptions:

M. S.

Viri clarissimi & Judicis integerrimi JOHANNIS SAVILE, Equitis Aurati, Scaccarii Regii Baronum unius,

unius, ac, ex fpeciali gratia Regis, in proprio Comitatu fuo Jufticiarii Affiz. Filii & Hæredis Henrici Savile, de Overbradley in Stainland, juxta Eland, in ifto agro Eboracenfi, Armig. ex antiqua Saviliorum profapia oriundi. Qui, fecundo die Februarii, anno Dom. 1606, ætatis 61. Londini (ubi corpus ejus in Ecclefia S. Dunftani in Occidente inhumatur, cor vero hic inter Anteceffores) placidiffime in Domino obdormivit.

Vir fuit pietatis zelo, ingenii perfpicacia, morum fvavitate, rerum Principis & Patriæ agendarum dexteritate variis & exquifitis animi dolibus undique confpicuus.

Ex Uxore prima, Jana, filia Ricardi Garth, de Moreden, in Com. Surr. Armig. habuit Henricum Savile, poftea Militem & Baronettum, in hoc tumulo repofitum ; Elizabetham, uxorem Johannis Jackfon, Militis, defuncti ; & Janam, uxorem Henrici Goodrick, Milit. modo viven. Ex Uxore fecunda, Elizabetha, filia Tho. Wentworth, de Elmfall, in Com. Ebor. Armig. habuit Johannem Savile fuperftitem præfati fratris fui defuncti fucceflorem, ac hæredem propinquum, & Helenam, quæ in minori ætate obiit. Patri pientiffimo, Filius obfequentiffimus, fuperftes fupradictus, hoc amoris memoraculo parentavit.

Spe Refurrectionis beatificæ hic jacet HENRICUS SAVILE, Miles & Baronettus, filius primogenitus & Hæres dicti Johannis Savile, etiam Militis, defuncti, una cum Conjuge fua chariffima, Maria, filia prima Johannis Dent, Civitat. London. Armigeri, per quam habuit Johannem Savile, fummæ fpei ac præclaræ indolis adolefcentem, in peregrinatione fua Lutetiæ in regno Galliæ anno ætat. fuæ 21, & Salutis noftræ 1631 extinctum. Habuit etiam filium fecundum Henricum Savile, & nonnullos alios qui obiere infantes.

Vir fuit paternarum virtutum hæres fplendidiffimus, qui poft multos in graviffimis Regiis & Reipub. negotiis feliciter expediendis laboris per fex luftra exantlatos, & diutinam cum morbo ingravefcente luctam,

tam, pro cælesti terrestrem tandem pie mutavit hæreditatem. Obiit in ædibus suis infra hanc villam 23° Junii, 1632, ætatis vero suæ 53.

Prædictus Johannes Savile, ad gratæ & perennnaturæ memoriæ testificationèm votivum hoc prædecessoribus tam bene merentibus dedicavit Monumentum.

To the Memory of CHARLES SAVILE, Esquire, and ALETHEIA his Wife.

He was descended from an illustrious Family in this county, whose antiquity cannot be traced, distinguished, in its several branches, by Persons of great abilities and eminence. He was the fifth in a lineal descent from that worthy Man, and great Honour of the Law, Sir John Savile, of this place, Knight, one of the Barons of the Exchequer in the time of Queen Elizabeth and King James the first; whose eldest son Henry was advanced to the Dignity of a Baronet in 1611, but died without issue; and whose brother, Sir Henry Savile, Knight, Provost of Eaton, will ever be remembered as an Ornament to Learning, to his Family, and to his Country. Aletheia was daughter and coheiress of Gilbert Millington, of Felley Abbey, in the county of Nottingham, Esquire. She enjoyed all the true comforts of the conjugal state with the best of Husbands till June 5th, 1741, when he departed this life, aged 65, leaving his only son John, to inherit the possessions and imitate the virtues of his ancestors.

She caused this Monument to be erected, that no instance might be omitted of her regard and gratitude to him, purposing and desiring that when she departs this life, her remains may be deposited with his in a Vault near this place prepared by her for that purpose, in hopes that they shall rise together to Glory and Honour, through the Mercies of God, and the Merits of Jesus Christ our Lord.

The above mentioned Aletheia died June the 24th, 1759, in the 77th year of her age, and was here interred.

EARL of WINTERTON.

Edward-Garth Turnour, Earl of Winterton, Viscount Turnour, and Baron Winterton, of Gorf, in the county of Galway, was raised to the dignity of a Baron, March 28, 1761, 1 Geo. III. and to those of a Viscount and Earl, on Dec. 27, 1765, 5 Geo. III, and is Member in the British Parliament for the borough of Bramber, in Sussex. On March 15, 1756, his Lordship married Anne, younger daughter of Thomas, Lord Archer, by whom he has issue three sons and six daughters, viz. Edward, Viscount Turnour; Arthur, Gerrard, Ladies Anne, Catharine; Sarah, who died in her infancy; Isabella, Maria, and Frances.

The ancestor of this noble Lord came from Normandy to England, with William the Conqueror, and got large possessions in this kingdom.

Creations.] *Ut supra.*
Arms.]
Crest.]
Supporters.]
Motto.] *Esse quam videri.*
Chief Seats.] Shillingleigh, Sussex; another in Norfolk.

EARL of ELY.

Nicholas-Hume Loftus, Earl of Ely, Viscount Loftus, and Baron Loftus, of Loftushall, in in the county of Wexford, was born Sept. 11, 1738, and succeeded his grandfather, Nicholas, the first Earl, in 1767.

Nicholas, the late Earl, was created a Baron Oct. 5, 1751, Viscount Loftus, of Ely, July 3, 1756, and Earl of Ely, Oct. 28, 1766. He married

married firſt, Anne, ſecond daughter of William, Viſcount Duncannon, and ſiſter of Brabazon Earl of Beſborough; by whom he had iſſue two ſons and three daughters that ſurvived their infancy; and, ſecondly, Letitia, daughter of John Rowley, of Caſtle-Roe, in the county of Derry, Eſq; and relict of Arthur, Viſcount Loftus, of Ely, by whom he had no iſſue. His children by the firſt venter were,

1. Nicholas, who was returned to Parliament for the borough of Bannow in Oct. 1739: and, Aug. 27, 1753, was appointed Deputy Governor of the county of Wexford: he married, Aug. 18, 1736, Mary, eldeſt daughter and co-heir of Sir Guſtavus Hume, of Caſtle-Hume, in the county of Fermanagh, Bart. and by her, who died in Oct. 1740, had an only ſon, Nicholas-Hume, the preſent Earl.

2. Henry of Richfield, who, in 1744, was Sheriff of the county of Wexford; and in Oct. 1747, choſen Member of Parliament for the borough of Bannow, and is Clerk of the Coaſt-permits. He married, in 1745, Frances, daughter of Henry Monro, of Roe's-hall, in the county of Downe, Eſq; but hath no iſſue.

3. Mary, married to William Alcock, of Welton, in the county of Wexford, Eſq; and is deceaſed.

4. Anne, married to Charles Tottenham, Eſq; Surveyor-general of the county of Leinſter.

5. Elizabeth, married to John Tottenham, of Tottenham-green, Eſq;

This noble family has been thrice advanced to the Peerage of Ireland, and is deſcended from Edward Loftus, of Swineſhead, in Yorkſhire, where the family had long reſided. His son Robert had three sons, of whom Adam the second was created Viscount Loftus, of Elye. He had three sons: 1. Sir Robert, whose daughter Anne married Richard-Lennard Barret, of Bellhouse, in Essex, Esq; whose grandson succeeded to the title of Lord Dacre, in July 1755. 2. Edward, the second Viscount, had a son Arthur, the third Viscount, who dying without issue male, the title became extinct; and his estate descended to Edward, Earl of Drogheda, son of his daughter Jane, who married Charles, Viscount Moore, of Drogheda. 3. Francis, who died young. Adam, the second son of Edward Loftus, of Swineshead, was advanced to the Archiepiscopal See of Dublin in 1562; in 1573, was made Keeper of the Great Seal; and, in 1577, Lord High Chancellor, in which office he continued till his death, April 5, 1605. He had, besides eight children who died young, five sons and seven daughters that survived him. His eldest son, Sir Dudley, had issue six sons; the eldest son, Sir Adam, had eight sons and nine daughters; his eldest son, Sir Arthur, had four sons and three daughters. Of the sons three died unmarried; and Adam, the second, was created Viscount Lisburne, and Baron of Rathfarnham, but was killed at the siege of Limerick, Sept. 15, 1691, leaving only one daughter and heir, Lucy, married to Thomas Lord Wharton.

Nicholas, the second son of Sir Dudley, had eight sons, six of which died young; and Nicholas, one of the two surviving sons, dying without issue male, the estate descended to his brother Henry Loftus, of Loftus-hall, who married first, Amy, daughter of John Gorges, of Cole-

Coleraine, Esq; by whom he had a son Gorges, who died young; secondly, Anne, daughter and heir to Henry Crewkerne, of Exeter, Esq; widow of Oliver Keating, of Ballynunry, Esq; by whom he had two sons, Nicholas, Earl of Ely, and Henry, who died unmarried.

Creations.] *Ut supra.*

Arms.] Quarterly, the 1st and 4th, diamond, a chevron engrailed, ermine, between three trefoils, flipped, pearl. 2d and 3d, gironny of eight pieces, pearl and diamond; a saltire, engrailed, between four fleurs de lis, all counterchanged.

Crest.] On a wreath, a boar's head erased, and erect, pearl, langued, ruby, with the words, *Loyal au mort*, over it.

Supporters.] Two eagles, pearl, with beaks and legs, topaz, each charged on the breast with a trefoil, flipped, emerald.

Motto.] *Prend moy tel que je sui.*

Chief Seat.] Loftus-hall, in the county of Wexford.

EARL BECTIVE.

THOMAS TAYLOR, Earl Bective, of Castle-Bective, in the county of Meath, Viscount and Baron Headfort, of Headfort, in the said county, was created a Baron, August 19, 1760, a Viscount March 24, 1762, and Earl of Bective, October 28, 1766. His Lordship was born Oct. 20, 1724, was elected to serve in Parliament for the borough of Kells, in the county of Meath, in October 1747, and on July 4, 1754, married Jane, eldest daughter of the Right Hon. Hercules Langford Rowley, of Summerhill, in the county of Meath, Efq; by whom he has had iſſue; Elizabeth, who died young; Thomas; Hercules Langford; Robert; Sarah; Clotworthy; Henrietta; Henry; all now living.

His Lordſhip's immediate anceſtor, Thomas Taylor, of Ringmere, in the pariſh of Battle, in the county of Suſſex, on Sept. 6, 1602, purchaſed, of John Page, and William Delves, Eſqrs, a large track of land, at Skir-corner, in the manor of Stonham, in the ſaid county, on which he lived, and died in Sept. 1629, aged ſeventy, leaving iſſue two ſons, John and Nicholas.

Nicholas, the younger ſon, of Watling, in the county of Suſſex, died in the year 1654, without iſſue, and left his brother John his heir to an eſtate that he had, near the village of Boreham, in the pariſh of Watling, in the ſaid county; alſo to a very profitable leaſe of the lands of Sharpſham, in the pariſh of Battle, hundred of Barfloe, and ſaid county.

John, his elder brother, on Aug. 13, 1627, bought of Robert James, of Hoe, the lands of Thorndance, in the pariſh of Battle, borough of Inlight, and county of Suſſex, which were mortgaged to his father: He died in the year 1658, aged 65, having had iſſue four daughters, who all died young; and one ſon, his ſucceſſor,

Thomas Taylor, Eſq; who went to Ireland in 1653, with Sir William Petty, between whom a great friendſhip ſubſiſted, which had been contracted at ſchool and college. They undertook and perfected the Down Survey of that kingdom, the Maps of which were publiſhed

lished in Sir William's name. In 1660, he disposed of his English estates, and purchased the town, and town-lands, of Kells, alias Kenlis, of Berfordstown, Brownstown, and others thereto belonging; with those of Armagh-Bregagh, and others thereto appertaining, in the county of Meath. After the restoration of King Charles II. he was appointed a Sub-commissioner in the Court of Claims, in 1664, 1665, and 1666. In 1669 and 1670 he was Deputy Receiver-general under Sir George Carteret; and in part of 1670, and 1671, under Lord Angier. He was a Sub-commissioner in the Court of Claims, held for persons transplanted into the province of Connaught and county of Clare, in 1675. He was also Treasurer of the Farmers of the Revenue in 1679, or 1680. He officiated as Vice-treasurer and Treasurer at War, during the suspension of the Lord Ranelagh in 1681, in which employment he died Aug. 1, 1682, of a dropsy and consumption, aged 51.

He married Anne, daughter of William Axtell, of Berkhampstead, in Hertfordshire, Esq; in 1658, and by her (who died June 4, 1687, and was buried by her husband, in St. Michael's church, in Dublin, in the middle isle) had issue three sons; John, and William, who both died young, and were buried in St. Michael's church; Thomas, who was the second son; and one daughter, Anne, wife of Sir Nicholas Acheson, of Market-hill, in the county of Armagh, Bart. He was succeeded by his only surviving son,

Thomas, who was born July 20, 1662, in St. Michael's lane, Dublin, elected to serve in
Parlia-

Parliament for the borough of Kells, in the county of Meath, in 1692, and created a Baronet of Ireland by Queen Anne. In 1726 he was appointed a Privy-counfellor, and died Aug. 5, 1736, aged 76. He married Anne, daughter of Sir Robert Cotton, of Combermeer, in Chefhire, Bart. on June 20, 1682, and by her (who died at Kells, Dec. 24, 1710) had iffue fix fons and five daughters; viz. 1. Henrietta, wife of Col. John Prefton, of Bellinter, in com. Meath, by whom fhe had one fon that died young, and three daughters, Henrietta, Sophia, and Sarah. 2. Thomas, born Nov. 20, 1686, of whom prefently. 3. Salifbury, wife of Dr. William Fitzgerald, Bifhop of Clonfert, and afterwards of General James Crofts, and died at Bath, Jan. 5, 1724, without iffue. 4. Robert, born May 22, 1689, at Combermeer, in Chefhire, and, taking holy orders, was Archdeacon of Kilmacduagh, Rector of Loughrea and Tinagh, in the diocefe of Clonfert, and in 1726 made Dean of Clonfert. He died unmarried in May, 1744. 5. Anne, wife of George Pepper, of Ballygarth, in the county of Meath, and died April 19, 1749, leaving iffue only one fon, Thomas. 6. Hefther, who died young. Henry, who died at fea, on his fifth voyage to the Eaft Indies, unmarried. 8. John; and 9. William, both died young. 10. James, born Jan. 20, 1700, and married Catharine, daughter of Thomas Meredyth, of Newtown, in the county of Meath, Efq; by whom he had feveral children, which died young, and died in 1747. 11. Emilia, who died young. He was fucceeded by his faid fon,

Thomas

[113]

Thomas Taylor, Efq; who was elected to ferve in Parliament for the borough of Kells, in 1711, and in 1753 was fworn of the Privy-council: He was alfo a Truftee for the Linen-manufacture, a Commiffioner of the Inland Navigation, and a Governor of the Workhoufe.

He married Sarah, fecond daughter of John Graham, of Plattin, in the county of Meath, Efq; on Nov. 18, 1714, and by her had iffue two fons, and four daughters, viz. 1. Anne; 2. Charity; 3. Thomas; and, 4. Sarah, who all died young; 5. Henrierta, married Feb. 24, 1741, to Richard Moore, of Barnes, in the county of Tipperary, Efq; by whom fhe had ten daughters and four fons, three of whom are now living, Thomas, Stephen, and Richard; and feven daughters, Henrietta, Salifbury, Jane, Elizabeth, Anne, Charity, and Mary; and 6. Thomas, the prefent Earl of Bective.

Title and Creations.] *Ut fupra.*
Arms.]
Creft.]
Supporters.] A lion and a panther.
Motto. *Confequitur quodcunque petit.*
Chief Seats] Headfort, in the county of Meath; Profpect, in the county of Dublin; and Virginia-park, in the county of Cavan.

COUNTESS GRANDISON.

ELIZABETH MASON, Countess and Viscountess GRANDISON, of Dromana, and Viscountess Villiers, was the only child and heir apparent of John, late Earl Grandison, and was created a Viscountess April 10, 1736, with remainder to the heirs male of her body for ever. In 1739 she married Aland-John Mason, of Waterford, Esq; by whom she had issue five sons, and one daughter; of whom are surviving, George, Viscount Villiers, born July 10, 1750, and Robert, born Dec. 14, 1751. On Dec. 20, 1766, her Ladyship was created Countess Grandison.

This illustrious family were possessed of a fair inheritance in the county of Leicester, for many ages, at Brookesby; but originally came from Normandy. Of this family is the present Earl of Jersey, (see that title, in my English Peerage,) as was George, Duke of Buckingham, the great favourite of James I. and Charles I. whose fate is well known. Also John, the late Earl Grandison, who was the fourth Viscount and first Earl Grandison, raised to the latter title Sept. 11, 1721, 8 Geo. I.

His Lordship married Frances, daughter of Anthony, the first Viscount Falkland, of Scotland, by whom he had issue,

1. James, Lord Villiers, whose only son, John, died in the lif-time of his grandfather.

2. William, Lord Villiers, a fine young nobleman, who also died before his father, Dec. 16, 1739.

3. Anne, who died young.

4. Lady

4. Lady Elizabeth, now Countess Grandison.
5. Lady Catharine, who died unmarried in 1738.

Titles and Creations.] *Ut supra.*
Arms.] Pearl, on a cross, ruby, five escallop shells, topaz.
Crest.] On a wreath, a lion rampant, pearl, ducally crowned, topaz.
Supporters.] On the dexter side, an horse, pearl; on the sinister, a lion, as the crest.
Motto.] *Fidei coticula crux.*
Chief Seat.] Dromana, in the county of Waterford.

EARL of HOWTH.

THOMAS ST. LAWRENCE, Earl of HOWTH, Viscount St. Lawrence, and Baron of Howth, in the county of Dublin, was born May 10, 1730, and succeeded his father, William, Lord Howth, April 4, 1748. On Nov. 17, 1750, he married Isabella, sister of Robert, Lord Kingsborough, by whom he hath issue, William, Viscount St. Lawrence, born Oct. 4, 1752; and a daughter, Lady Isabella, born Aug. 30, 1751, with other children since. In 1767 he was created Earl of Howth, and Viscount St. Lawrence.

William, the late and twenty-sixth Baron of Howth, succeeded his father Thomas, in Aug. 1727; and, Aug. 2, 1728, married Lucy, younger daughter of Lieutenant general Richard Gorges, of Kilbrue, in the county of Meath, by whom he had two sons, Thomas, the present Earl; and William, born June 1, 1732, and died April 10, 1749; and a daughter, Mary, married, Aug. 15, 1750, to Richard, son and heir of of Sir Richard Gethin, Bart. Thomas, the twenty fifth Lord, fucceeded his father William; and, Sep. 23, 1687, married Mary, eldeſt daughter of Henry, Lord Viſcount Kingſland, by whom he had ſix ſons, and three daughters. viz.

1. William, the late Lord.
2. Charles, who died an infant.
3. Henry, who died Jan. 7, 1735, unmarried.
4. Nicholas, who died Oct. 29, 1747, unmarried.
5. Oliver, who died young.
6. Mark, married to Mary, daughter of Mr. Travers.
7. Elizabeth, born Oct. 26, 1690, was married, firſt, Feb. 21, 1716, to Edward Rice, of Mount-Rice, in the county of Kildare, Eſq; and ſecondly, in 1721, to Dominick Quin, of Quinsborough, in the ſame county, Eſq;
8. Mary; and 9. Mabel, died both unmarried.

Hiſtory informs us, that the name of this antient and noble family, which is of Engliſh extraction, was originally Triſtram, till, on St. Lawrence's day, Sir Almericus Triſtram, being to command an army againſt the Danes near Clantarffe, made a vow to that Saint, that if he got the victory, he and his poſterity, in honour of him, ſhould bear the name of St. Lawrence, which has ſo continued to this time; and the ſword wherewith he fought is now hanging up at the great Hall of Howth, the ſeat of the preſent Lord; and what is very remarkable in this family is, that the eſtate and Barony they now enjoy has been in the poſſeſſion of the family ſix-hundred years, without any increaſe or diminution;

minution; during which time, there never was an attainder in it. The valour and conduct of Sir Almericus were fo remarkable in this battle againſt the Danes, that the victory obtained over them was, in a great meaſure, attributed to him and his family, having loſt ſeven ſons, uncles, and nephews, in the engagement: whereupon he had the land and title of Howth allotted to him; and in 1189, upon the removal of Sir John Courcy from the government, by King Richard I. and fubſtituting Hugh Lacy in his room, the Iriſh reſolved to recover their country from Courcy now diveſted of his power; Sir Almericus being then in Connaught with thirty Knights and two-hundred foot, was defired to repair to the affiſtance of Courcy; but O Connor, King of Connaught, oppoſing his march, all the horſemen killed their horſes, that they might not be tempted to fly, and engaging the enemy, which confiſted of twenty-thouſand men, killed one-thouſand of them: but being overwhelmed by numbers, they all periſhed to a man. He married the fiſter of Sir John de Courcy, Earl of Ulſter, by whom he had Sir Nicholas, the ſecond Lord Howth.

Robert, the fifteenth Lord, was, in 1483, appointed Lord Chancellor of Ireland; and married Joan, ſecond daughter of Edmund Beaufort Duke of Somerſet, by whom he had Thomas, who was Attorney-general, and afterwards Juſtice of the King's Bench in Ireland; and his eldeſt ſon Sir Nicholas was the ſixteenth Lord, who was entirely devoted to the houſe of Lancaſter, and diſcovering the deſigns of the impoſtor Lambert Simnel, imparted them to King

King Henry VII. who presented him with a gift worth three-hundred pounds in gold, in testimony of his favour.

Sir Christopher, the twenty second Baron of Howth, was Colonel of foot, and behaved with great bravery at the remarkable siege of Kingsale; and his son and successor Nicholas was a great sufferer for his loyalty to King Charles I.

Creations.] Baron of Howth, originally by Tenure, temp. Hen. II. by King John's Patent of confirmation; and again, March 4, 1489, 4 Henry VII. Earl of Howth, and Viscount St. Lawrence, Aug. 15, 1767, 6 Geo. III.

Arms.] Ruby, two swords in saltire, the pomels and hilts topaz, between four roses, pearl, barbed, and seeded, proper.

Crest.] On a wreath, a sea-lion, party per fess, pearl, and proper.

Supporters.] On the dexter side, a sea-lion, party per fess, as the crest. On the sinister, a mermaid holding in her exterior hand a mirror, all proper.

Motto.] *Que pance;* or, *Que pense.*

Chief Seat.] At Howth, in the county of Dublin.

EARL of BELLAMONT.

Sir CHARLES COOTE, Knight of the Bath, Lord Collooney, Baron Coote, of Collooney, on the demise of the late Earl of Bellamont, his relation, had revived in his person the title of Lord Collooney, and was created Earl of Bellamont, Aug. 15, 1767. His Lordship's bravery, conduct, and great services in the East

East Indies, particularly in the reduction of Pondicherry, are too well remembered to require recapitulation here.

This noble Lord is descended from Sir Charles Coote, Baronet, whose third son, Richard, was, for his services, rewarded with the title of Baron Coote, of Colloony, by King Charles II. He was father of Richard, created Earl of Bellamont; of Chidley Coote, of Cootehall, in the county of Roscommon, Esq; and of Thomas, of whom presently. (See Earl of Mountrath.)

Richard, the eldest son, and second Lord Colloony, was by King William, Nov. 2, 1689, created Earl of Bellamont. He was father of Nanfan, the second, and Richard, the third, and late Earl of Bellamont, whose children all deceasing before him, and his Lordship himself dying in 1766, the title became extinct.

I now return to Thomas Coote, of Cootehill, youngest son of Richard, the first Lord Colloony, and brother of Richard, the first Earl of Bellamont.

Which Thomas was, after the Revolution, chosen Recorder of Dublin, and in 1693, appointed one of the Justices of the King's Bench, which he resigned on the death of Queen Anne. He married Frances, daughter and coheir of Col. Christopher Copley, and had issue a son, Col. Chidley Coote, who died in 1719, unmarried. His second wife was Eleanor, daughter and coheir of Sir Thomas St. George, of Woodford, in Essex, Knt. by whom he had a son, Thomas, that died without issue, and a daughter Eleanor. His third wife was Anne, daughter of Christopher Lovat, Alderman of Dublin,

Dublin, by whom he had three sons and six daughters, whereof two sons and two daughters died young; Charles, of whom presently; Frances; Elizabeth, wife of Mervyn Pratt, of Cabragh, in the county of Cavan, Esq; who had issue the Rev. Joseph Pratt, and other children; Catharine, wife of James Macartney, Esq; who left issue two sons and two daughters; and Anne, wife of Samuel Bindon, of Rockmount, Esq; He died on April 24, 1741, and was succeeded by his eldest surviving son,

Charles Coote, Esq; High Sheriff of the county of Cavan, in 1719, who married Prudence, second daughter of Richard Geering, Esq; and dying Oct. 19, 1750, left issue, Charles, now Earl of Bellamont, born in April 1738; Anne, wife of William Anketell, of Anketell's grove, in the county of Monaghan, Esq; who had issue; Frances; Catharine; Caroline; Elizabeth, and two other children.

Creations.] Baron of Colloony, in the county of Sligo, Sept. 6, 1660, 12 Charles II. Earl of Bellamont, in the same county, Aug. 15, 1767, 6 George III.

Arms.] The same as the Earl of Mountrath, with a crescent for difference.

Crest.] On a wreath, a coote, proper.

Supporters.] Two wolves, ermine, *i. e.* black powdered with white.

Motto.] *Vincit Veritas.*

Chief Seat.] Coote-hill, in the county of Cavan, &c.

VISCOUNTS.

VISCOUNTS.

VISCOUNT MOUNTGARRET.

THE Right Hon. EDMUND BUTLER, Viscount MOUNTGARRET, and Baron of Kells, premier Viscount of the kingdom of Ireland, succeeded his father, Edmund, the ninth Viscount, on March 6, 1750-1, and was sworn a Barrister at Law, Nov. 25, 1749. In 1744 his Lordship married Charlotte, second daughter of Simon Bradstreet, Esq; Counsellor at Law, by whom he has issue one son, the hon. Edmund Butler, and one daughter, Eleanor.

Edmund, the sixth Viscount Mountgarret, succeeded his father, Richard, in Feb. 1706-7; and married, first, Mary, daughter of —— Buchanan, of Londonderry, Esq; who died without issue; and, secondly, Elizabeth, relict of Oliver Grace, of Shanganagh, in Queen's-county, Esq; (which Lady died June 13, 1736) and he dying in 1735, left a daughter, married to Hugh Reilley, of Ballintough, in the county of Meath, Esq; and three sons, viz.

1. Richard, the seventh Viscount, who succeeded him July 25, 1735, but died without issue, May 14, 1736.

2. James, the eighth Viscount, who served many years in the Emperor's army; and, in the campaign of the Rhine, in 1735, signalized himself

himself by his bravery and conduct; but died without issue, May 13, 1749.

3. Edmund, his only surviving brother, succeeded, and was the ninth Viscount, who, on Nov. 7, 1736, conformed to the established church of Ireland, and in October 1749, took his seat in the House of Peers. He married Anne, eldest daughter of Major Toby Purcell, of Ballymartin and Cloghpooke, in the county of Kilkenny; by whom he had issue Edmund, the tenth and present Viscount.

This great and illustrious family of the Butlers, so renowned for the many valiant and loyal persons it has produced, is descended from the ancient Counts of Brion in Normandy. Their first residence in England was in the county of Norfolk, where, in the reign of William the Conqueror, lived Herveius Walter, whose son Hubert built a monastery, encompassed with a strong wall and moat: he became the first Dean of York; King Richard I. advanced him to the see of Salisbury; and, in 1193, to the see of Canterbury. He was afterwards made Lord Chancellor and Lord High Treasurer of England; and on his son Theobald King Henry II. conferred the office of Chief Butler of Ireland, from whence he and his successors assumed the name of Butler. But the more immediate ancestor of this noble Lord was Sir Richard Butler, younger son of Pierce, Earl of Ossory and Ormond, who was created Viscount Mountgarret by Edward the sixth.

Creations.] Viscount Mountgarret and Baron of Kells, in the county of Wexford, Oct. 23, 1550, 5 Edw. VI.

Arms.]

Arms.] Topaz, a chief, indented, sapphire, a crescent for difference; or, within a border, gules, at pleasure.

Crest.] In a ducal coronet, topaz, a plume of five ostrich feathers, and thence a falcon rising, all pearl.

Supporters.] On the dexter side, a falcon with wings expanded, pearl, beaked and membered, topaz. On the sinister, a male gryphon, pearl; his horns, beak, fore legs, rays, plain collar, and chain, topaz.

Motto.] *Depressus extollor.*

Chief Seat.] At Ballyconragh, in the county of Kilkenny.

VISCOUNT VALENTIA.

An account of this noble family will be found in my English Peerage, under the title of Earl of ANGLESEA.

VISCOUNT NETTERVILLE.

JOHN NETTERVILLE, Viscount NETTERVILLE, of Douth, in the county of Meath, was born in 1744, and succeeded his father, Nicholas, the sixth Viscount, on March 19, 1750-1.

Nicholas, the late and sixth Viscount, born in 1708, succeeded his father, John, Dec. 12, 1727; and in 1731 married Catharine, only daughter of Samuel Burton, of Burton-hall, in the county of Carlow, Esq; by whom he had issue John, the present Viscount; another son, born in 1745; and two daughters, Frances and Anne.

* A 2   This

This ancient and noble family derive their pedigree, according to the Irish Annals, from Charles Duke of Normandy; and in the year 1169, Sir Formal Netterville, coming to Ireland, and marrying Philadelphia, daughter of William Lord Vesey, had a son Richard, from whom, in a direct male line, descended Sir Robert Netterville, who was created Viscount Netterville by James I.

Creations.] Viscount, *ut supra*, Apr. 3, 1622, 20 James I.

Arms.] Pearl, a cross, ruby, fretté, topaz.

Crest.] On a wreath, a demi-lion, rampant, ruby, bezantée.

Supporters.] On the dexter side a sea-horse, party per fess, ruby, and proper; his mane, legs, fins, and tip of the tail, topaz. On the sinister, a lion, guardant, ruby, bezantée.

Motto.] *Cruci dum spiro fido.*

Chief Seat.] At New Grange, in the county of Meath.

VISCOUNT KILMOREY.

THOMAS NEEDHAM, Viscount KILMOREY, in the county of Clare, succeeded his brother, Robert, the seventh Viscount, Feb. 19, 1716-17, and married Lady Mary, third daughter and co-heir of Washington, Earl Ferrers (by his wife, Mary, daughter of Sir Richard Levinge, Bart. Justice of the Court of King's Bench in Ireland) by whom he has issue.

Robert, the sixth Viscount, succeeded his father, Thomas, the fifth Viscount, and married Mary, daughter of John Offley, of Crew, in Cheshire, Esq; by whom he had issue,

1. Ro-

1. Robert, the late Viscount, who died unmarried. 2. Thomas, the present Viscount. 3. Francis; and 4. John, who in 1737, was Captain and Colonel of grenadiers in the second regiment of Foot-guards, which he resigned in 1748; he married, in 1738, ——, relict of Peter Shakerly, of Chester, Esq; 5. Anne; 6. Mary; 7. Elizabeth; 8. Henrietta.

Thomas, the fifth Viscount, married Frances, daughter and heir of Francis Leveson Fowler, of Harnidge-Grange, in Shropshire, Esq; (by his wife, Anne, second daughter of Peter Venables, Baron of Kinderton) and by her (who on May 2, 1690 re-married with Theophilus, Earl of Huntingdon, being his second wife, and after with the Chevalier Ligonday) had issue, Robert, the sixth Viscount, father of the late and present Viscounts.

This antient and noble family hath been of great note in the counties of Salop and Chester; and is derived from William de Needham, or Nedeham, Lord of Staunton in the last mentioned county in 1102, 3 Henry I. and from him descended

Sir Robert Needham, who was Sheriff of the county of Salop in 1606; and was created Viscount Kilmorey, by Charles I.

Creations.] Viscount, *ut supra*, April 18, 1625, 1 Charles I.

Arms.] Pearl, a bend, sapphire, between two bucks-heads, cabossed, and attired, diamond.

Crest.] On a wreath, a phœnix in flames, proper.

Supporters.] On the dexter, a horse, pearl. On the sinister, a stag, proper.

A 3 *Motto.*]

Motto.] *Nunc aut nunquam.*
Chief Seat.] At Shenton-hall, in Shropshire.

VISCOUNT MAYO.

John Bourke, Viscount Mayo, and Baronet, succeeded his brother, Sir Theobald, the seventh Viscount, Jan. 7, 1741-2, and married Catharine, daughter and heir of Major Whitgift Aylmer, of the West-Indies, descended from Dr. John Aylmer, Bishop of London, and from Dr. John Whitgift, Archbishop of Canterbury, temp. Eliz. and relict of —— Hamilton, of the county of Galway, Esq; by whom he had issue, Aylmer, born Nov. 17, 1743, and died July 21, 1748; and Bridget, married, on May 11, 1758, to Edmund Lambert, of Boyton, in the county of Wilts, Esq;

Theobald, the sixth Viscount Mayo, born Jan. 6, 1681, conformed to the established church on June 19, 1709; and married first, July 8, 1702, his cousin Mary, daughter of John Brown, of West-Port, Esq; by whom he had issue three sons and five daughters, viz.

1. Theobald, the late Viscount, who married Alice, eldest daughter of James Agar, of Gowran, in the county of Kilkenny, Esq; and by her, (who afterwards married Francis Lord Athenry, and is now Countess of Brandon,) had two sons, who died infants.
2. Miles, who died young.
3. John, the present Viscount.
4. Jane, wife of Murrough O'Flaherty, of Lemon-field, in the county of Galway, Esq;
5. Maud, who died young.

6. Eli-

6. Elizabeth, married to William Mitchel, of Carshalton, in the county of Surry, Esq.
7. Mary, who died young.
8. Bridget, married, in Oct. 1731, to John Gunning, Esq; son and heir of Bryan Gunning, of Castle-Coote, in the county of Roscommon, Esq; by whom she had a son John, and four daughters; Mary married, in March 1752, to George-William, Earl of Coventry, and deceased without issue. Elizabeth, married, in Feb. 1752, to James the late Duke of Hamilton, by whom she had the present Duke; and, March 3, 1759, to Colonel John Campbell, now Marquis of Lorn, and Baron Sundridge; Catharine; and Lissy, who died Jan. 1, 1753.

His Lordship married, secondly, Margaret, daughter of the said Bryan Gunning, Esq; but by her had no issue.

This family is a branch of the antient and noble family of Clanrickard, whereof Theobald Bourke, in the reign of Queen Elizabeth, commanded a company in her Majesty's guards; and, upon the King of Spain's landing forces, in conjunction with the Pope's Nuncio, at Kinsale, he levied, at his own expence, 160 men, and fought at the head of them, under the Lord Montjoy; where a glorious victory near Kinsale being obtained, he was knighted for his gallant behaviour, and, by Charles I. was created a Viscount.

Creations.] Baronet of Nova Scotia, by Charles I. and Viscount of the county of Mayo, June 21, 1627, 3 Charles I.

Arms.] Party per fess, topaz and ermine, a cross ruby; the first quarter charged with a lion rampant; and the second with a dexter hand,

hand, couped at the wrift, and erect, both diamond.

Creft.] On a cap of maintenance, a lion fejant, pearl, gorged with a ducal collar, topaz.

Supporters.] On the dexter fide, a harpy guardant, with wings, and a lion's body, topaz; a human face, neck, and breaft, proper, and armed ruby. On the finifter, a man in armour to the middle of his thighs; having a fword proper in a belt ruby; and about his neck a fquare white band, his hands naked, fandals diamond, and in his exterior hand a battle-ax proper.

Motto.] *A cruce Salus.*

Chief feat.] At Caftle-Bourke, in the county of Mayo.

VISCOUNT LUMLEY of WATERFORD.

See an account of this noble family, under the title of Earl of SCARBOROUGH, in my Englifh Peerage.

VISCOUNT STRANGFORD.

PHILIP SMYTH, Vifcount STRANGFORD, and Dean of Derry, fucceeded his father Endymion, the fifth Vifcount, Sept. 8, 1724, and in 1741, married Mary, daughter of Anthony Jephfon, of Mayallow, in the county of Cork, Efq; by whom he has iffue a fon, the Hon. ——— Smythe, born May 19, 1758, and two daughters, Mary and Anne.

Endymion, the late Vifcount, fucceeded his father Philip, the fourth Vifcount, in 1715; and

and married Elizabeth, daughter of Mr. de Larget, of St. Martin's, London, by whom he had issue the present Viscount, and a daughter.

Philip, the fourth Viscount, by his wife Mary, daughter of George Porter, of Middlesex, Esq; had issue

Endymion, the late Viscount, and several daughters, whereof Catharine was the first wife of Henry Lord Teynham, and mother of Philip and Henry, successively Lords Teynham; Elizabeth, of Henry Audley, of Bear-church, in Essex, Esq; and died in Jan. 1732; and Olivia, of John Davell, of Calehill, in Kent, Esq; and died Jan. 15, 1753, aged eighty-two.

John Smythe, Esq; who resided at Corsham, in Essex, in the reign of Henry the eighth, had Thomas his heir, who removed to Westenhanger, in Kent; and being Farmer of the Customs, acquired a very considerable estate; by Alice, daughter and heir of Sir Andrew Judd, of Ashford, he had two sons, John, and Sir Thomas, who was also Customer to Queen Elizabeth after his father's death; and was, by King James I. sent Ambassador to the Empress of Russia. He was succeeded by his son Sir John in his estate at Bidborough, in Kent, who was also Farmer of the Customs, and ancestor of Sir Sidney-Stafford Smythe, now one of the Barons of the Exchequer in England, and F. R. S. John, the eldest son of the said Thomas and Alice Judd, was High Sheriff of the county of Kent; in the 42d of Queen Elizabeth; and marrying Elizabeth, daughter and heir of John Phineux, of Hawhouse, in Kent, Esq; left issue Sir Thomas,

mas, his heir, made a Knight of the Bath by King James I. at the creation of Charles Prince of Wales, and created a Viscount.

Creations.] Viscount Strangford, of the county of Downe, July 17, 1628, 4 Cha. I.

Arms.] Pearl, a chevron ingrailed, between three lions passant, diamond.

Crest.] On a wreath, a leopard's head erased, pearl, gorged with a plain collar and chain affixed, diamond.

Supporters.] On the dexter side a lion topaz, guttée de larmes. On the sinister a leopard pearl, collared and chained as the crest.

Motto.] *Virtus incendit vires.*

VISCOUNT WENMAN.

PHILIP WENMAN, Viscount and Baron WENMAN, and Baronet, succeeded his father, Philip, the sixth Viscount, Aug. 16, 1760, and on July 7, 1766, married Lady Eleanor, daughter of Willoughby, Earl of Abington, and sister of the present Earl.

Philip, the late Viscount, succeeded his father Richard the fifth Viscount, Nov. 27, 1729, and on July 13, 1741, married Sophia, eldest daughter and coheir of James Herbert, of Tythorpe, in the county of Oxford, Esq; descended from James Herbert, second son of Philip, fourth Earl of Pembroke and Montgomery, by whom he had four sons and three daughters.

1. Philip, born April 18, 1742, the present Viscount.

2. Thomas-Francis, born Nov. 18, 1745.

3. Richard, born Nov. 13, 1746, who died in his infancy.

4. Her-

4. Herbert-Henry, born July 18, 1749, who died young.
5. Sophia, born Aug. 17, 1743.
6. Susanna, born Nov. 10, 1744, who died young.
7. Mary, born March 27, 1748, and died July 5, 1755.

His Lordship represented the city of Oxford in Parliament, from 1749 to 1754, and then was returned for the county of Oxford.

This family of Wenman has been long seated in the counties of Oxford and Berks, of which was Henry Wenman, of Bluebury, in the county of Berks, who married, in 1482, Emmote, daughter and heir of Symkin Hervey, of Herefordshire, Esq; by whom he had Richard, his eldest son, whose son Thomas was knighted by Queen Elizabeth, and married Ursula, daughter and heir of Thomas Gifford, Esq; of Twyford, in the county of Bucks, by whom he had the manors of Twyford, Pounden, and Charndon, in the said county. His eldest son, Sir Richard, was Sheriff of the county of Oxford, in 1562; and married Isabel, eldest daughter and coheir of John, Lord Williams, of Thame, by whom he had Sir Richard his heir; whose eldest son and successor, Sir Richard, was Sheriff of the county of Oxford in 1627, was honoured with knighthood for his gallant behaviour at the taking of Cadiz, in 1596, where he served as volunteer, and was created a Viscount by Charles I. whose service he promoted to the utmost of his power, during the Civil-war; and was succeeded by his son Thomas, who was one of the adventurers in Ireland, when that Kingdom was reduced by the English Parliament;

*A 6
and

and subscribing the sum of 600*l.* had an allotment of 617 Acres, 1 Rood, and 15 Perches, of land, plantation measure, in the barony of Garry-Castle, and King's county. His Lordship was appointed by the Parliament one of the Commissioners to carry the Propositions for Peace to the King at Oxford in 1644, and was again appointed Commissioner for the treaty at Uxbridge, in 1644; for the treaty at Newport in 1648; and was one of the forty one members who, for giving their vote, " That " the concessions of his Majesty to the proposi-" tions upon the treaty at Newport, were suf-" ficient grounds for the house to proceed upon " for the settlement of the Peace of the King-" dom," were seized by the Army, and committed to close imprisonment. In the year 1645, he was considered as one of the sufferers, and received four pounds per week, by order of the Parliament, for damages he suffered on his estates in the county of Oxford, by the King's forces. His Lordship dying without issue male surviving him, was succeeded by his uncle, Philip, the third Viscount, who having no male issue, procured from King Charles II. Jan. 30, 1683, a new entail of the honours on his next heir, Sir Richard Wenman, Bart. in reversion after his own death, with the same precedency he enjoyed, who, accordingly, succeeded to the title; which

Sir Richard, the fourth Viscount Wenman, was the youngest and only surviving son of his niece Mary, the sixth and youngest daughter of his brother Thomas, who married Sir Francis Wenman, of Caswell, by which marriage the two families of Caswell and Thame-Park were united;

united; and this Richard, the fourth Viscount Wenman, succeeded, upon the death of his father, to the title of Baronet, and was grandfather to the present Viscount.

Creations.] Baron Wenman, of Kilmaynham, in the county of Dublin, and Viscount Wenman, of Tuam, in the county of Galway, July 30, 1628, 4 Charles I. Baronet Nov. 29, 1662, 14 Charles II.

Arms.] Party per pale, ruby and sapphire, a cross patonce, topaz.

Crest.] On a wreath, a cock's head erased, sapphire, crested and jelloped, topaz.

Supporters.] Two greyhounds ruby, gorged with a plain collar, topaz, unguled, sapphire.

Motto.] Omnia bona Bonis.

Chief Seats.] Thame Park and Wickham, Oxfordshire; and Twyford, in the county of Buckingham.

VISCOUNT TAAFE.

NICHOLAS TAAFE, Viscount TAAFE, Baron of Ballymote, and Count of the Roman Empire, succeeded to the estate (and title of Viscount and Baron,) of Theobald, fifth Viscount Taafe, and fourth Earl of Carlingford, which last title became extinct by his death, on Nov. 24, 1738, O. S. he dying without issue. His Lordship was the son of Francis Taafe, Esq; son of William, eighth son of John, the first Viscount Taafe. His Lordship had two sisters, 1. Anne, wife of John Brett, of Rathdooney, in the county of Sligo, Esq; by whom he had several sons, all deceased, and four daughters, Anne,

Anne, wife of Roger Irwin, of Lisballan, in Sligo, Efq; Sarah, Mary, and Elizabeth. 2. Mary, wife of Theodore Verdun, of Clunigafhill, Efq; who died without iffue. His Lordfhip married Mary-Anne, Countefs of Spendler, daughter and heir of Count Spendler, of Lintz, in Upper Auftria, of a moft ancient and illuftrious family in Germany, and by her (who is Lady of the Bed-chamber to the Emprefs-dowager, Queen of Hungary,) has iffue two fons, John and Francis. His Lordfhip was Chamberlain to the late Emperor, and is now a Lieutenant-general, and Colonel of a regiment in the Auftrian fervice: He is poffeffed of a large eftate in Silefia, and by the name of Count Taafe has diftinguifhed himfelf in the feveral wars of Hungary and Germany.

3. Of this noble and ancient family was Richard Taafe, who lived in 1282; as, in 1306, did John Taafe, who was Archbifhop of Armagh; and, in 1479, the Order of the Garter being eftablifhed in Ireland, Sir Nicholas Taafe was one of the firft members. In the reign of Queen Elizabeth this family was in good repute in the county of Louth, where they have refided ever fince; of whom Sir William Taafe was one who affifted to reduce the Irifh to the Queen's obedience, when they were in arms under the rebellious Earl of Tyrone.

John, his fon and heir, was created a Baron and Vifcount, by K. Charles I. and he marrying Anne, daughter of Theobald, the firft Vifcount Dillon, by her had fourteen fons and three daughters.

Of

Of the sons, Theobald, the eldest, was created Earl of Carlingford, and was succeeded by his son, Nicholas, the second Earl, and third Viscount, who was slain in behalf of King James II. to whom he was a Colonel of Foot at the battle of the Boyne; and was succeeded by his brother Francis, the famous Count Taafe, who was many years in the Imperial service, where he was Colonel of the Royal Cuirassiers, and Lieutenant-general of Horse; and upon the decease of Nicholas, the second Earl, was, by a particular clause in the English Act of Parliament, 1689, 1 Will. & Mar. exempted from forfeiture; and he dying without issue, in 1704, was succeeded by his nephew, Theobald, son of his brother John, who dying without issue, in Nov. 1738, the title of Earl of Carlingford became extinct; but the titles of Viscount and Baron devolved upon Nicholas, as above mentioned, the present Viscount.

Creations.] Baron of Ballymote and Viscount Taafe, of Corren, both in the county of Sligo, Aug. 1, 1628, 4 Charles I.

Arms.] Ruby, a cross, pearl, frettée, sapphire.

Crest.] On a wreath, a dexter arm in armour, embowed, brandishing a sword, pearl, all proper.

Supporters.] On the dexter side, an horse, pearl, femée of estoils, diamond. On the sinister, a wyvern, or sea-dragon, with wings expanded, proper.

Motto.] *In hoc signo spes mea.*

VISCOUNT RANELAGH.

CHARLES JONES, Baron Jones of Navan, and Viscount RANELAGH, upon proof of his descent, as hereafter, was allowed those titles, Oct. 7, 1759, and is the fourth Viscount. He married Sarah, daughter of Thomas Montgomery, Esq; Member in Parliament for the borough of Lifford, by whom his Lordship has issue three sons and two daughters, viz. Charles, born Oct. 29, 1761; Thomas, Richard; Mary, and Sarah.

This noble family is descended from Thomas Jones, Esq; an Alderman of London, father of the Rev. Dr. Thomas Jones, Bishop of Meath, and afterwards Archbishop of Dublin. His Grace was also Lord Chancellor, and Lord Justice of Ireland, and married Margaret, daughter of Adam Purdon, of Lurgan-race, Esq; and by her (who deceased Dec. 15, 1618) had issue one son, Sir Roger, and two daughters; Margaret, wife of Gilbert Domville, Esq; Clerk of the Hanaper, ancestor of Sir Compton Domville, Bart. and Jane, wife of Henry Piers, of Tristernagh, in the county of York, Esq; ancestor of Sir Pigot-William Piers, Bart. His Grace died on April 10, 1619. His son,

Sir Roger Jones, Knt. married to his first wife, Frances, daughter of Sir Gerald Moore, first Viscount Drogheda, by whom he had issue,

1. Arthur, of whom presently.
2. Thomas, of whom hereafter.
3. Margaret, wife of Sir John Clotworthy, Viscount Massareene.
4. Mary,

4. Mary, wife of John Chichester, Esq;

His second wife was Catharine, daughter of Sir Edward Longueville, of Wolverton, in the county of Bucks, Knt. by whom he had issue one daughter, Elizabeth, wife of Sir Robert Sands, of Marbourne, in Kent, Knt. He was created Baron Jones of Navan, and Viscount Ranelagh, and dying in 1628, was succeeded by his eldest son,

Arthur, the second Viscount, who married Lady Catharine Boyle, daughter of Richard, Earl of Cork, by whom he had issue,

1. Richard, of whom presently.
2. Catharine, wife of Sir William Parsons, Knt. and afterwards of Hugh, Earl of Mount-Alexander.
3. Elizabeth, of ——— Malster, Esq; and
4. Frances, who died unmarried.

His Lordship dying on Jan. 7, 1669, was succeeded by his only son,

Richard, the third Viscount, who, on Dec. 11, 1677, was created Earl of Ranelagh, and represented the boroughs of Castle-rising, in the county of Norfolk, and Westloe, in the county of Cornwall, in the English Parliament. His Lordship was Vice-treasurer of Ireland, Constable of Athlone, several years Pay-master of the Army, and a Lord of the Privy-council. He married Elizabeth, daughter of Francis, Lord Willoughby, of Parham, by whom he had issue Arthur and Edward, who both died before they came to years of maturity; and three daughters, viz. 1. Elizabeth, wife of John, Earl of Kildare; 2. Frances, of Thomas, Earl of Coningsby, and mother of Margaret,

garet, late Countefs of Coningfby; and, 3. Catharine, who died unmarried. His Lordfhip deceafing on Jan. 3, 1711, without furviving male iffue, the title of Earl became extinct; but thofe of Vifcount and Baron reverted to the iffue of Thomas Jones, fecond fon of Sir Roger Jones, the firft Vifcount. Which Thomas married Elizabeth, daughter of John Harris, of Winchefter, Efq; by whom he had iffue two fons, Roger; and Thomas, who died without iffue.

Roger Jones, Efq; the eldeft, married Martha, daughter of the Rev. Mr. Gulfton, Rector of Waltham, and Prebendary of Winchefter, by whom he had one fon, and three daughters; Elizabeth, wife of William Whitaker, Efq; Martha, of Jofeph Etherfea, Efq; and Anne, of John Devile, Efq. The fon, Charles Jones, Efq; married Elizabeth, daughter of James Douglas, of Haddington, in North Britain, Efq; by whom he had iffue three daughters; Martha; Margaret, wife of Thomas Garden, Efq; and Wilimina, of Dr. John Hill, of London; and one fon, Charles, the prefent, and fourth Vifcount Ranelagh.

Creations.] Baron Jones, of Navan, Aug. 5, 1628; and Vifcount Ranelagh, Aug. 12, the fame year, by Charles I.

Arms.]
Creft.]
Supporters.]
Motto.]
Chief Seat.]

VISCOUNT MOLYNEUX.

RICHARD MOLYNEUX, Viscount MOLYNEUX, of Maryborough, and Baronet, succeeded his father Caryl, the late and sixth Viscount, in Nov. 1645, and is an Ecclesiastic of the Romish Church.

Caryl, the late and sixth Viscount, succeeded his brother Richard in Dec. 1738; and left two sons, Richard the present Viscount, and Robert, who, July 20, 1746, married the widow of ———— Errington, of Lancashire, Esq; by whom he hath a son.

In the year 1066, when William Duke of Normandy invaded England, among his noble attendants was William de Molines, a person not less famous for his virtues than for his noble extraction, as appears from the Roll of Battle-abbey, in which list his name stands the eighteenth in order; and to the said William, Roger Pictaviensis (of Poictiers) by consent of the Conqueror, gave the manors of Sephton, Thornton, and Kuerdon, in the county of Lancaster, among which Sephton became his chief-seat. From him descended, in a direct male line of illustrious ancestors,

Richard, who eminently distinguished himself at the battle of Agincourt, where he was knighted; he was in great favour with King Henry VI. who, by his letters patent, gave to him and his heirs the Forestership of the forests and parks in West-Derbyshire; also the Stewardship of Staffordshire, and the office of Constable of Liverpool. He was succeeded by his eldest son,

Sir

Sir Richard, who was in such favour with his Prince, and had so much honour done him by his country, that in the act of Resumption, the thirty-sixth of Henry VI. there was this provisional clause in his behalf, "Provided always that this act extend not, nor in any wise be prejudicial unto, Richard Molyneux, of Sephton, Esq; one of the Ushers of our Privy-chamber, in, of, or to, the Constableship of our castle of Liverpool, the Stewardship of West-Derbyshire and Staffordshire, the Foresterhip of our forest of Symond's wood, and of our parks of Croxtath, &c." He was afterwards knighted, and slain at the battle of Bloreheath, in Staffordshire, Sept. 23, 1459, fighting for the house of Lancaster.

From him descended Sir William, who, in the reign of King Henry VIII. was a great commander in the county of Lancaster, and at the battle of Flodden-field, took there, with his own hand, two streamers, which are still in the family.

Richard, his great grandson, was, by Queen Elizabeth, made a Knight, and by James I. created a Baronet, and his third son, Richard, succeeding him, was created a Viscount, by Charles I. and was succeeded by Richard the second Viscount; who, at the breaking out of the rebellion, took up arms for the King, together with his brother Caryl; and for that service raised a regiment of horse, and another of foot, with which he served all the time of that unnatural war, and were in Oxford when it surrendered to the rebels. They afterwards

were

were with Charles II. when he marched out of Scotland; and were with him at the battle of Worcester, after which they lived in retirement for some time. He was succeeded by his brother Caryl, the third Viscount, who was outlawed, and by the rebels excepted from compounding; but at last had his estate, after paying an excessive fine.

He lived to a very great age, being, by James II. appointed Lord Lieutenant and Custos Rotulorum of Lancashire, and Admiral of the Narrow-Seas. He died on Feb. 2, 1698-9, and was succeeded by his only surviving son, William the fourth Viscount, who, on March 8, 1717, was succeeded by his eldest son, Richard, the fifth Viscount, who married Mary, eldest daughter of Francis Lord Brudenell, by whom he had one son, that died in his lifetime, and two daughters; Mary, wife of Thomas Clifton, of Latham, and after of William Anderton, of Luxton-hall, in the county of Lancaster, Esq; and Dorothy. He was succeeded by Caryl, the late Viscount his brother.

Creations.] Baronet, May 22, 1611, 9 James I. Viscount Molyneux, of Maryborough, in the Queen's county, Dec. 22, 1628, 4 Charles I.

Arms.] Sapphire, a cross, moline, topaz.

Crest.] Out of a chapeau, ruby, turned up, ermine, a peacock's tail, in pride, proper. And sometimes on a wreath a lion's head erased, sapphire, ducally crowned topaz.

Supporters.] Two lions sapphire.

Motto.] *Vivere sat vincere.*

Chief Seat.] Croxtath-hall, and Sephton, in the county of Lancaster.

VIS-

VISCOUNT FAIRFAX.

CHARLES-GREGORY FAIRFAX, Viscount Fairfax, of Emely, succeeded his father, William, the late and ninth Viscount, in 1738, and on Nov. 17, 1720, married, first, Elizabeth, eldest daughter of Hugh, Lord Clifford, of Chudleigh, relict of William Constable, Viscount Dunbar, who died April 25, 1721; and, secondly, Mary, daughter of Nicholas, the sixth Viscount Fairfax, and by her, who died July 1, 1741, his Lordship had issue four sons and five daughters, whereof only are surviving Anne and Elizabeth.

William, the late Viscount, married Elizabeth, daughter of Capt. Gerard, son of Lord Gerard, by whom he had two sons, Charles-Gregory, the present Viscount, and George.

At the time of the Conquest, this noble family was seated at Torcester, in Northumberland, and from thence removed into Yorkshire, where, in the sixth of King John, Richard Fairfax, being possessed of the lands of Askam, and several others, was therein succeeded by William his son, who was father of another William, who purchasing the manor of Walton, in the county of York, the same has continued in the family to the present time.

From him descended Thomas, who marrying the daughter and heir of Sir Ivo Juan, or John de Etton, Lord of Gilling, brought that estate long after into the family in the reign of Henry VII. and from him descended Richard, who was Chief Justice in England in the reign of Henry VI. He had six sons, of which Sir Guy, the

the third, was Justice of the King's-bench, and progenitor of the Lord Fairfax of Scotland, (see my Peerage of that Kingdom,) and Nicholas, the fifth, was a Knight of Rhodes. From him descended Sir Thomas, who was knighted, and served Sheriff of Yorkshire in the third of Charles I. and by that Prince was advanced to the Peerage. He was succeeded by his son, Thomas, the second Viscount, whose sons, William and Charles, were successively Viscounts, and the latter dying in his infancy, was succeeded by his uncle Charles, second son of Thomas, the second Viscount; who dying without issue male, was succceeded by his nephew,

Nicholas, the sixth Viscount, eldest son of Nicholas, fourth son of Thomas, the second Viscount. His Lordship married Mary, daughter of William Weld, of Lulworth-Castle, in Dorsetshire, Esq; (who married 2dly, Sir Francis Hungate, of Seaton, Bart.) and had issue a daughter, Mary, wife of Nicholas, Viscount Fairfax; and mother by him of the present Viscountess, and a son Charles, the seventh Viscount, who died young, and was succeeded by his uncle Charles, the eighth Viscount, who dying unmarried, was succeeded by William, the ninth Viscount, eldest son of William, third son of Thomas, the first Viscount, by his wife Mary, daughter of Marmaduke Constable, of Brandsby, in Yorkshire, Esq; and was father of the present Viscount.

Creations.] Viscount Fairfax, of Emely, in the county of Tipperary, Febr. 10, 1628, 4 Charles I.

Arms.]

Arms.] Pearl, three bars gemelles, ruby; surmounted by a lion rampant, diamond.
Cr. st.] On a wreath, a lion passant-guardant of the latter.
Supporters.] Two lions, as in the coat
Motto.] *Je la feray durant ma vie.*
Chief Seats.] At Gilling-castle and Walton, both in the county of York.

VISCOUNT FITZ-WILLIAM.

See partly, an account of the descent of this noble family, in my Peerage of England, under Earl FITZ-WILLIAM.

RICHARD FITZ-WILLIAM, Viscount FITZ-WILLIAM, of Meryon, and Baron Fitz-William, of Thorn-castle, in the county of Dublin, a Privy-counsellor, Knight of the Bath, and F. R. S. succeeded his father, Richard, the fifth Viscount, June 20, 1743, and on May 3, 1744, married Catharine, daughter of Sir Matthew Decker, of Richmond, in Surry, Bart. by whom his Lordship has issue three sons, Richard, born in Aug. 1745; William, and John.

Richard, the late Viscount, was appointed one of the Privy-council to George I. and II; was twice chosen Member in the British House of Commons for Fowey in Cornwall; and marrying Frances, only daughter of Sir John Shelley, of Michael grove, in Sussex, Bart. had issue three sons and two daughters, viz.

1. Richard, the present Viscount.
2. William, who, in 1747, was made Usher of the Black-rod, in Ireland; and, Dec. 4, 1750, married

married the only daughter of Thomas Bouchier, Efq;

3. John, a Lieutenant-general, Colonel of the fecond regiment of foot, and Member in the prefent Parliament for Windfor, in May, 1738, married the daughter of James Lanoy, of Hammerfmith, Efq;

4. Mary, appointed one of the Maids of Honour to the late Queen, when Princefs of Wales, and after fhe was Queen; and on Aug. 28, 1733, was married to Henry, Earl of Pembroke, and was by him mother of the prefent Earl; and, fecondly, in Sept. 1751, to North-Ludlow Bernard, Efq; Major of Dragoons.

5. Frances, married, May 18, 1732, to George Evans, Lord Carbery, and mother of the prefent Lord.

Of this antient and noble family, who were faid to be coufin in blood to King Edward the Confeffor, was Sir William Fitz-William, Knt. who attended King William, called the Conqueror, as Marfhal of the army, when he entered England; and his defcendants being afterwards Lords of Sprotborough and Emely, in the county of York; from thence a branch went into Ireland with King John, when Earl of Mortagne, where his pofterity has remained ever fince.

In 1348, King Edward III. pardoned William, the fon of Richard Fitz-William, all tranfgreffions, &c. and the faid William having built the Caftle of Wicklow, he became Conftable thereof, and in the forty-ninth year of that reign was Commander in chief of all thofe parts.

* B

In 1381, his son William was Sheriff of the county of Meath, and had a grant to be Seneſchal of all the temporalties in the ſaid county, with power to appoint his Deputy, &c. Some time after this, he was made Keeper of the Peace in the county of Dublin, with power to arm the county at his will and pleaſure, for defence of the ſame; to puniſh all evil doers; and to do all things that he ſhould judge convenient for the good of the ſaid county. From him deſcended

Richard, who was one of the Gentlemen of the Bed-Chamber to Henry VIII. to whom that Prince granted, during life, the Seneſchalſhip of the King's four manors, which were Newcaſtle, near Lions, Eſher, Caſſagard, and Cromlin, with power to appoint his deputies, without yielding any account ; and his ſon

Sir Thomas, in the reign of Queen Elizabeth, was appointed Seneſchal, or Chief ruler over the Marches of Dublin, together with the Barony of Rathdown, and over the Sept of the Archbolds, with power to him, his deputy or deputies, to ſummon all the forces under his Government, at will and pleaſure, and to take ſuch order for the proſecuting of rebels, and puniſhing malefactors, as he, his deputy, or deputies, ſhould think fit.

His grandſon, Sir Thomas Fitz-William, Knt, was made Sheriff of the county of Dublin, and created a Baron and Viſcount. In recompence of the ſervices of himſelf and his two ſons, during the Civil-wars of King Charles I. he obtained a Privy-Seal to paſs letters patent under the Great Seal, to be made an Earl of England; and a patent was accordingly drawn, dated

dated at Oxford May 1, the 20th of Charles I. but the Great Seal not being then in the power of that unfortunate Prince, this patent was deferred; and after the Restoration, the family having unhappily a great man to their enemy, was never perfected.

His son, Oliver, the second Viscount, stipulated with the French King, to carry three-thousand men out of England and Ireland into France, for the said King's service; and he commanded them there as Colonel. In the reign of King Charles I. he was, by articles, concluded in France with that Prince's wife, the Queen of England, made General of ten thousand foot, and three thousand horse, which were to come out of Ireland, to serve his Majesty in the Civil-wars of England, but the fatal success of the battle of Naseby, where he served his Majesty, put a stop to his proceedings. He was also Lieutenant-general to the Marquis of Ormond, and General in Ireland, at which time he won the battle of Roscommon, and reduced the Province of Connaught to the King's service; and was created Earl of Tyrconnel; but dying without issue, in 1667, the title of Earl became extinct; but in those of Baron and Viscount he was succeeded by his brother,

William, the third Viscount, who was also Lieutenant-colonel of the three thousand men the said Oliver carried into France; and in the time of the Civil-wars of England, was Governor of Whitchurch, in the county of Salop, and Lieutenant-general of the county of Chester.

B 2   *Creations.*]

Creations.] Viscount and Baron, *ut supra*, Aug. 5, 1629, 5 Charles I.

Arms.] Lozengy, pearl, and ruby.

Crest.] In a ducal coronet, topaz, a double plume of five ostrich feathers, pearl.

Supporters.] Two ostriches, pearl, each holding in its beak a horse-shoe, topaz.

Motto.] *Deo adjuvante, non timendum.*

Chief Seats.] Mount Merion, in the county of Dublin; Thorpe, in the county of Surry.

VISCOUNT CULLEN.

CHARLES COCKAINE, Viscount CULLEN, was born Sept. 2, 1710, succeeded his father, Charles, the fourth Viscount, and on May 4, 1732, married his first cousin, Anne, daughter of Borlace Warren, Esq; by which Lady (who died in 1754) his Lordship has issue.

Charles, the third Viscount, succeeded his father Bryen, the second Viscount, and by his wife, Catharine, daughter of William, Lord Willoughby of Parham, had issue,

Charles, the fourth Viscount, who married Anne, sister of Borlace Warren, of Stapleford, in the county of Nottingham, Esq; and by her had issue the present Viscount.

Of this ancient family was Andreas Cockaine, of Ashburne, in the county of Derby, whose son and heir, William Cockaine, was father of another William, who had a son Roger, father of William Cockaine, of Ashburne, who lived in the 28th year of Edward I. From him descended

Sir William Cockaine, merchant, and in 1619 Lord Mayor of London; who, about the 10th of James I. was sent first Governor into the Province of Ulster, when about three hundred persons, of all sorts of handicrafts, went thither; which Sir William bought the manor of Elmsthorp, in the county of Leicester. He died in 1626, leaving issue six daughters, four of which were married to Peers of England; and two sons, whereof Charles, the eldest, succeeded him, and was created Viscount Cullen, by Charles I. He was succeeded by his son,

Brien, the second Viscount, who marrying Elizabeth, daughter and sole heir of Francis Trentham, of the county of Stafford, Esq; with her had the rich Lordship of Rosceter, in that county, and Castle-Heviningham, in the county of Essex, by whom he had issue Charles, the third Viscount, Trentham, George, Elizabeth, and Mary.

Creation.] Viscount Cullen, in the county of Donegal, Aug. 11, 1642, 17 Charles I.

Arms.] Pearl, three cocks, ruby, crested and jelloped, diamond; a crescent upon a crescent, for difference.

Crest.] On a wreath, a cock's head erased, ruby, crested and jelloped, as those in the coat.

Supporters.] None; nor ever had a grant of any.

Motto.] *Virtus in arduis.*

Chief Seat.] At Rushton, in the county of Northampton.

VISCOUNT TRACY.

Thomas-Charles Tracy, Viscount Tracy, succeeded his father Thomas-Charles, the fifth Viscount, June 4, 1756, and on Feb. 6, 1755, married Harriot, daughter of Peter Bathurst, of Clarendon-Park, in the county of Wilts, Esq; by his second wife, Lady Selina, daughter of Robert, Earl Ferrers.

This noble family is maternally descended of the royal blood of the Saxon Kings of England; and take their name from the town of Traci, in the duchy of Normandy; of which, in the reign of King Stephen, was Henry de Traci, who was possessed of the Honor of Barnstaple, in the county of Devon, by the gift of that King; and, being a valiant and expert soldier, did his Majesty great service in those western parts. To him succeeded William, his son, who was possessed of the manor of Toddington, in the county of Gloucester, and was an eminent soldier; and to him succeeded Sir Oliver, his son, who was High Sheriff of the county of Gloucester; and his son, Sir William, was made High Sheriff of the same county by the Barons in 1263; and, in 1289, is said to command under King Edward I. in his expedition to Scotland. All his successors served the office of High Sheriff of the county of Gloucester down to Sir William, who was Sheriff of this county in the fifth of Henry VIII. and was one of the first who embraced the reformed religion in England, as appears by his last will, which was condemned as heretical; and his body was taken up and burnt. He was suc-

succeeded by his son William, whose son and successor, Sir John, was knighted, in 1574, by Queen Elizabeth; in the 20th of her reign was High Sheriff of the county of Gloucester, and Knight of the Shire; and his son and successor, Sir John, was knighted by James I. and created a Baron and Viscount by Charles I.

Robert, the second Viscount, was knighted by Charles I. married Bridget, third daughter of John Lyttelton, of Frankley, in Worcestershire, Esq; (who died in 1601,) by whom he had issue, John, his successor, and Anne, wife of William Somerville, of Edston, in Warwickshire, Esq; by whom she had eleven sons and five daughters. He married, secondly, Dorothy, daughter of Thomas Cox, of Castleditch, in Herefordshire, Esq; and by her had issue Robert, one of the Justices of the King's-bench to William III. and of the Common-pleas in the reign of Queen Anne. In 1710, he was one of the Commissioners of the Great Seal, and again in 1718, with Sir John Pratt and Sir James Montague. Being obliged, through ill health, to quit his Employments, he had, in 1726, a pension settled upon him of 1000l. per ann. for life, and died Sept. 11, 1735. This upright magistrate married Anne, eldest daughter of William Dowdeswell, of Poole-court, in Worcestershire, Esq; by whom he had three sons and two daughters; Robert, Richard, and William, all deceased, the eldest of whom left a son, heir to his grandfather, whose son and heir was named Dowdeswell. Of the daughters, Anne was wife, first, of Charles Dowdeswell, of Northampton-court in Gloucestershire, Esq; and, secondly, of Thomas

mas Wylde, Efq; Commiffioner of Excife, and Member in feveral Parliaments for the city of Worcefter; and Dorothy, of John Pratt, Efq; eldeft fon of Sir John Pratt, Chief-juftice of the King's-bench, and died March 23, 1726, in child-birth.

John, the third Vifcount, married Elizabeth, eldeft furviving daughter of Thomas, the firft Lord Leigh, of Stone-leigh, by whom he had iffue two fons, 1. William, the fourth Vifcount. 2. Ferdinando, who being left by Sir John Tracy, Bart. heir of his eftate, became feated at Stanway; and marrying ———, daughter of Sir Anthony Keck, Commiffioner of the Great Seal, was therein fucceeded by John, his only fon, poffeffor of a large eftate, who married Anne, daughter of Sir Robert Atkyns, of Saperton, in the county of Gloucefter, Chief Baron of the Exchequer (who died in 1710; by his fecond wife, Anne, daughter of Sir Thomas Dacres, of Hertfordfhire) and dying April 19, 1735, left feveral children, of whom Robert, the eldeft fon, was, in April, 1734, elected to Parliament for Tewkfbury, and in 1747 for Worcefter, and on Aug. 7, 1735, married ———, eldeft daughter of Sir Roger Hudfon, Knt. John, the fecond fon, Curfitor Baron of the Exchequer, married Catharine, daughter of —— Lindfey, Efq; on Oct. 8, 1735. Anthony Tracy Keck, the third fon, in Aug. 1736, married the Lady Sufan, fifter of James, Duke of Hamilton, and dying in June, 1767, left iffue by her, Charlotte, Maid of Honour to the Queen; and Sufan. Thomas, the fourth fon, one of the Reprefentatives in Parliament for the county of Gloucefter, married,

ried, in 1746, Mary, only daughter of Sir William Dodwell, Knt. by whom he has one son. Anne, the eldeſt daughter, married John Travell, of Swerford, in Oxfordſhire, Eſq; And Frances, the youngeſt daughter, is the wife of Guſtavus Guydickens, Eſq; a Captain in the third regiment of Foot-guards.

William, the fourth Viſcount, married, firſt, Frances, daughter of Leiceſter Devereux, Viſcount Hereford, by whom he had an only daughter, Elizabeth, wife of Robert, ſon and heir apparent of Sir Robert Burdett, of Brumeſh, in Warwickſhire, Bart. who dying Jan. 7, 1715, a fortnight before his father, left her with child of Sir Robert Burdett, Bart. born May 28, 1716, and who, in Nov. 1739, married the only daughter of the late Sir Charles Sedley, of Nuthall, in Nottinghamſhire, Bart. and, in 1748, was choſen to Parliament for the borough of Tamworth. His Lordſhip married, 2dly, Jane, third and youngeſt daughter of Sir Thomas Leigh (who died before his father, Thomas, ſecond Lord Leigh, by his ſecond wife, Jane, daughter of Patrick, the nineteenth Lord of Kerry) and by her had iſſue, Thomas-Charles, the fifth Viſcount, and one daughter, Anne, married Nov. 23, 1710, to Sir William Keyt, of Old Stratford upon Avon, in Warwickſhire, Bart. Member for Warwick, (whoſe anceſtor, Sir John Keyt, of Ebrington, in Glouceſterſhire, was advanced to that dignity Dec. 22, 1660) and is mother of the preſent Sir Robert Keyt, Bt. and a daughter, wife of ——— Gibbs, of Warwickſhire, Eſq.

Thomas-Charles, the fifth Viſcount, married, firſt, Elizabeth, eldeſt daughter of William

liam Keyt, Efq; (who died before his father, Sir William Keyt, of Ebrington, Bart.) and by her, (who was born Sept. 11, 1689, and died in 1720) had iffue, William, who left no children; Thomas-Charles, the prefent and fixth Vifcount; and Jane, relict of the late Capel Hanbury, of Pontypool, in Monmouthfhire, Efq; by whom fhe had one fon and two daughters. His Lordfhip, in 1721, married, secondly, Frances, daughter of Sir John Packington, of Weftwood, in the county of Worcefter, Bart. (by his firft wife, Frances, eldeft daughter of Sir Henry Packer, of Honington, in Warwickfhire, Bart.) by whom he had three fons and four daughters: John, Warden of All Souls college, Oxford; Henry, a Captain in the Army; ——, who died without iffue; Frances, Woman of the Bed-chamber to the Queen; Anne, wife of John Smith, of Combhey, in Somerfetfhire, Efq; Member in the prefent Parliament for Bath, by whom fhe left one fon, and died in the year 1763. The other daughters died without iffue.

Creations.] Vifcount Tracy, of Rathcoole, in the county of Dublin, Jan. 12, 1642, 18 Ch. I.

Arms.] Topaz, an efcallop in the chief point, diamond, between two bends, ruby.

Creft.] On a cap of maintenance, ruby, an efcallop fhell, as in the coat, between two wings erect, topaz.

Supporters.] Two falcons proper, beaked, and belled, topaz.

Motto.] *Memoria pii æterna.*

Chief Seat.] Toddington, in the county of Gloucefter.

VISCOUNT BULKELEY*.

Thomas-James, Viscount Bulkeley, was born Dec. 12, 1752, and succceeded his father, James the late and sixth Viscount, and is at Westminster-School.

James, the late Viscount, married Emma, daughter and sole heir of Thomas Rowlands, of Cayrea, in the county of Anglesea, Esq; by whom he had issue two daughters, Bridget, born in 1749, and died July 13, 1766; and Eleonora-Maria, born 1750, and died the same year. And his Lordship deceasing on May 23, 1752, left his Lady with child, who was brought to bed, on Dec. 12, following, of the present Viscount. Her Ladyship, his mother, married, secondly, in 1760, Sir Hugh Williams, Bart. by whom she has issue two sons and two daughters.

This noble Lord is lineally descended from Robert Bulkeley, Esq; who was Lord of the manor of Bulkeley, in the county of Chester, in the reign of King John; another of his ancestors was Sir William Bulkeley, Knt. Chief Justice of Chester, in the reign of Henry IV.

Sir Richard Bulkeley was knighted, and appointed Chamberlain of North-Wales, in 1534, 26 Henry VIII. Sir Richard, his eldest son, was knighted in 1576, served in Parliament for the county of Anglesea in the reigns of the Queens Mary and Elizabeth, to the

---

* Principally from the kind information of John Lewis, of Beaumaris, in the Island of Anglesea, Esq;

last of which he was a faithful soldier and servant, and was Chamberlain of North-Wales. His sixth son, by his second wife, Lancelot, was in 1619, Archbishop of Dublin; Sir Richard, his eldest son by his first wife, was knighted, and appointed of Council to William, Lord Compton, President of Wales. His second wife was Mary, daughter of William, Lord Borough, of Gainsborough, by whom he had issue, *inter alia*,

Thomas, his second son, who was seated at Bawn-Hill, near Beaumaris, and by Charles I. was created Viscount Bulkeley. He was succeeded by his eldest surviving son,

Robert, the second Viscount, who in 1658, was Sheriff of the county of Anglesea, and Member of Parliament for the same, at the Restoration and continued to represent that county till his death, Oct. 18, 1688. He married Sarah, daughter of Daniel Hervey, of Cromlee, in Surry, Esq; by whom he had issue,

1. Richard, the third Viscount.
2. Robert, LL.D. Member in Parliament for Beaumaris.
3. Thomas, Member for Caernarvon.
4. Elizabeth, wife of John Griffith, of Glyn, in Caernarvonshire, Esq;
5. Martha, wife of Roger Price, of Rules, Esq;
6. Penelope. 7. Lumley.
8. Eleanor, wife of Sir William Smith, of Vinall, Bart. and 9. Catharine.

Richard, the third Viscount, born in 1658, represented the county of Anglesea, in all the Parliaments from 1680, to his death, and in 1701, was Vice-Admiral of North-Wales. He married,

married, firft, Mary, eldeft daughter of Sir Philip Egerton, of Egerton and Oulton, in the county of Chefter, Knt. and fecondly ———, daughter of Henry White, of Hawthlin, in the county of Pembroke, Efq; and deceafing Aug. 9, 1704, was fucceeded by his fon and heir,

Richard, the fourth Vifcount, who ferved for the county of Anglefea in feveral Parliaments, in the reigns of Queen Anne and King George I. which honour, together with that of Conftable of Beaumaris-caftle, and Chamberlain of North-Wales, have been, almoft without interruption, in this noble family, from the reign of Q. Elizabeth. On Sept. 2, 1713, he was conftituted Conftable of Caernarvon-caftle; but in 1714, was fucceeded therein by the Earl of Radnor, and died on June 24, 1724, at Bath. He married the Lady Bridget, eldeft daughter of James, the firft Earl of Abingdon, (by his firft wife, Eleonora, eldeft daughter and coheir of Sir Henry Lee, of Ditchley, in Oxfordfhire, Bart.) and by her Ladyfhip (who died in June 1753) left iffue two fons; Richard; James; and four daughters, Bridget; Eleonora-Maria; Anne; and Elizabeth.

Richard, the eldeft fon, fifth Vifcount, born in 1708, and elected March 24, 1730, Member for Beaumaris, was Conftable of the Caftle of that place, and Chamberlain of North-Wales, and married, in Jan. 1731, ———, daughter and heir of Lewis Owen, of Penierth, in Merionethfhire, Efq; (who remarried with Edward, third fon of John Williams, of Chefter, Efq;) by whom, having no iffue, he was fucceeded by by his brother, James, the sixth and late Viscount.

Creation.] Viscount Bulkeley, of Cashell, in the county of Tipperary, Nov. 10, 1644, 19 Charles I.

Arms.] Quarterly, first, diamond, a chevron between three bulls, their heads caboshed, pearl, armed the same; second, pearl, a fesse dancette, ruby; third, diamond, a cross pattee, pearl, in the sinister chief, an escallopshell, topaz; fourth, pearl, a chevron and half, between three chaplets, ruby.

Crest.] In a ducal coronet, topaz, a bull's head pearl, armed topaz.

Supporters.] Two bulls pearl, armed and unguled, topaz, each gorged with a collar dancette, ruby.

Motto.] *Nec temere, nec timide.*

Chief Seat.] Baron-hill, in the county of Anglesea.

VISCOUNT KINGSLAND.

HENRY-BENEDICT BARNEWALL, Viscount KINGSLAND, and Baron of Turvey, was born Feb. 1, 1708, succeeded his father, Nicholas, the late and third Viscount, June 14, 1725, and the last day of the session of Parliament, in April, 1739, delivered his Writ of Summons, and took the Oath of Allegiance; but his Lordship professing the Roman-catholic religion, is disqualified from sitting in the House of Peers, or enjoying the Privileges of Parliament. On May 12, 1735, his Lordship married Honora, eldest daughter of Peter Daly, of Quansbury, in the county of Galway, Esq;

Counsellor at Law, by his wife Elizabeth, daughter of Richard Blake, of Ardfry, in that county, Esq; but has no issue.

Nicholas, the late and third Viscount, succeeded his father Henry; and married Mary, daughter of Frances, Duchess of Tyrconnel, by her first husband George, Count Hamilton: and by her, who died Feb. 15, 1735-6, had issue two sons, Henry-Benedict, the present Viscount, and George; and four daughters, three whereof died young; but Frances, the second, married Richard Barnewall, Esq; third son of John Lord Trimleston.

Henry, the second Viscount, and grandfather of the present, succeeded his father, Aug. 20, 1663; and married first, Mary, daughter of John, the second Viscount Netterville, by whom he had a daughter, Marian, who married Thomas Nugent, Lord Riverston; and by his second wife, the Lady Mary Nugent, daughter of Richard, the second Earl of Westmeath, he had four sons and three daughters, viz.

1. Nicholas, the late Viscount.
2. Richard, born Aug. 7, 1675, and died June 4, 1746, unmarried.
3. Joseph, born April 25, 1677.
4. Christopher, born Feb. 22, 1680.
5. Mary, born July 20, 1670, and married, Sept. 23, 1687, to Thomas, Lord Howth, and died Oct. 16, 1715.
6. Bridget, born June 6, 1672, married to ———— Macmahon, Esq;
7. Mabel, born Nov. 24, 1673, first married to Oliver, the eighth Lord Louth, who died in 1707, leaving an only son, usually called Lord

Lord Louth; and, secondly, Stephen Taafe, of Dowanftown, Efq;

This antient and noble family is of French extraction, and allied to the Dukes of Little-Bretaigne, where the name continues ftill in great repute; and thence the progenitor of this noble Lord attended William Duke of Normandy, in his expedition to England. Upon the firft arrival of this family in Ireland, temp. Hen. II. they fettled at Beerhaven, in the county of Cork, and there obtained great poffeffions: but at length, by a confpiracy of the Irifh, headed by the Sullivans, were all flain, except the chief of the family's wife, who being big with child, and making her efcape towards Dublin, was kindly received, and foon after delivered of a fon, who refided at Drumnagh in the county of Dublin; and marrying a great heirefs, by her had two fons, Hugh, who died without iffue, in 1237, and Reginald, who was heir to his brother, from whom defcended Sir Nicholas, who had two fons.

1. Sir Chriftopher, from whom defcended the family of the Barnwalls of Crickftown, and the Lords Trimlefton.

2. John, anceftor of the Lord Kingfland, who was Sheriff of the county of Meath in 1433. From him defcended Sir Patrick Barnewall, who was Sollicitor-general and Mafter of the Rolls in Ireland in 1550. He was fucceeded by his fon and heir, Sir Chriftopher, who was very eminent in the profeffion of the law: he was fucceeded by his eldeft fon Sir Patrick, who was father of Nicholas, whom King Charles I. in regard to his fervices, was pleafed to create a Baron and Vifcount. He married Bridget, eldeft

dest daughter and coheir of Henry the twelfth Earl of Kildare, widow of Rory Odonnel, Earl of Tyrconnel, by whom he had five sons and four daughters, viz.
1. Christopher, who died unmarried.
2. Col. Patrick, who performed many great services for King Charles I, and died unmarried.
3. Henry, the second Viscount, already treated of.
4. Francis, of Beggstown, and Wood Park, in com. Meath, who had a numerous posterity, many of whom settled in foreign parts.
5. Matthew, who died unmarried.
6. Mary, wife of Nicholas, the sixth Viscount Gormanstown, and mother of Jenico, the seventh Viscount, and of Nicholas, whose sons succeeded to the honours.
7. Mabel, wife of Christopher, the second Earl of Fingal, mother of Luke, the third Earl.
8. Eleanor, wife of Charles White, of Leixlip Esq;
9. Frances, who died unmarried.

Creation.] Viscount Barnewall, of Kingsland, and Baron of Turvey, both in the county of Dublin, June 29, 1646, 22 Charles I.

Arms.] Ermine, a bordure ingrailed, ruby.

Crest.] On a wreath, a plume of five feathers, topaz, ruby, sapphire, emerald, and pearl; and thereon a falcon with wings disclosed of the last.

Supporters.] On the dexter, a griphon, pearl; On the sinister, a lion, ruby.

Motto.] *Malo mori quam fœdari.*

Chief Seat.] At Turvey, in the county of Dublin.

VISCOUNT KELLS.

See an account of this noble family, in my Peerage of England, under the title of Earl of CHOLMONDELEY.

VISCOUNT DOWNE.

JOHN DAWNAY, Viscount DAWNAY, of Downe, and Baronet, Member in the present Parliament for Cirencester, in Gloucestershire, (for which he was also elected in the last Parliament,) was born April 9, 1728, succeeded his brother, Henry-Pleydell, the late and third Viscount, on Dec. 9, 1760, and in 1763, married Lora, only daughter and heir of William Burton, of Luffenham, in the county of Rutland, Esq; by whom he has issue one son, the Hon. John-Christopher-Burton, born Nov. 15, 1764.

Sir Paine Dawnay, of Dawnay-castle, in the Duchy of Normandy, Knt. was one of those Generals that accompanied William the Conqueror, in his expedition to England, and was amply rewarded for his great services. From him descended, in a direct male line, Sir Nicholas Dawnay, of Shunock, in the county of Cornwall, who was summoned, amongst the Barons, to Parliament, 1 Edw. III. He was succeeded by Sir Thomas Dawnay, his eldest son, who settled at Cowick-hall, in the county of York, in 1334.

From him lineally descended Sir Christopher Dawnay, who was created a Baronet by King Charles I, May 19, 1642. He died in 1644, and was succeeded by his brother,

Sir

Sir John Dawnay, Knt. and Bart. created Vifcount Downe by Charles II. He reprefented the county of York, in the Convention-Parliament, 1660, and ferved for that county, and the borough of Pontefract, during the reigns of Charles II. and James II. He died in 1695, and was fucceeded by his fon,

Sir Henry Dawnay, the fecond Vifcount, who was a burgefs for the borough of Pontefract, in 1690, and reprefented the county of York, during the reigns of King William, Queen Anne, and King George I. He had iffue feveral fons and daughters.

John Dawnay, Efq; the eldeft fon, was chofen burgefs for Pontefract and Aldborough, 1713, and again for Pontefract, 1715. He married Charlotta-Louifa, daughter and fole heir of Robert Pleydell, of Ampney, in the county of Gloucefter, Efq; by whom he had iffue, Henry-Pleydell, the late Vifcount, and John, the prefent Vifcount. Dying in 1740, before his father,

Sir Henry-Pleydell, his eldeft fon, born Ap. 8, 1727, fucceeded his grandfather, in 1741, and was the third Vifcount. He reprefented the county of York, 1749, and again in 1754; was a Lord of the Bed-chamber to his Majefty, both when King and Prince of Wales, F. R. S. Colonel by brevet, Colonel of the Yorkfhire Militia, and Lieutenant-colonel of the twenty-fifth regiment of Foot; which regiment he commanded at the glorious battle of Minden, 1759, and which was one of thofe four regiments, whofe intrepidity determined the fate of that day; and again at the battle of Campen, October 16, 1760, where being mortally wounded,

wounded, he died the 9th of December following, and was succeeded by his only brother, Sir John, the fourth and present Viscount.

Creations.] Baronet, May 19, 1642, 18 Ch. I. Viscount Dawnay, of the county of Downe, Feb. 19, 1680, 33 Charles II.

Arms.] Pearl, on a bend cottised, diamond, three annulets of the field.

Crest] On a wreath, a Saracen in armour, couped at the thighs, and wreathed about the temples, proper, holding in his right hand, a ring, topaz, stoned, sapphire; and in his left a lion's gamb, erased, gold, topaz, armed, ruby.

Supporters.] Two lions, topaz, collared with the coat, and ducally crowned, pearl.

Motto.] *Timet pudorem.*

Chief Seats.] Cowick-hall, Dawnay-lodge, and Danby-castle, all in the county of York.

VISCOUNT LISBURNE.

WILMOT VAUGHAN, Viscount LISBURNE, Lord Vaughan, Baron of Fethers, succeeded his father, Wilmot, the late and third Viscount, on Jan. 6, 1766, and married, first, in July, 1754, Elizabeth, sole daughter of Joseph-Gascoyne Nightingale, of Mamhead, in the county of Devon, and of Enfield, in the county of Middlesex, Esq; (by the Lady Elizabeth Shirley, his wife, daughter and coheir of Washington, Earl Ferrers) sister, and at length coheir to her brother, Washington-Gascoyne Nightingale, Esq; who died in 1754, and by her Ladyship (who died May 19, 1755) had issue one son, the Hon. Wilmot Vaughan, born May 9, 1755.

His

His Lordship married, secondly, April 19, 1763, Dorothy, eldest daughter of John Shafto, of Whitworth, in the county of Durham, Esq; who represented that city in several Parliaments, and sister of Robert Shafto, Esq; Representative in the present Parliament for that county, and by her Ladyship has issue two daughters, Dorothy-Elizabeth, born May 13, 1764; and Mallett, born July 30, 1765.

In 1750, his Lordship was appointed an Ensign in the Coldstream regiment of Foot-guards, which he resigned in 1754. In 1755, he was chosen to represent the county of Cardigan, and upon the accession of his present Majesty was appointed Lord Lieutenant of that county, in the room of his father, who resigned. He was elected, Dec. 26, 1765, to represent the borough of Berwick upon Tweed, in the room of his uncle, Thomas Watson, Esq; who dying Jan. 6, 1766, bequeathed to his Lordship his whole estate.

Wilmot, the late Viscount, succeeded his brother, John-Edward, the second Viscount, and also as Lord Lieutenant of the county of Cardigan, and died at Trawscoed, Jan. 6, 1766. He married Elizabeth, eldest daughter of Thomas Watson, of Berwick upon Tweed, Esq; (who died Jan. 7, 1764) and by her left two sons, and one daughter, Elizabeth, wife of Thomas Lloyd, Esq; of Abertrenant, in the county of Cardigan, Esq. Of the sons, John the youngest, is Lieutenant-colonel of the 46th regiment of Foot, and Wilmot, the eldest, is the present Viscount.

This ancient family, which derives its descent, in a paternal line, from Collwyn ap Tagno,

Tegno, one of the fifteen tribes of Gwynydd, (who flourished about the year of our Lord 875) has been seated at Trawscoed (Crosswood) in the county of Cardigan, for sixteen generations. Of whom, John Vaughan, Esq; the son of Edward, and Lettice, daughter of John Stedman, of Strata-Florida, in the county of Cardigan, Esq; proved a very learned Lawyer, and eminent patriot. In the Parliament of 1640, he was chosen to represent the borough of Cardigan, and acted firmly with Selden, Pym, Hampden, and other patriot leaders, in their noble and spirited opposition to the measures of Charles I. But upon the breaking out of the civil war, he retired to his family seat, and remained there twenty years, till upon the return of Charles II. being elected to represent the county of Cardigan, in the Parliament held in the year 1660, he appeared again, amongst the most considerable men of those times. On May 20, 1668, he was appointed Lord Chief-Justice of the Common-Pleas, and died in that office, Dec. 3, 1674. He was buried in the Temple church, London, near the grave of his dearest friend, the learned Selden, who dedicated to him his *Vindiciæ*, and bequeathing his fortune amongst his four executors, appointed him one of them. A marble monument was erected on the south-west end of the said church, to his memory, thus inscribed:

Hic situs est, JOHANNES VAUGHAN, *Eques Auratus, Capital. Justiciar. de Commun. Banco; Filius Ed. Vaughan, de Trawscoed, in agro Dimætarum, & Letitiæ Uxoris ejus, Filiæ Johan. Stedman de Strata-Florida, in eodem Com.*

Com. Arm. Unus e quatuor perdocti Seldeni Executoribus, & stabili amicitia, studiorumque communione, a Tyrocinio intimus ac percarus. Natus erat xiii. die Sept. anno Dom. 1603, *& denatus x. die Dec.* 1674, *qui juxta hoc marmor depositus, adventum Christi propitium expectat, multum deploratus.*

He married Jane, eldest daughter and co-heir of John Stedman, of Kilkennin, in the county of Cardigan, Esq; by whom he had one son, Edward, and one daughter, wife of Richard Herbert, of Swansea, in the county of Glamorgan, Esquire. His said son,

Edward, served in several Parliaments for the county of Cardigan, and distinguished himself by his learned Speeches against a corrupt and arbitrary Court. He joined the Lords Russel and Cavendish in the Bill of Exclusion, and in all other measures tending to secure the Protestant Religion and the Liberty of the Subject. Many of his Speeches, upon the most interesting points, are extant in the Parliamentary Debates, and Anchitel Grey's Collection. Bishop Burnet, in his History of his Own Times, ranks him amongst those eminent men, who preserved the Constitution at that critical season, and bears testimony to his great integrity, and his public services*. He was, for some time, one of the Lords of the Admiralty, and published the Reports of his Father, with a learned Preface, written by himself. He died at Ludlow, in Shropshire, in 1683, leaving issue by Letitia, his wife, daughter of Sir William

---

* Burnet's Hist. Vol. i. p. 389.

Hooker,

Hooker, Knt. sometime Lord Mayor of London, two sons and three daughters. Of the daughters, the eldest became the wife of Robert Davies, of Llaneth, in the county of Flint, Esq; and, secondly, of —— Pennant, Esq; the second was the wife of John Owen, of Cundover, in the county of Salop, Esq; and the youngest died unmarried. Of the sons, Selden, the youngest, died unmarried, and

John, the eldest, was by King William, of glorious memory, created a Baron and Viscount. He represented the county of Cardigan in several Parliaments, and was appointed Lord Lieutenant and Custos Rotulorum thereof, in 1715.

His Lordship married Lady Mallett Wilmot, third daughter of John, Earl of Rochester, and sister and coheir to her brother, Charles, Earl of Rochester, and by her had issue three sons and four daughters, whereof Elizabeth and Mallett died unmarried; and Anne was the wife of Sir John Prideaux, of Netherton, in the county of Devon, Bart. Of the sons, Henry died unmarried, and John-Edward, the eldest succeeded his father, who died in 1721. The said

John-Edward, the second Viscount, was, in 1721, appointed Lord Lieutenant of the county of Cardigan, and elected to represent that county in Parliament in 1727. He died Jan. 15, 1740, without surviving issue. His first wife was ——, daughter of Sir John Bennet, Knt. Serjeant at Law; but by her, who died July 31, 1723, he had no children. His second was Dorothy, daughter of Richard Hill, of Henblas, in the county of Montgomery, Esq;

by

by whom he had one daughter, Mallett, deceased. He was succeeded by his next brother, Wilmot, the late Viscount, father of the present, as above recited.

Creation] Viscount and Baron, *ut supra*, June 25, 1695, 7 William III.

Arms.] Diamond, a chevron between three fleurs de lys, pearl, the arms of Collwyn.

Crest.] On a wreath, an armed hand, bent at the elbow, brandishing a fleur de lys, all proper.

Supporters.] On the dexter a dragon, with wings expanded, reguardant, emerald, gorged with a plain collar, diamond, edged pearl, and charged with three fleurs de lys, as in the coat, having a golden chain thereto affixed. On the sinister, an unicorn, reguardant, pearl, his horn, tufts, mane, and hoofs topaz, gorged and chained as the dexter.

Motto.] *Non revertar inultus.*

Chief Seats.] Trawscoed (Crosswood) in Cardiganshire; Mamhead, in the county of Devon; and Grindon-Ridge, in the county of Durham.

VISCOUNT HOWE.

RICHARD HOWE, Viscount HOWE, Baron of Clenawly, and Baronet, Treasurer of the Navy, and a Captain therein, Colonel of the Chatham division of Marines, a Lord of the Privy-council, and Member in the present Parliament for the borough of Clifton-Dartmouth-Hardness, in the county of Devon, succeeded his brother, George-Augustus, the third and late Viscount, on July 5, 1758, and on March

10, 1758, married Miſs Hartopp, daughter of —— Hartopp, Eſq; Lieutenant-governor of Plymouth, by whom he has iſſue one daughter. His Lordſhip's great and eminent ſervices to his country, in the late war, will hand down his name with honour to poſterity.

George-Auguſtus, the third and late Viſcount, ſucceeded his father, Emanuel-Scrope, March 29, 1735; and, in 1747, was choſen Member of Parliament for the town of Nottingham; as he alſo was in 1754. His Lordſhip, taking to a military life, was appointed Colonel, Sept. 28, 1757; and afterwards Brigadier-general, in which capacity he commanded under General Abercrombie, in North America; where his Lordſhip was killed in a ſkirmiſh as he was marching on the attack of Ticonderoga, July 5, 1758.

Sir Emanuel-Scrope, the ſecond Viſcount, and father of the late and preſent Viſcounts, ſucceeded his father Scrope, Jan. 26, 1712-13; and was choſen Knight of the ſhire for the county of Nottingham, in the ſecond Parment of King George I. re-choſen for the ſame in 1727; and in 1732 was appointed Governor of Barbadoes, where he died. On April 8, 1719, his Lordſhip married the Lady Maria-Sophia-Charlotte, eldeſt daughter of the Baron Kielmanſegg, a Count of the Empire of Germany, and Maſter of the Horſe to King George I. as Elector of Hanover (by the Lady Sophia-Charlotte, his wife, daughter of Count Platen, of the Empire of Germany; which Lady Sophia-Charlotte, Sept. 3, 1721, was created Counteſs of the Province of Leinſter, in Ireland; and, on April 10, 1722, was created

created Baronefs of Brentford, and Countefs of Darlington, in England, and was Countefs of Platen and Baronefs Kielmanfegg in Germany; and died April 20, 1725;) and by her, who is Lady of the Bed-chamber to the Princefs Dowager of Wales, his Lordfhip had four fons, viz. George-Auguftus, the late Vifcount; George-Scrope, who died without iflue; Richard, the prefent Vifcount; and William, Colonel of the 46th regiment of Foot, and Member in the prefent Parliament for the town of Nottingham. Alfo fix daughters.

The name of Howe frequently occurs in the antient Englifh writers, and has been of long continuance in the counties of Nottingham, Somerfet, Wilts, and Gloucefter.

Of this family was Sir John Howe, of Bifhop's Lydiard, in the county of Somerfet, Efq; who marrying Jane, daughter of Nicholas, and fifter of Sir Richard Grubham, who died in 1629, by her had three fons, of whom John and Sir George became poffeffed of vaft real and perfonal eftates, by the gift of their uncle, the faid Sir Richard Grubham. Sir George-Grubham Howe was feated at Cold-Berwick, or Berwick St. Leonard's, in Wilts; and had a fon, George, who was created a Baronet, June 20, 1660; whofe only fon, Sir James Howe, dying without iflue, Jan. 19, 1735, the title of Baronet became extinct.

Sir John, the eldeft of the two fons, by the fifter of Sir Richard Grubham, became feated at Compton, in the county of Gloucefter, and at Wifhford, near Salifbury; and, Sept. 22, 1660, was created a Baronet. He had three fons, Sir Richard-Grubham Howe, Bart. John-

* C 2   Grubham

Grubham Howe, and Sir Thomas Howe. S
Richard, the eldeſt, was ſucceeded by his on[ly]
ſon, Sir Richard, the third Baronet, who d[y]ing without iſſue, in 1730, his title deſcende[d]
to Scrope, Viſcount Howe.

John-Grubham Howe, the ſecond ſon, b[e]came poſſeſſed of the manor of Langar, in t[he]
county of Nottingham, by his wife, Lady A[n]nabella, third natural daughter and co-heir [of]
Emanuel, Earl of Sunderland; by which Lad[y]
who died March 21, 1703, he had four ſo[ns]
and five daughters, viz.

1. Sir Scrope, Groom of the Bed-chamber [to]
King William, by whom he was created Bar[on]
and Viſcount; and by his wife, Lady An[n]
Manners, ſixth daughter of John, the eigh[t]
Earl of Rutland, had two daughters; and [by]
his ſecond wife, Juliana, daughter of Willia[m]
Lord Allington, of Horſeheath, had a ſo[n]
Scrope, who was the ſecond Viſcount, a[nd]
three daughters; Mary, wife of Thomas, E[arl]
of Pembroke, and after of John Mordaun[t],
Eſq; brother of Charles, Earl of Peterboroug[h];
Judith, of Thomas Page, Eſq; ſecond ſon [of]
Sir Gregory Page, Bart. and Anne, of Colo[nel]
John Mordaunt.

2. John Grubham Howe, Eſq; who marri[ed]
Mary, daughter and co-heir of Humphry B[ac]kerville, Eſq; by whom he had iſſue Jo[hn]
Howe, late Lord Chedworth, who was fath[er]
of John-Thynne Howe, the late, and Fred[e]rick-Henry-Thynne, the preſent Lord Che[d]worth.

3. Charles, ſeated at Gritworth, in t[he]
county of Northampton, who left an on[ly]
daught[er]

daughter, married to Peter Bathurst, Esq; brother of Allen, Lord Bathurst.

4. Emanuel, who was Brigadier and Major-general in the armies of Queen Anne, Colonel of a regiment of Foot, and her Majesty's Envoy extraordinary at the Court of Hanover. He was Member of Parliament for Morpeth in 1701, and married Ruperta, natural daughter of Prince Rupert, Count Palatine of the Rhine, &c. by whom he had three sons and a daughter.

5. Bridget, wife of John Bennet, Lord Ossulston, and mother of Charles, Earl of Tankerville.

6. Elizabeth, married to Sir John Guise, of Elmore, in the county of Gloucester, Bart.

7. Diana, married to Sir Francis Molyneux, of Teversfelt, in the county of Nottingham, Bart.

8. Annabella; and

9. Mary, who died unmarried.

Creations.] Baronet, Sept. 22, 1660, 12 Cha. II. Viscount Howe, and Baron of Clenawly, in the county of Fermanagh, May 16, 1701, 13 William III.

Arms.] Topaz, a fess between two wolves heads, couped, diamond.

Crest.] In a ducal coronet, topaz, a plume of five feathers, sapphire.

Supporters.] Two Cornish choughs, proper; beaked, and membered, ruby.

Motto.] *Utcunque placuerit Deo.*

Chief Seat.] At Langar-castle, in the county of Nottingham.

VISCOUNT STRABANE.

An account of this noble family will be found in my Peerage of Scotland, under the title of Earl of ABERCORN.

VISCOUNT MOLESWORTH.

RICHARD-NASSAU MOLESWORTH, Viscount MOLESWORTH, and Baron of Philipstown, was born Nov. 4, 1748, succeeded his father, Richard, the third and late Viscount, Oct. 13, 1758, and is in his minority.

Richard, the late and third Viscount Molesworth, succeeded his brother John, Feb. 17, 1725-6, and, Nov. 10, 1714, was made Lieutenant of the Ordnance in Ireland, and a Colonel of Dragoons at Preston, in 1715; on March 19, 1724-5, he succeeded Major-general Witham in the command of his regiment of Foot in Ireland, where he was Member of Parliament for the borough of Swords : he also commanded a regiment in Flanders, and greatly distinguished himself at the battle of Ramillies, when he remounted the Duke of Marlborough on his own horse, by which means he rescued that great General from being taken prisoner, at the manifest hazard of his own life. After that, he had been advanced through several military employments; and at his death was Colonel of the Royal Irish regiment of Dragoons, Master-general of the Ordnance, General of Horse, Commander in chief of the Army in Ireland, and Field-marshal of his Majesty's forces; he was also one

one of his Majesty's Privy-council, and F. R. S. His Lordship married, first, Jane, daughter of Mr. Lucas, of Dublin; and by her, who died April 1, 1742, had a son, who died an infant, and three daughters, viz.

1. Mary, married, Aug. 7, 1746, to Robert Rochfort, Lord Bellfield, now Earl of Belvedere.
2. Letitia, married, Oct. 1753, to Lieutenant-colonel James Molesworth.
3. Amelia.

His Lordship married, secondly, Febr. 7, 1742-3, Mary, daughter of the Rev. Mr. William Usher, Archdeacon of Clonfert, by whom he had issue one son and six daughters, viz.

1. Richard-Nassau, the present Viscount.
2. Mary, born Sept. 14, 1744, and died soon after her birth.
3. Henrietta, born in July, 1745.
4. Melosina, born Dec. 27, 1746.
5. Mary, born Nov. 30, 1747.
6. Louisa, born Oct. 23, 1749.
7. Elizabeth, born Sept. 17, 1751.

Another of these Ladies died Jan. 30, 1758.

Of this noble family, which, in the reign of Edward I. flourished in the counties of Northampton and Bedford, was Sir Walter de Molesworth, Knt. who was of great note in the reign of that King; and, in 1290, accompanied that Prince in his expedition to the Holy Land against the Infidels; and from the 25th to the 34th of that King's reign was Sheriff for the counties of Bedford and Bucks, an office, in those early times, of great trust and authority.

In 1306, on a great festival at Whitsuntide, when King Edward I. to adorn his court with greater splendor, and augment the glory of his intended expedition into Scotland, knighted Edward, Earl of Caernarvon, his eldest son; the Prince, immediately after that ceremony, at the altar in Westminster-abbey, conferred the same honour on near three hundred gentlemen, the sons of Earls, Barons, and Knights; of which was Sir Walter de Molesworth; and that Prince succeeding to the throne, July 7, 1307, directed a summons to Sir Walter and his Lady, to attend at his coronation; and appointed him that year, with Gilbert de Holme, Sheriff of the aforesaid counties; and in 1313, sole Sheriff of the same; and in the fifth year of King Edward II. he and Gerard de Braybrooke had their writs of expence issued for their service as Knights of the Shire for Bedford, in the first Parliament of that King, which met at Westminster.

To this Sir Walter succeeded Hugh, who, in the eighth of Edward II. with Henry de Tilley, served as Knight of the Shire for the county of Huntingdon, in a Parliament held at York. To him succeeded Sir Walter, whose son and heir, Richard, is mentioned in the Pipe-rolls of Northamptonshire in 1339.

From him descended Robert Molesworth, of Edlington, in the county of York, and Bracken's-town, in the county of Dublin, who, upon the Revolution, in 1688, distinguished himself by an early and zealous appearance in the defence of the religion and liberty of his country, and enjoyed no small share of the esteem of King William III. by whom he was sent Envoy extraordinary to Denmark, at which court he refided for feveral years; and foon after his return obliged the public with an account of that kingdom; which is generally efteemed one of the beft works of that kind that has appeared in our language, from whence it has been tranflated into feveral foreign ones; he was the author of feveral other pieces in defence of liberty and the common rights of mankind, for which he will always continue to be highly efteemed, on account of his great judgment, force of reafoning, and mafculine eloquence. He was member of the Privy-council to Queen Anne, till the latter end of her reign, when parties running high, he was difmiffed from that Board, in Jan. 1714, upon a complaint againft him from the lower Houfe of Convocation, to the Houfe of Peers, charging him with faying, in the hearing of a great many perfons, the following words, " They " that have turned the world upfide down are " come hither alfo;" and for affronting the clergy in convocation, when they prefented their addrefs in favour of Lord Chancellor Phipps: but his Majefty, K. George I. in the firft year of his reign, reftored him to the Privy-council, made him one of the Commiffioners of Trade and Plantations, and created him Baron and Vifcount as above. He married Letitia, daughter of Richard Coote, Baron of Colloony, by which Lady, who died Mar. 18, 1729, he had feven fons, and four daughters, viz.

1. John, who fucceeded him, in May 1725, and was by her Majefty Queen Anne appointed
her

her Envoy extraordinary to the Grand Duke of Tuscany; and, in 1720, was, by K. George I. appointed Envoy extraordinary and Plenipotentiary to the King of Sardinia; as he was afterwards to the States of Venice and Switzerland. He married Mary, one of the five daughters and coheirs of Thomas Middleton, of Stansted-mountfitchet, in the county of Essex, Esq; by whom he had an only daughter, born after his decease, and married, in 1751, to Frederick Gore, Esq; Clerk of the Quitrents, and Member for the borough of Tulske.

2. Richard, the late Viscount, who succeeded his brother John.

3. William, Surveyor-general of the lands in Ireland, and Member of Parliament for the borough of Philipstown; who married Anne, eldest daughter of Robert Adair, of Holybrook, in the county of Wicklow, Esq; and had issue Robert, Lieutenant of a troop of Dragoons; John; Richard; Letitia, wife of Captain Johnston; Elizabeth, Juliana, Jane, Amelia, and Isabella.

4. Edward, an Officer in the army, who had a son, Nicholas, deceased, and one daughter.

5. Walter, also an Officer in the army.

6. Coote, M. D. in 1735, appointed Physician to the garrison at Minorca.

7. Byrie, Member of Parliament for the borough of Swords; who, by Elizabeth, daughter of John Cole, of Enniskellin, Esq; had seven sons and two daughters.

8. Margaret, who died young.

9. Mary, married to George Monk, of Stephen's-green, Esq; and dying, left behind her a collection of excellent Poems, which her father

ther publiſhed, and dedicated to her late Majeſty Queen Caroline. She had iſſue Henry-Stanley Monk, Eſq; Sarah, wife of Robert Maſon, Eſq; and Margaret, of Henry Butler, Eſq;

10. Charlotta-Amelia, married to Captain William Tichburne, ſecond ſon of Henry, Lord Farard, by whom ſhe had one ſon and three daughters.

11. Letitia, married to Edward Bolton, of Brazile, in the county of Dublin, Eſq; and Member of Parliament for Swords, by whom ſhe had four ſons and five daughters.

Creations.] Viſcount Moleſworth, of Swordes, in the county of Dublin, and Baron of Philipſtown, in the Queen's county, July 16, 1716, 2 Geo. I.

Arms.] Vaire, on a bordure, ruby, eight croſlets, topaz.

Creſt.] On a wreath, an armed arm embowed at the elbow, proper, holding a croſlet, topaz.

Supporters.] Two pegaſuſſes, the dexter, pearl, crined, winged, and unguled, topaz. The finiſter, ruby, alike crined, winged, and unguled, and femée of croſlets, topaz.

Motto.] *Vincit amor patriæ*; and, *Sic fidem teneo.*

Chief Seats.] Breckdenſtown, in the county of Dublin; and Edlington, in the Weſt-riding of Yorkſhire.

VISCOUNT CHETWYND.

WILLIAM CHETWYND, Viscount CHETWYND, and Baron of Rathdowne; Masterworker of his Majesty's Mint, and Member in Parliament for Stafford, succeeded his brother, John, the late and second Viscount, in 1767, and has issue, by his Lady, who died in childbed Sept. 5, 1726, William, late Member for Stockbridge, Hants, (who married on Nov. 16, 1751, the youngest daughter of Sir Jonathan Cope, Bart. by whom he had a son born in 1753,) and three daughters.

John, the late Viscount, succeeded his brother, Walter, the first Viscount, Feb. 21, 1735-6; on Nov. 8, 1714, he was made a Commissioner of Trade and Plantations: In May 1717, he was appointed his Majesty's Envoy Extraordinary to the Court of Spain. In the first Parliament of George I. he was elected for St. Maw's, in Cornwall; and in the two succeeding ones for Stockbridge, in Hampshire. He was elected for Stafford in 1738, and again in 1741. His Lordship had several children, of whom his eldest son died abroad in 1741. William-Richard, the second, was chosen Member of Parliament for Stafford in 1754, and died also *vita patris*; and his eldest daughter married, in Aug. 1748, to the Hon. John Talbot, Esq; brother of Earl Talbot.

Of this family, which hath been of great antiquity in the county of Salop, taking their surname from Chetwynd in that county, was Adam de Chetwynd, who married Agnes, daughter of John, Lord Lovel, Baron of Dockinges,

Inges, and Lord of Minster-Lovel in Oxfordshire; and by her had issue Sir John de Chetwynd, who, in the 37th of Henry III. had a charter of free-warren throughout all his demesne in the counties of Salop, Stafford, and Warwick; for the manor of Baxterly, in the county of Warwick, he had a grant of John Lovel, his kinsman, paying to him and his heirs a pound of pepper yearly at Easter; and, in 1280, it was found that the same Sir John had certain customary tenants there, who did suit twice a year at his leet. He married Isabel, daughter and heir of Phil'p de Mitton, with whom he had the Lordships of Ingestree, Salte, and Gretwiche, in the county of Stafford; and to him succeeded William his son, whose seat was at Oddeston, in the county of Leicester. From him descended Sir William Chetwynd of Ingestree, who, in the reign of King Edward III. was, by indenture, retained with John of Gaunt, Duke of Lancaster, to serve him, as well in times of peace as war, for ten merks per annum, which indenture being lost was again renewed by the said Duke, whereby he increased his fee to ten pounds per annum; and in the 10th of Richard II. recounting his faithful services, gave him the sum of ten pounds more per annum, to be received out of the issues of his Honor at Tetbury. Richard, his son and successor, was, in the 7th and 15th of Henry VI. Sheriff of Staffordshire; in the 17th of that reign, was employed in the dutchy of Guienne for the King's service; and in the 20th constituted Governor of the city of Baion in Normandy, being allowed nine hundred and forty merks to retain as many Archers,

for

for the safeguard thereof, as might be therewith hired for a quarter of a year. In the 22d of the same reign, he was retained by Humphry, Earl of Buckingham, to do service during life, according to his degree, as well in times of peace as war, with as many men and horses as the said Earl should appoint.

From him descended Walter, the eldest son of John Chetwynd, of Mare and the Ridge, in the county of Stafford, who succeeded to the estate of Sir Walter Chetwynd, of Ingestree, was made Master of her Majesty Queen Anne's Hart and Buck-hounds; and was Member of Parliament for Stafford, from 1702 to 1734. In 1715, he was appointed Ranger of St. James's Park; and was created a Peer; and, Jan. 18, 1717, was elected High Steward of the borough of Stafford. He married Mary, daughter and coheir of John Berkley, Viscount Fitz-Harding, by which Lady, who died June 3, 1741, he had no issue, and was succeeded by his brother the late Viscount.

Creations.] Viscount Chetwynd, of Bearhaven, in the county of Kerry; and Baron of Rathdowne, in the county of Dublin.

Arms] Sapphire, a chevron between three mullets, topaz.

Crest.] On a wreath, a goat's head erased, pearl, attired, topaz.

Supporters.] Two unicorns, pearl, each gorged with a chaplet of red roses, barbed and seeded, proper, and thereto affixed a chain of the same.

Motto.] *Probitas verus honos.*

Chief Seats.] At Hazelar, near Litchfield.

VISCOUNT MIDLETON.

George Brodrick, Viscount Midleton, and Baron Brodrick, was born Nov. 1, 1754, and succeeded his father, George, the late and third Viscount, Sept. 22, 1765. His Lordship is a minor.

George, the late Viscount, was born Oct. 3, 1730, and succeeded his father Alan, the second Viscount, June 8, 1747. He married Albinia, daughter of Thomas Townshend, Esq; brother of Charles, Viscount Townshend, by whom he had issue, George, the present Viscount, and Thomas, born Dec. 1, 1758, in which year his Lordship was chosen Member for Ashburton, in Devonshire. His Lordship had seven children besides, of whom five are living; Mary, Henry, Charles, William, and John.

Alan, the second Viscount, succeeded his father Alan, Aug. 29, 1728; and, in May 1729, married the Lady Mary Capel, one of the Ladies of the Bed-chamber to the Princess Royal, and sister to William, Earl of Essex, by whom he had two sons, George, the late Viscount, and another son, who died an infant. His Lordship, in 1727, was appointed a a Commissioner of the Customs in England, which he held till Aug. 1730, when, in conjunction with Sir Philip Meadows, he was appointed Comptroller for the Accounts of the Army.

Of this family, which is lineally descended from George de Brodrick (who came into England in the reign of William II.) was Sir Thomas Brodrick, of Richmond, in Yorkshire,

and

and Wandsworth, in Surry, Knt. who died in 1641, whose son and heir, Sir Alan, was Surveyor-general of Ireland, and Member of Parliament for Dungarvan in 1661, and died in 1680. Sir St. John, third son of the said Sir Thomas Brodrick, dwelt at Midleton, in the county of Cork, and in the first Parliament after the Restoration, was Member for Kingsale. His son and heir, Thomas, was one of the Privy-council to King William, and Member for Cork, and was Joint-comptroller of the Accounts of the Army with Sir Philip Meadows, which he resigned in 1711, and was Comptroller of the Salt-duties. In the last Parliament of Queen Anne, and the first of King George I. he represented the borough of Stockbridge; in the following Parliament was elected for Guilford; and was appointed Member of the Privy Council to K. George I. but died in 1730. He married Anne, daughter to Alexander Pigott, of Innishannon, in the county of Cork, Esq; by whom he had issue,

1. Laurence Brodrick, who, in Jan. 1735-6, was appointed Joint-register of all Deeds and Conveyances in Ireland.
2. Alan, created Lord Midleton.
3. St. John, Serjeant at Law, died in 1707, unmarried.
4. Randal, died also unmarried.
5. William, appointed Attorney-general of the Island of Jamaica, and a Serjeant at Law, 1692; and,
6. Laurence, who was Chaplain to the House of Commons in England, and Prebendary of Westminster, died in 1740, leaving a daughter, wife of Benjamin Bathurst, Esq; brother of Allen,

Allen, Lord Bathurst; and one son, Laurence, Treasurer of Lismore, &c. &c.

Alan, the second son, was appointed by King William, Sollicitor-general of Ireland, in which post he was continued by Queen Anne, and, in 1703, was chosen Speaker to the Irish House of Commons. In 1707 he was made Attorney-general of Ireland; and, in 1709, was made Lord Chief-justice of the Queen's-bench there. In the first of George I. he was declared Lord Chancellor of Ireland, and continued in that trust till 1725. He was created a Baron and Viscount; and in 1717 was made one of the Lords Justices of Ireland, as he was again in 1724. In 1716 he was chosen to serve in the British Parliament, for Midhurst, in Sussex, which place he represented till his death. He married to his first wife, Catharine, second daughter of Redmond Barry, of Rath-cormuck, in the county of Cork, by whom he had issue one daughter, who died an infant; and a son, St. John, who was chosen Member of Parliament for Beer-Alston, in the county of Devon, and was appointed of his Majesty's Privy-council in Ireland, where he was also chosen Knight of the shire for the county of Cork. He married Anne, sister of Trevor, first Viscount Hillsborough, but died before his father, in Feb. 1727-8, leaving issue five daughters. To his second wife, the said Alan, Viscount Midleton, married Alice, daughter of Sir Peter Courthorp, of the Little-Island, in the county of Cork, Knt. by whom he had two sons, Courthorp, who died young, and Alan, the second Viscount; and a daughter, Alice, wife of the Rev. John Castleman. He married, thirdly,

thirdly, Anne, daughter of Sir John Trevor, Master of the Rolls, in England, but by her, who died in Jan. 1747-8, had no issue.

Creations.] Baron Brodrick, of Midleton, in the county of Cork, April 13, 1715, 1 George I. Viscount Brodrick, August 15, 1717, 3 George I.

Arms.] Pearl, on a chief, emerald, two spears, heads erect, of the field, the points imbrued, ruby.

Crest.] Issuing out of a ducal coronet, a spear, proper, imbrued, as in the coat.

Supporters.] Two men in complete armour, each holding in his exterior hand a spear, as the crest.

Motto.] *A cuspide corona.*

Chief Seat.] At Pepper-harrow, in the county of Surry.

VISCOUNT BOYNE.

FREDERICK HAMILTON, Viscount BOYNE, and Baron Hamilton, was born in Nov. 1718, succeeded his cousin, Gustavus, the second Viscount, April 20, 1746, and in Oct. 1747, took his seat in the House of Peers.

Claud, the first Lord Paisley, had five sons (See my Peerage of Scotland, under the title Earl of ABERCORN) of whom Sir Frederick, the youngest, served under Gustavus Adolphus, King of Sweden; after which he had a regiment in the wars of Ireland, in the reign of King Charles II. He married Sidney, daughter and sole heir of Sir John Vaughan, Knt. by whom he had three sons and one daughter. Of the sons, Gustavus, the youngest, had a regiment

ment given him by King William in 1689, which he headed at the battle of the Boyne, where he narrowly efcaped being killed. After this victory, ftorming the town of Athlone, he was made Governor thereof; and was in all the battles fought by General Ginckell for the reduction of Ireland; upon the accomplifhment whereof, he was fworn of the Privy-Council, and made a Brigadier-general. In 1704, he was Knight of the fhire for the county of Donegall, of which county he was alfo Cuftos Rotulorum, and Vice-admiral of the Province of Ulfter; and was of the Privy-council to Queen Anne, and King George I. being by the former made a Major-general; and by the latter created a Baron and Vifcount, as above. He married Elizabeth, fecond daughter of Sir Henry Brooke, of Brooke's-borough, in the county of Fermanagh, Knight, and by her had three fons, and a daughter, viz.

1. Frederick, who died before his father; and having married Sophia, eldeft daughter of James Hamilton, of Tullimore Efq; and fifter of James, Vifcount Limerick, left two fons, Guftavus, who fucceeded his grandfather, and James, an Officer in the navy, who died in 1744; and two daughters, Anne and Elizabeth, who died young.

2. Guftavus, who was Knight of the fhire for Donegall, and married Dorothy, only daughter of Richard Lord Bellew; and dying in 1734-5, left two fons, and five daughters, viz. Frederick, the prefent Vifcount; and Richard, born March 24, 1724-5, whom Guftavus, Vifcount Boyne, made his heir. He married Jane, daughter of William Bury, of Shannon-grove,

in the county of Limerick, Efq. Of the daughters, Frances the eldeſt, Elizabeth the ſecond, and Sophia the fourth, died unmarried. Catharine, the third, married, Dec. 26, 1744, to Edward Lovibond, of Hampton, in Middleſex, Efq; and Dorothea.

3. Henry was Knight of the ſhire for the county of Donegall, and married Mary, eldeſt daughter of Joſhua Dawſon, of Caſtle-Dawſon, in the county of Derry, Efq; and dying in 1743, left five ſons and two daughters, viz.

The Rev. Guſtavus, who married Letitia, eldeſt daughter of Edward Bolton, of Brazeil, Efq; Joſhua, Land-waiter in the Port of Cork, who married the eldeſt daughter of Sir Richard Cox, Bart. Sackville, Clerk in the Secretary's Office of the Revenue; Henry; Edward; Anne, and Mary.

4. Elizabeth, married to Charles Lambert, of Pean's-town, in the county of Meath, brother to the firſt Earl of Cavan.

Guſtavus, eldeſt ſon of Frederick, ſucceeded his grandfather, Sept. 16, 1723, and was the ſecond Viſcount: in 1736, he was choſen Member of Parliament for Newport, in the Iſle of Wight; and in 1737, made a Commiſſioner of the Revenue in Ireland, having been ſworn of his Majeſty's Council the preceding year, and died unmarried.

Creations.] Baron Hamilton, of Stackallan, in the county of Meath, Oct. 20, 1715, 2 Geo. I. Viſcount Boyne, of the river Boyne, Aug. 20, 1717, 4 Geo. I.

Arms.] Ruby, three cinquefoils, pierced, ermine.

Creſt.] In a ducal coronet, topaz, an oak, fructed,

fructed, and penetrated tranfverfely in the main ſtem, by a frame-ſaw, proper, the frame, topaz.

Supporters.] Two mermaids, proper, their hair diſhevelled, topaz, each holding in her exterior hand, a mirror of the latter.

Motto.] *Nec timeo, nec ſperno.*

Chief Seat.] Redwood, in King's county.

VISCOUNT ALLEN.

JOSHUA ALLEN, Viſcount and Baron ALLEN, Captain in the firſt regiment of Foot-guards, with the rank of Lieutenant-colonel, and Member of Parliament for the borough of Eye, in Suffolk, ſucceeded his brother, John, the fourth Viſcount, on Nov. 10, 1753, and is unmarried.

This family, which was originally Engliſh, ſettled in Holland about two hundred years ago, of whom John Allen, Eſq; was ſent to Ireland, as a Factor for the Dutch, in the latter end of the reign of Queen Elizabeth; and being a ſkilful Architect, was conſulted by moſt of the Nobility in their buildings, and left a large fortune to his ſon, Sir Joſhua, who was a merchant; in 1664, Sheriff; and, in 1673, Lord Mayor of the city of Dublin: but was involved in the general attainder in 1689. He was ſucceeded by his only ſurviving ſon John, who bore a Captain's Commiſſion in the reign of King William, and in that and the ſucceeding reign repreſented the county of Wicklow in Parliament, as he did the county of Dublin in the reign of K. George I. when he was ſworn of his Majeſty's Privy-council, and created a Peer. He married Mary, ry, eldeſt daughter of Robert Fitzgerald, Eſq; and ſiſter of Robert, the nineteenth Earl of Kildare; dying Nov. 8, 1726, he left three ſons, viz.

1. Joſhua, who ſucceeded him, and was the ſecond Viſcount.

2. Robert, Knight of the ſhire for the county of Wicklow, from the time that he came of age till his death: he was alſo Sheriff of that county in the years 1720 and 1721. He died in 1641, leaving iſſue by Frances, daughter of Robert Johnſon, Eſq; Baron of the Exchequer, two ſons, who both died unmarried, and three daughters.

3. Richard, who ſerved in Parliament for the borough of Athy, in the reign of K. George I. and married Dorothy, one of the five daughters and coheirs, of Major Green, of Killaghy, in the county of Tipperary, by whom he had iſſue five ſons and four daughters, all deceaſed, except Joſhua, the preſent Viſcount Allen, Richard, Jane, and Elizabeth.

Joſhua, the ſecond Viſcount Allen, born in 1685, married Margaret, daughter of Samuel Dupaſs, of Epſom, Eſq; by whom he had two ſons and five daughters, and was ſucceeded, Dec. 5, 1742, by his only ſurviving ſon, John, the third Viſcount, who having the misfortune to be inſulted in the ſtreets, April 26, 1745, by three Dragoons, his Lordſhip received a wound in his hand, which threw him into a fever, of which he died, May 25th following, and was ſucceeded by

John, the fourth Viſcount, eldeſt ſon of Richard Allen, the youngeſt ſon of the firſt Viſcount,

count, who, dying unmarried, was succeeded by his brother, the present Viscount.

Creation.] Viscount Alien, of the county of Kildare, and Baron Allen, of Stillorgan, in the county of Dublin, Aug. 28, 1717, 4 Geo. I.

Arms.] Pearl, two bars wavey, and a chief sapphire; on the latter, an estoile between two escallop shells, topaz.

Crest.] On a wreath, a bezant, charged with a talbot's head erased, diamond.

Supporters.] Two talbots of the last.

Motto.] *Triumpho morte tam vita.*

Chief Seats.] Puncheftown, in the county of Kildare; and Stillorgan, in the county of Dublin.

VISCOUNT GRIMSTON.

JAMES GRIMSTON, Viscount GRIMSTON, Baron of Dunboyne, and Baronet, was born Oct. 9, 1711, succeeded his father, William, the late and first Viscount, Oct. 15, 1756, and married Mary, daughter of William Bucknall, of Oxhey, in the county of Hertford, Esq; (which Lady was born April 28, 1717) by whom he has issue, 1. The Hon. James-Bucknall, born May 9, 1747; 2. Jane, born Sept. 18, 1748; 3. William, born June 23, 1750; 4. Harbottle, born April 14, 1752; 5. Mary, born May 28, 1753; 6. Susanna-Askell, born Sept. 28, 1754; 7. Francis-Cook, born Mar. 27, 1757; 8. Joanna, born Sept. 10, 1759.

This ancient family took their firname from their lands in the county of York, and are descended from Sylvester de Grimston, who attended William I. in his conquest of England,

as

as his Standard-bearer. When the Conqueror was settled on the throne, he was constituted his Chamberlain, and did homage and swore fealty for Grimston, Hoxton, Tonsted, and other lands, which he held of the Lord Roos, of his honor of Roos, in Holdernesse, in the county of York. He was succeeded at Grimston, by his son Daniel, father of Sir Thomas Grimston, living in the reign of King Stephen, father of John, father of Sir William, father of Sir Roger, who was Under-sheriff of the county of Kent, to Hubert de Burgh, from 1223 to 1228. He had issue two sons, Walter; and Sir Gervaise Grimston, who had no issue.

Walter, who succeeded, had three sons; 1. William, some of whose posterity are still seated in Yorkshire; 2. Robert; and, 3. John, Dean of Windsor, probably, in 6 Hen. V.

Robert, the second son, became seated in Suffolk, in the reign of Henry V. and marrying the daughter of Sir Anthony Spilman, was father of Edward, his successor in the lands at Rishangles, and Ipswich, in that county, who married, first, Philippa, daughter of John, Lord Tiptoft, sister and co-heir of John, Earl of Worcester, and relict of Thomas, Lord Roos, by whom he had no issue. His second wife was Mary, daughter of William Drury, of Rougham, in Suffolk, Esq; by whom, amongst other children, he had issue, John, ancestor of the Grimstons of Norfolk and Essex; and Edward, his eldest son, who was father of Edward, father of another Edward, who served in several Parliaments in the reign of Queen Elizabeth, for Ipswich, was knighted, and sworn of that Princess's Privy-council; he was also continued

tinued Comptroller of Calais, to which he had been appointed by Edward VI. He was ninety-eight years of age at the time of his death, and was succeeded by his son, Edward Grimston, Esq; who was seated at Bradfield, in Essex, and 31 Eliz. was Member for Eye, his father being then living. He greatly enlarged his estate by his marriage with Joan, daughter and co-heir of Thomas Rysby, of Lavenham, in Suffolk, Esq; and had issue by her two sons, Harbottle, and Henry, who were both knighted. He deceased Aug. 15, 1610. His sons married two sisters, and Sir Henry had a son, Edward, who died March 17, 1656.

Sir Harbottle, the elder son, was created a Baronet, Nov. 25, 1612, and was Sheriff of Essex, in 1614. He represented that county in three Parliaments, in the reign of K. Charles I. married Elizabeth, daughter of Ralph Coppinger, of Stoke, in Kent, Esq; and dying about 1640, left issue five sons; Edward, who, had no issue; Harbottle, Henry, Thomas, and William. He was succeeded by his second son,

Sir Harbottle, the second Baronet, well remembered in history for his honest and constitutional behaviour during the civil wars in the reign of Charles I. But he did not approve of all the measures of the Long Parliament, and therefore was, by force, excluded from his seat in the House of Commons, imprisoned and hardly dealt by. He was afterwards very instrumental in the Restoration of Charles II. and returning to the House, was chosen Speaker, Ap. 25, 1660. He was of the Privy-council to that Prince, and Master of the Rolls, and was also Recorder of Harwich, and High-steward of St.

* D   Alban's.

Alban's. He deceased in Jan. 1683, age eighty-two. He married Mary, daughter of Sir George Crooke, Knt. Justice of the Common pleas, by whom he had six sons and two daughters: Of the sons, five died before him, and of them, George, the eldest, in the 23d year of his age, without issue. The daughters were Mary, wife of Sir Capel Luckyn, Knt. and Bart. and Elizabeth, of Sir George Grubham Howe, of Cold-Barwick, in Wiltshire, Bart. His second wife was Anne, elder daughter, and at length heir, of Sir Nathanael Bacon, of Culford-hall, in Suffolk, Knight of the Bath, by whom he had an only daughter, Anne, who died young; and his Lady having the manor of Gorhambury and Kingsbury, near St. Alban's, settled upon her for life, he purchased the reversion thereof from Mr. Hercules Meautys, nephew of Sir Thomas Meautys, her first husband, the former of which, Sir Samuel Grimston, his only surviving son, made the chief place of his residence. Which

Sir Samuel served in six Parliaments for St. Alban's, in the reigns of Charles II. and William III. He married, first, Elizabeth, eldest daughter of Heneage Finch, Earl of Nottingham, Chancellor of England, by whom he had an only daughter, Elizabeth, the first wife of William Saville, Marquis of Halifax, who had by her a daughter, Anne, the first wife of Thomas Lord Bruce, son of Thomas, Earl of Aylesbury. His second wife was Lady Anne Tufton, youngest daughter of John, second Earl of Thanet, by whom he had a son, Edward, and a daughter, Mary, who both died young; whereupon the title of Baronet became extinct, upon his death

death, in 1700; but he bequeathed his great estate, under certain limitations, to William Luckyn, Esq; second son of Sir William Luckyn, of Miffing-hall, in Essex, Knt. and Bart. son and heir of Sir Capel Luckyn, before mentioned, by Mary, Sir Samuel's eldest sister.

Which family of Luckyn, the paternal ancestors of the present Lord, were of great antiquity in Essex, Robert Luckyn being Sheriff of that county, 16 James I. as Sir William Luckyn, of Little-Waltham, Knt. was in 13 Charles I. and was created a Baronet in 1628. He was father of Sir Capel, above mentioned, and of Sir William, created a Baronet in 1661, who leaving only a daughter, the title expired.

The said Sir Capel, by his said wife, Mary Grimston, (who died March 18, 1718, aged eighty-six) had a numerous issue, of whom Sir William, the second son, succeeded to the title and estate, and marrying Mary, daughter of William Sherrington, Esq; Alderman of London, had ten sons and five daughters, viz. 1. Sir Harbottle, his successor, Cup-bearer to Queen Anne, and King George II. who died unmarried; 2. William, adopted heir of Sir Samuel Grimston; 3. Capel; 4. Henry, both deceased; 5. Charles, Rector of Peelmarsh and Messing, in Essex; 6. Edward; 7. Samuel, deceased; 8. George, who died in 1733; 9 & 10. Sherrington and James, both deceased: Mary, Elizabeth, Sarah, Mildred, and Martha, all deceased.

The second son, Sir William, assumed the name of Grimston, and in 1713, 1714, and 1727, was Member for St. Alban's, and was created Viscount Grimston.

His Lordship married Jane, daughter of James Cooke, citizen of London, by whom he had many children; whereof, 1. Samuel, the eldest son, in Nov. 1730, married Mary, daughter and heir of Henry Lovel, Esq; a Turkey-merchant, youngest son of Sir Salathiel Lovel, Baron of the Exchequer, by whom he had issue a daughter, that died in her infancy; and deceasing himself, June 19, 1737, his widow afterwards remarried with William-Wildman, the present Viscount Barrington. 2. William, who died young. 3. James, the second and present Viscount. 4. Harbottle, born Dec. 2, 1712, deceased. 5. George, born Aug. 12, 1714. 6, 7. Edward, and Edward, both died young. 8. William, born Jan. 3, 1719, deceased. 9. Edward, died young. 10. Henry, born Mar. 21, 1727. Of the daughters, Jane and Frances, both died in their infancy; Jane was born Dec. 20, 1718, married Thomas Gape, of St. Alban's, Esq; and is deceased; and Frances, born Sept. 15, 1725, died young.

Creations.] Baronet, March 2, 1628, 4 Cha. I. Viscount Grimston, and Baron of Dunboyne, in the county of Meath, Jun. 3, 1719, 5 Geo. I.

Arms.] Quarterly, the first and fourth pearl, on a fess, diamond, three mullets, of six points, pierced, topaz, and in the dexter chief an ermine spot, for Grimston. The second and third diamond, a fess dancette, between two leopards faces, topaz, for Luckyn.

Crest.] On a wreath, a stag's head couped, proper; attired, topaz.

Supporters.] On the dexter a stag, reguardant, proper, attired as the crest; on the sinister, a gryphon, reguardant, topaz.

Motto.]

Motto.] *Mediocria firma.*
Chief Seats.] Gorhambury, in the county of Hertford; Miffing-hall, in Effex.

VISCOUNT BARRINGTON.

WILLIAM-WILDMAM BARRINGTON, Vifcount and Baron BARRINGTON, was born in the year 1717, and fucceeded his father, John, the late Vifcount, in 1734. In Sept. 1740, his Lordfhip married Mary, daughter and heir of Henry, youngeft fon of Sir Salathiel Lovel, Baron of the Exchequer, and relict of Samuel Grimfton, eldeft fon of William, late Vifcount Grimfton, which Lady died in Sept. 1764, without leaving any furviving iffue.

His Lordfhip has been a Member of the Britifh Parliament ever fince 1739, either for Berwick on Tweed, or Plymouth, which laft borough he now reprefents. In 1746, he was appointed a Lord Commiffioner of the Admiralty, in 1754, Mafter of the Great Wardrobe, and in March the following year, was fworn of the Privy Council. In Nov. of the fame year, he was conftituted Secretary at War. In March, 1761, he was appointed Chancellor and Under-Treafurer of the Exchequer, in the room of the Right Hon. Henry-Bilfon Legge, and in June 1762, furrendering that Office into his Majefty's hands, was conftituted Treafurer of the Navy, in the place of the Right Hon. George Grenville, then appointed Secretary of State. On July 19, 1765, he was a fecond time appointed Secretary at War.

It appears by the Records in the Herald's Office, that the family of Shute is originally

* D 3   Norman,

Norman, and was settled in that Dutchy, while the English Kings were in possession thereof. They served those Princes with reputation and success, both in the field and as Governors of fortresses committed to their charge, and were possessed of a castle called after their name; some remains of which castle, with the arms of Shute, painted on the windows, and monuments of that family, in several towns in Normandy, were to be seen in the reign of Queen Elizabeth. It also appears, that Christopher Shute, of Hockington, in the county of Cambridge, Esq; a descendant of the Norman family, was father of Robert, who being bred to the Law, was a Judge in that reign. He was created Serjeant in Michaelmas term, 1577, was Recorder of Cambridge, and served in several Parliaments for that town, till 1579, when he was made a Baron of the Exchequer, and afterwards, in 1585, he was appointed one of the Justices of the King's-Bench. He married Thomasine, daughter of Christopher Burgoine, of Long Staunton, in Cambridgeshire, Esq; by whom he had four sons, Francis, John, Christopher, Thomas, and a daughter, Jane, married to John Hatton, Esq; father of Sir Christopher Hatton, Knt. of the Bath.

Francis, the eldest son, had a son of his own name, by his wife, Frances, daughter of Hercules Mewtays, of West-ham, in Essex, Esq; (who re-married with Robert Ratcliffe, Earl of Sussex.) Which second Francis resided at Upton, in Leicestershire, and had three sons, James, Samuel, and Benjamin. James, the eldest, had two sons, James and Joseph; Samuel, the second, had three sons, Francis, Joseph, and Caryl,

who

who all died young, and two daughters, his co-heirs; 1. Elizabeth, married to Francis Barrington, of Tofts, in Effex, Efq; 2. Anne, firft married to Thomas Andrews, of Langdon-hills, in Effex, Efq; and afterwards to Dr. Knightley Chetwoode, of Tempsford, in Bedfordfhire, Dean of Gloucefter.

Benjamin Shute, Efq; the youngeft fon, died in 1683, and having married Elizabeth Caryl, had iffue three fons, and three daughters, viz.

1. Samuel, Colonel of Horfe, and afterwards Governor of New England, who died unmarried in 1742.
2. Benjamin, who died alfo unmarried in 1714.
3. John, of whom prefently.
4. Mary, wife of Henry Yeamans, Efq;
5. Martha, wife of Henry Bendifh, Efq; and,
6. Mary, wife firft of Richard Offley, of Norton-hall, in Derbyfhire, Efq; and afterwards of Gervafe Scrope, of Cockrington, in Lincolnfhire, Efq;

John Shute, Efq; the third fon, was made a Commiffioner of the Cuftoms, in 1708, being then a young Barrifter of the Inner-Temple, and fucceeded to the eftate of Francis Barrington, Efq; beforementioned, who married his firft coufin; in confequence of whofe will he took the name and arms of Barrington, a family of great note and antiquity in Effex, which has the honour of being defcended from George, Duke of Clarence, brother of King Edward IV. by his daughter the Countefs of Salifbury. In the year 1710, he alfo came into a large eftate in Berkfhire, bequeathed to him by John Wildman, of Becket, Efq; no way related

* D 4

lated or allied to him, who, in his will, dated four years before his death, declared his only reason for making Mr. Shute his heir, was, that he thought that Gentleman the most worthy to be adopted by him. On June 20, 1720, he was created Viscount and Baron Barrington, and at the same time, had a reversionary grant of the Office of Master of the Rolls, in Ireland, then in the possession of the late Lord Berkeley, of Stratton. He was twice chosen Representative for the town of Berwick upon Tweed, and married Anne, eldest daughter and coheir of Sir William Daines, Knt. (which Lady died Feb. 8, 1763,) by whom he had issue six sons and three daughters, viz.

1. William Wildman, the present Viscount.
2. Francis, who died in his minority.
3. John, a Major-general, and Colonel of the 8th regiment of foot, endeared to his country by his gallant behaviour in the late war, who married Elizabeth, daughter of Florentius Vassal, Esq; by whom he had three sons and one daughter, William, Richard, George, and Louisa, and he died in 1764. In 1759, succeeding General Hopson, deceased, in his command, as senior Officer, he reduced the Island of Guadalupe to his late Majesty's obedience, after an obstinate resistance, which was the first important acquisition of the late war, and by his moderation, and strict execution of the terms of capitulation, after the surrender of that Island, did not inconsiderably contribute to our future successes in those parts.
4. Daines, Barrister at Law, one of the Welsh Judges.

5. Sa-

5. Samuel, Captain in the Navy, who has distinguished himself in the two last wars, particularly, by taking singly, the St. Florentine, a 60 gun ship of war, in the French service, when he commanded the Achilles, which was, in every respect, inferior in force to the enemy.

6. Shute, LL. D. Chaplain in Ordinary to his Majesty, and Canon of Christ-Church, who married Lady Diana, daughter of Charles, late Duke of St. Albans, who died in 1766, without issue.

7. Sarah, deceased, who in 1759, married Robert Price, of Foxley, in Herefordshire, Esq;

8. Anne, wife of Thomas, son and heir of the late Sir Thomas Clarges, Bart. and

9. Mary, who died unmarried in 1743.

His Lordship died on Dec. 14, 1734, in the 56th year of his age, and was succeeded by his son, the present Viscount, as before recited.

Creation] Baron Barrington, of Newcastle, in the county of Dublin, and Viscount Barrington, of Ardglass, in the county of Downe, July 1, 1720, 6 George I.

Arms.] Pearl, three chevronels, ruby, a label of three points, sapphire.

Crest.] On a wreath, a Capuchin Friar, proper, with black hair, a band about his neck, argent, vested, pally of six, pearl and ruby, with a cap, or cowl, of the same.

Supporters.] Two gryphons, with wings expanded, topaz, and gorged with labels, as in the coat.

Motto.] *Honesta, quam splendida.*

Chief Seats.] Becket-house, in Berkshire; Totts, in Essex.

VISCOUNT VANE.

WILLIAM VANE, Viscount VANE, and Baron Vane, of Dungannon, in the county of Tyrone, born in 1714, succeeded his father, William, the first Viscount, on May 20, 1734, and in 1735, married Anne, daughter and heir of Francis Hawes, of Perley-hall, in Berkshire, Esq; one of the South-sea Directors, in the year 1720, and relict of Lord William Hamilton, by whom he has no surviving issue.

Of the family of Vane, which were antiently seated in Wales, and thence transplanted into Kent, where they have continued many years, was Sir Henry Vane, Knt. who, in 1330, was so made by the Black Prince at the battle of Poictiers; and from him descended Ralph Vane, who was knighted by Henry VIII. at the siege of Boulogne; and afterwards, being involved in the misfortunes of the Duke of Somerset, he was beheaded Feb. 26, 1551, and his estate was lost to the family. John, his brother, married Joan, daughter and coheir of Edward Hault, and had two sons, Henry and Richard; from which Richard are descended the present Earl of Westmoreland and Lord Catherlogh, and the Viscount Fane; and Henry, the eldest, continuing the line in Kent, from him descended Sir Henry Vane, Knt. who was so made by K. James I. and by Charles I. sent Ambassador extraordinary, first to the States of Holland; secondly to the Queen of Bohemia; and afterwards to Gustavus Adolphus, King of Sweden. He was also, by that King, made Comptroller and Treasurer of the Houshold, and Secretary

of

of State; and when the civil wars broke out, he so heartily concurred with the measures of the Parliament, that, in Dec. 1645, on a treaty with the King, he was nominated by both Houses to be created a Baron. He died before the Restoration, leaving two sons, Sir Henry, and Sir George, both of whom were knighted by King Charles I.

Sir Henry, the eldest, was made Treasurer of the Navy, by patent, for life: but in the first wars between the English and the Dutch, when the fees of the office, which were fourpence per pound, amounted to near thirty thousand pounds per annum, he looked upon it as too much, and generously gave up his patent to the Parliament, desiring but two thousand pounds per annum for an agent he had bred up to the business; and the remainder to go to the public.

The title of Baron Raby (the house and land of Vane, which title Sir Henry had promised himself,) being unluckily given to the Earl of Strafford, in contempt of Vane, his father, and himself, he joined with Mr. Pym, and other discontented persons, and acted very strenuously against the King in the civil-war. Upon the Restoration he was imprisoned, and after two years confinement was beheaded on Tower-hill, for high treason, June 4, 1662. His eldest son,

Thomas Vane, of Raby-castle, dying without issue, was succeeded by his brother, Sir Christopher Vane, Knt. who was created Baron Bernard, of Bernard-castle, in the bishopric of Durham; and dying Oct. 28, 1723, left issue by Elizabeth, eldest daughter of Gilbert Holles,

Holles, Earl of Clare, and sister and co-heir of John, Duke of Newcastle, four sons, and four daughters; Albinia, Elizabeth, and Mary, who died young, and Grace. The sons were, 1. Henry; 2. Christopher; who died young. 3. Gilbert, second Lord Bernard, father of Henry, late Earl of Darlington. (See Earl of DARLINGTON, in my Peerage of England.) 4. William, who, Sept. 13, 1720, 7 Geo. I. was created Baron of Dungannon, and Viscount Vane. He was chosen Representative for the Bishopric of Durham, in 1708, for Steyning in 1727, and for the county of Kent a few days before he died. He married Lucy, daughter of William Jollife, of Carefwell, in the county of Stafford, Esq; and by her, who died March 27, 1742, had three sons, viz.

1. Christopher, who died July 19, 1721, aged seventeen years.

2. John, who died Feb. 5, 1724, at the age of seventeen.

3. William, the present Viscount.

Creations.] *Ut supra.*

Arms.] Sapphire, three sinister gauntlets topaz, on a canton, ermine, a pile, diamond, charged with a mullet of five points, pearl.

Crest.] On a wreath, a dexter hand couped above the wrist, and erect, in a gauntlet, topaz, brandishing a sword, proper.

Supporters.] On the dexter, a bay horse: On the sinister, a buck, proper, both reguardant.

Motto.] *Pulchra pro libertate.*

Chief Seats.] Fairlawn, in the county of Kent; and Carefwell, in the county of Stafford.

VISCOUNT GAGE.

WILLIAM-HALL GAGE, Viscount and Baron GAGE, and Baronet; Pay-master of the Pensions, Member in Parliament for Seaford, in Suffex, and Fellow of the Royal Society, succeeded his father, Thomas, the late and first Viscount, in 1754, and in Jan. 1757, married Miss Elizabeth Gideon, daughter of the late Sampson Gideon, Esq; and sister of the present Sir Sampson Gideon, of Spalding, in Lincolnshire, Bart. but has not yet any issue.

This noble family is of Norman extraction, and derives its descent from de Gaga, or Gage, who attended William I. in his expedition to England; and after the conquest thereof, was rewarded with large grants of lands in the Forest of Dean, and county of Gloucester, near which Forest he fixed his residence, by building a seat at Clerenwell, in the same place where the house of Gage now stands: he also built a great house at the town of Cirencester, at which place he died; and was buried in the Abbey there.

Of this family there were Barons in Parliament in the reign of King Henry II. and Members of Parliament in the reigns of Edward III. and Henry IV. for Tavistock in Devonshire, and Basingstoke in Hampshire.

Sir John Gage distinguished himself in an extraordinary manner at the siege of Terouenne, under King Henry VIII. and was thereupon made Captain of the Castle of Calais; soon after that he was sent for home, knighted, made one of the Privy-council, Vice-chamberlain, and Captain of the Guards. A few years after, for services done on the Borders of Scotland, he was made Comptroller of the Houshold, and Chancellor of the Dutchy of Lancaster in one day. He was also made Constable of the Tower of London, and Knight of the Garter, of which noble Order he was installed, May 22, 1541. He was one of the Knights, who, with the two Archbishops and the principal Nobility and Clergy, signed that memorable letter to Pope Clement VII. desiring his Holiness to comply with the King in his divorce.

At the taking of Boulogne, 36 Henry VIII. he was in joint Commission with Charles Duke of Suffolk, Lord Lieutenant of his Majesty's Camp; and was made Captain of the band of Horsemen. At the death of the King, he was left one of his Executors; and, as a token of his royal favour, he left him a legacy of two thousand marks. In the reign of Edward VI. he was one of the Supreme Council; and in that of Queen Mary, he was made Lord Chamberlain of the Houshold.

His eldest son and heir, Sir Edward Gage, was made a Knight of the Bath in the reign of Queen Mary, in the life-time of his father; and was Sheriff of Surry and Sussex, in the fourth of her reign; and his son John Gage succeeded to fifteen manors, besides divers messuages, lands, &c. in Sussex: but dying without issue, he was succeeded by John Gage, his nephew, eldest son of Thomas, his third brother, who was created a Baronet; and was succeeded by his son Sir Thomas Gage, of Firle, whose eldest son and successor, Sir Thomas, dying on his travels without issue, was succeeded by his brother, Sir John, who was the fourth Baronet.

Sir

Sir William Gage, the seventh Baronet, was created a Knight of the Bath in May 1725, and was elected to Parliament for Seaford, which he reprefented till he died, Apr. 23, 1744, and dying unmarried, the title defcended to Thomas, fourth fon of Jofeph, fourth fon of the fecond Baronet, who was created Vifcount Gage, to whofe fons he left the bulk of his fortune.

Which Jofeph Gage, above-mentioned, the fourth fon of Sir Thomas Gage, the fecond Baronet, inherited his mother's eftate of Shirburn-caftle, in the county of Oxford; and got a great eftate with his wife, Elizabeth, daughter of George Penruddock, of the county of Southampton, Efq; by whom he had iffue two fons and two daughters; Elizabeth, wife of John Wefton, of Sutton, in Surry, Efq; and Anne, married to Richard-Arundel Bealing, of Langhern, in Cornwall, Efq.

The fecond fon, Jofeph, being concerned in the Miffiffippi fchemes in France, in 1719, acquired a fortune computed at twelve or thirteen millions fterling, which fo intoxicated him, that he made an offer to Auguftus, then King of Poland, of three Millions for that Crown, which his Majefty refufing, he purpofed to purchafe the Ifland of Sardinia from that King, which project was alfo rejected. But the next year being reduced to great poverty, by the fall of that bubble, he fought new adventures in Spain, where, in Feb. 1727, he obtained a grant from the crown of working and draining all the Gold Mines in Old Spain, and fifhing for all wrecks on the coaft of Spain and the Indies. In 1741, the King prefented him with a Silver Mine of immenfe value, to him and his heirs,

by

by patent, with the title of Count, or Grandee, of the third clafs; after which, he was conftituted General of his Majefty's army in Sicily; and, in March 1743, honoured with the title of Grandee of Spain of the firft clafs, and Commander in chief of the army in Lombardy; being alfo prefented by the King of Naples with the Order of St. Januarius, and a yearly penfion of four thoufand ducats. He married the Lady Lucy Herbert, fourth daughter of William, the firft Marquis of Powis, and died in May, 1766.

Thomas, the eldeft fon of the faid Jofeph and Elizabeth, and the eighth Baronet, was created a Baron and Vifcount by George I. and reprefented the borough of Tewkfbury in Parliament from October 1721, to his death, was Verdurer of the Foreft of Dean, Steward of the Houfhold to Frederick, Prince of Wales, and F. R. S. On March 31, 1732, he received the Thanks of the Houfe of Commons, for his great fervice in detecting the fraudulent fale of the Earl of Derwentwater's eftate. He married firft Beata-Maria-Therefa, fole daughter and heir of Benedict Hall, of High Meadow, in the county of Gloucefter, Efq; and by her, who died July 25, 1749, had iffue,

1. William-Hall, the prefent Vifcount.
2. Thomas, Colonel of the twenty-fecond regiment of Foot, a Major-general, and Commander of the Forces in America, who married an American Lady, and has iffue two fons, Henry and William; and two daughters.
3. Therefa, married Mar. 6, 1755, to George Tafburgh, of Bodney, in Norfolk, Efq;

His

His Lordship married, 2dly, Dec. 26, 1756, Mrs. Jane Godfrey, widow of Henry-Jermyn Bond, of St. Edmund's-bury, Efq; by which Lady, who died Oct. 8, 1757, he had no iffue.

Creations.] Baronet, March 26, 1622, 24 James I. Vifcount Gage, of Caftle-Ifland, in the county of Kerry, and Baron Gage, of Caftlebar, in the county of Mayo, Sept. 14, 1720, 7 George I.

Arms.] Per faltire, fapphire and pearl, a faltire, ruby.

Creft.] On a wreath, a ram, proper, armed and unguled, topaz.

Supporters.] Two greyhounds, tenné, each gorged with a coronet, compounded of fleurs de lys, topaz.

Motto.] *Courage fans peur.*

Chief Seats.] High-meadow, in Gloucefterfhire; Firle, and Eaft-Grinftead, in Suffex.

VISCOUNT PALMERSTON.

Henry Temple, Vifcount Palmerston, and Baron Temple, one of the Lords Commiffioners of the Admiralty, and Member of Parliament for Eaftloe, in Cornwall, was born Dec. 4, 1739, fucceeded his grandfather Henry, the late and firft Vifcount, on June 10, 1757, and married the daughter of the late Sir Henry Poole, Bart.

Leuric, or Leofric, Earl of Chefter, living in the time of King Ethelbald, anno 716, is faid to be the anceftor of the family of Temple; from whom defcended Leofric, who is by fome affirmed to be the firft Earl of Leicefter, in the time of Edward the Confeffor; and was chiefly inftrumental strumental in raising that Prince to the Throne, as he was also of his successor Harold Harefoot. He founded that great monastery at Coventry, which he endowed with no less than twenty-four Lordships; and married the famous Godina, who rode naked through Coventry, by day, to regain the Citizens their privileges, which they had forfeited by offending their Lord her husband, and to free them from the taxes with which they were oppressed: he died Aug. 31, 1057, and was buried in his monastery. Algar, his son, succeeded to the Earldom of Mercia, who, in 1053, was Earl of the East-Saxons. His son Edwin, disliking the government of the Normans, was deprived of his Earldom by the Conqueror, and lost his life defending himself with only twenty horsemen, against a superior force, anno 1071. He left a son Edwin, sometime stiled Earl of Leicester and Coventry, who is said to assume the surname of Temple, from the Manor of Temple, in the hundred of Sparkenhoe, standing in Wellesborough, so denominated from the Knights Templars, to whom it was granted by the old Earls of Leicester.

Peter Temple, of Stow, in the county of Buckingham, had two sons, John, who succeeded him, and from him descended, in a direct line, the late Viscount Cobham, and present Earl Temple in England, who is still possessed of the Estate of Stow, in the county of Bucks, and others in the county of Warwick. The second son of the said Peter Temple was Anthony, father of Sir William, who became a Fellow of King's College, in Cambridge; and by the uncommon progress he made in his studies, recommended himself to the acquaintance and friendship

friendship of the famous Sir Philip Sidney, who took him into the Low Countries, and there expired in his arms. By the said Sir Philip he was recommended to the great Earl of Essex, whose Secretary he afterwards was, till that Earl's fall; and then retiring into Ireland, became Provost of Trinity College, in Dublin, where he died in 1626.

His eldest son and heir, Sir John, was knighted by Charles I. to whom he was one of the Privy-council, and Master of the Rolls in Ireland; and wrote the History of the Irish Rebellion. He married Mary, daughter of John Hammond, of Chertsey, and sister of that famous and great Divine, Dr. Hammond; by whom he had four sons and three daughters.

Sir William, the eldest, so well known by his many foreign negociations, from 1665 to 1679, and esteemed for his just and elegant writings, was created a Baronet.

Sir John, second son of Sir John Temple, Knt. and brother of Sir William Temple, Bart. was knighted by King Charles II. and was Speaker of the House of Commons in Ireland before the age of thirty; he was also, by the said King, made Sollicitor, and afterwards Attorney-general, in which station he continued most of the reign of King James, and in those of King William and Queen Mary. He married Jane, daughter of Sir Abraham Yarner, of Dublin, Knt. by whom he had four sons and seven daughters. Of the sons only two, Henry and John, lived to be men. John married Mrs. Elizabeth Temple, grand-daughter of the famous Sir William Temple before-mentioned, by whom he had eleven children, of which only four

four daughters furvived, and died at Moore-Park, in Surry, in Feb. 1752.

Henry, the eldeſt brother, was created Baron Temple, and Viſcount Palmerſton, and was Chief Remembrancer of his Majeſty's Court of Exchequer in Ireland. In 1727 he was choſen Member of Parliament for Eaſt Grinſtead; in 1734 for Boſſney; and in 1741 for Weobly. He married, firſt, Anne, daughter of Abraham Houblon, of London, Eſq; and by her, who died in December 1735, had five children, viz.

1. Henry, married, firſt, the only daughter of Colonel Lee, who died in 1736, without iſſue; and, ſecondly, Sept. 12, 1738, Jane, the youngeſt daughter of Sir John Barnard, Knt. then Lord Mayor of London, by whom he had Henry, the preſent Viſcount; and himſelf died in Auguſt, 1740.

2. John, who died an infant.

3. Richard, who married Henrietta, daughter of James Pelham, of Crowhurſt, in Suſſex, Eſq; by which Lady, (who married, ſecondly, George, Lord Abergavenny, in Feb. 1753,) he left a ſon, born Feb. 18, 1748-9, and died in Auguſt following.

4. Jane, who died Dec. 23, 1728.

5. Elizabeth, who died June 3, 1737.

His Lordſhip married, ſecondly, Iſabella, daughter of Sir Francis Gerrard, of Harrow on the hill, Bart. widow of Sir John Fryer, Bart. Lord Mayor of London in 1721, but had no iſſue by her.

Creation.] Viſcount Palmerſton, of Palmerſton, in the county of Dublin; and Baron Temple,

Temple, of Mount Temple, in the county of Sligo, March 12, 1722, 9 Geo. I.
Arms.] Quarterly, first and fourth, topaz, an eagle displayed, diamond. Second and third, Pearl, two bars, diamond, on each three martlets, topaz.
Crest.] On a wreath, a talbot sejant, diamond, gorged with a plain collar, topaz.
Supporters.] On the dexter side, a lion, reguardant, pean, viz. black powdered with yellow. On the sinister, a horse, reguardant, pearl, his main, tail, and hoofs, topaz.
Motto.] *Flecti, non frangi.*
Chief Seats.] East-Sheen, in the county of Surrey; and Palmerston, in the county of Dublin.

VISCOUNT BATEMAN.

JOHN BATEMAN, Viscount BATEMAN, and Baron of Culmore, one of the Lords of the Privy-council, Master of the Buck-hounds, Chief Steward of Leominster, and Member in the British Parliament for New Woodstock, in Oxfordshire, succeeded his father, William, the late and first Viscount, in Dec. 1744, and on July 10, 1748, married Miss Sambroke, daughter and co-heir of John Sambroke, Esq; and neice of Sir Jeremiah Sambroke, of Gubbins, in Hertfordshire, Bart.

Of this noble family, which was anciently seatted at Halesbrook, near St Omer's, in Flanders, was Giles Bateman, Esq; whose son Joas was a Merchant of London; and was father of Sir James Bateman, Knt. who, in 1712, was chosen Member of Parliament for Ilchester, in the county

county of Somerset, and re-chosen in 1713; and, in 1715, was Member for Eastlow, in Cornwall. In 1717, he was Lord Mayor of London, and, in 1718, was appointed Sub-governor of the South-sea Company; but dying Nov. 10, the same year, left issue, by Esther, youngest daughter and co-heir of John Searl, of Finchley, in Middlesex, Merchant of London, four sons and three daugters, viz. William, James, Richard, Henry, Anne, Judith, and Elizabeth.

William, the eldest, succeeded his father, and was elected Member of Parliament for Leominster in 1721; and in 1727. He was created a Peer as above; and, in 1731, he was made a Knight of the Bath. His Lordship married the Lady Anne Spencer, only daughter of Charles, Earl of Sunderland, by the Lady Anne Churchill, second daughter and coheir of John, Duke of Malborough; and by her had two sons, John, the present Viscount, and William, a Captain in the Navy, who, in 1752, was chosen Member of Parliament for Gatton, in Surrey; and, Feb. 17, 1755, married Miss Hedges, of Finchley.

Creation.] Baron of Culmore, in the county of Londonderry, and Viscount Bateman, July 12, 1725, 11 Geo. I.

Arms.] Topaz, on a fess, diamond, between three Muscovy ducks, proper, a rose of the field.

Crest.] On a wreath, a duck's head and breast, between two wings erect, proper.

Supporters.] Two lions, pearl, gorged with plain collars, diamond, charged with a rose between two fleurs de lys, topaz, and to each collar is a chain affixed, of the latter.

Motto.]

Motto.] *Nec prece, nec pretio.*
Chief Seats.] At Shobdon-court, in the county of Hereford; and at Upper-Tooting, in Surrey.

VISCOUNT GALWAY.

WILLIAM MONCTON, Viscount GALWAY, and Baron of Killard, Master of the Staghounds, Receiver of the Crown and Fee-farm Rents of Durham, Northumberland, &c. and Member in the British Parliament for the borough of Pontefract, in Yorkshire, succeeded his father, John, the late and first Viscount, on July 15, 1751, and on Aug. 12, 1747, married Miss Villa Real, a Lady of a very large fortune, by whom he has several children.

This noble family is descended from Simon Moncton, whose family had in possession the Lordship of Moncton, in the county of York, till it was made a Nunnery in the 20th Edw. II. 1326; and since called Nun-Moncton; after which time, the Monctons were seated at Cavil, in the said county, of which Lordship Thomas Moncton became possessed, by marrying the heiress of Cavil, about the 33d of Henry VI. and his posterity have been in possession of it ever since.

Sir Philip Moncton, of Cavil, was father of Sir Francis Moncton, who was knighted at York, Jan. 25, 1641, by Charles I. and had Sir Philip, who was knighted at Newcastle, in 1643; and underwent two banishments for King Charles I. as also several imprisonments during the civil-war for Charles II. when he and his father and grandfather were all at once under seque-

sequestration by Oliver Cromwell. He married Anne, daughter and heir of Robert Eyre, of Highlow, in the Peak of Derbyshire, Esq; and by her had Robert his heir, and William, an Officer in the Navy, killed before Barcelona in 1706. Robert, who succeeded his father, being one of those Gentlemen who went into Holland, and came over with King William, at the Revolution, was afterwards, for several years, one of the Commissioners of Trade. In 1695 he was chosen Member of Parliament for Pontefract; and, in 1701, for Aldborough, in Yorkshire. He married Theodosia, daughter and coheir of John Fountain, of Melton super montem, in the county of York, Esq; and by her had two sons, John and Robert, whereof the latter died unmarried.

John the eldest, had a warrant for the dignities of Baron and Viscount from King Geo. I. but his patent not passing the Seals in Ireland before that King's death, his warrant was renewed by K. George II. on his coming to the Crown. He was elected to Parliament for Clithero in Lancashire, in 1727; for Pontefract, also in 1734, 1741, and 1748. He married Lady Elizabeth, daughter of John, Duke of Rutland, by which Lady, who died March 22, 1729-30, he had three sons and one daughter, viz.

1. William, the present Viscount.
2. Robert, a Major-general, and Colonel of the 17th regiment of foot, and Governor of Berwick and Holy Island, whose services in the late war are too well remembered to need farther mention here.
3. John, died Oct. 2, 1728.

4. Eli

4. Elizabeth, died July 23, 1732.

His Lordship married, secondly, Jane, sister of Warner Westenrae, of Queen's county, Esq; by whom he had three sons, Philip, born July 27, 1738; ———, born in Aug. 1739; ———, born in Feb. 1701-2; and a daughter, born in April, 1747.

Creations.] Baron of Killard, in the county of Clare, and Viscount of the town of Galway, July 17, 1727, 1 George II.

Arms.] Diamond, on a chevron, between three martlets, topaz, as many mullets of the field.

Crest.] On a wreath, a martlet as in the coat.

Supporters.] Two unicorns, ermine, each gorged with an Eastern crown, topaz.

Motto.]

Chief Seat.] At Serlby, in the county of Nottingham.

VISCOUNT POWERSCOURT.

RICHARD WINGFIELD, Viscount POWERSCOURT, succeeded his brother Richard, the late and second Viscount, and was born in the year 1730.

This noble family is denominated from the manor of Wingfield, in Suffolk, where they had a seat before the Norman conquest, called Wingfield-castle; for we find that Robert Wingfield was Lord of Wingfield-castle so early as the year 1087, and left the same to his son, John de Wingfield, the father of another Robert, Lord of Wingfield. From him descended Sir Anthony Wingfield, Knight of the Garter, Vice-chamberlain of the Houshold, Captain of the Guards, and Executor to K. Henry VIII. He was father of Robert, whose son, Sir Thomas, had a son, Sir Anthony, of Goodwin, in Suffolk, created a Baronet, May 27, 1627, from whom descended Sir Mervin, who leaving an only daughter, the title of Baronet became extinct. Richard, the youngest of five sons of Sir Anthony Wingfield, Knight of the Garter, was father of Sir John, who lost his life in the expedition to Cales, in 1596.

Lewis, uncle to the said Sir Anthony, Knight of the Garter, and the ninth of twelve sons of Sir John Wingfield and Elizabeth Fitz-Lewis, settled in Hampshire, and was father of Sir Richard, who was Governor of Portsmouth in the reign of Queen Elizabeth; and was father of Sir Richard, who, by that Queen, was constituted Mareshal of Ireland; and by King James I. one of the Lords Justices, by whom also, on Feb. 1, 1618, he was created Viscount Powerscourt; but he dying without issue, the title became extinct.

George, the third son of Lewis, before mentioned, had a son Richard, whose son, Sir Edward, became heir to Lord Powerscourt: he was bred a soldier, and was Commander at the siege of Kingsale. His son, Sir Richard, had his house at Powerscourt burnt down, and lost his life in the service of King Charles I. He left a son, Folliott, born in 1642, who, in 1661, was returned to Parliament for the county of Wicklow, though under age, and, in 1665, was created Viscount Powerscourt; but dying without issue, in 1717, the title became again extinct; we therefore return to

Lewis,

Lewis, his uncle, the third of the six sons of Sir Edward Wingfield, who became heir to the first Lord Powerscourt, married Sidney, daughter of Sir Paul Gore, of Manor-Gore, in the county of Donegal, Bart. and had three sons, Edward, his heir, Thomas, and Richard, who left no issue.

Edward, the eldest, succeeded to the estate at Powerscourt, and married Eleanor, second daughter of Sir Arthur Gore, of Newtown-Gore, in the county of Mayo, Bart. by whom he had issue Richard his heir, and two daughters; Isabella, married to Sir Henry King, and was mother of Robert, Lord Kingsborough; and Sidney, married, in 1723, to Acheson Moore, of Aghnecloy, in the county of Tyrone, Esq. The said Edward Wingfield married, secondly, a daughter of William Lloyd, Bishop of Killala, and died in 1729.

Richard, his only son, was created a Viscount, and married, first, Aug. 30, 1721, Anne, daughter of Christopher Usher, of Usher's-quay, in Dublin, Esq; by whom he had no issue; and, secondly, on April 13, 1727, Dorothy, daughter of Hercules Rowley, of Summer-hill, in the county of Meath, Esq; by whom he had two sons, and two daughters, viz.

1. Edward, his successor, the late Viscount.
2. Richard, the present Viscount.
3. Frances, married, in 1747, to John Gore, Esq; Member in Parliament for Jamestown.
4. Isabella.

Creations.] Baron Wingfield, of Wingfield, in the county of Wexford, and Viscount Powerscourt, of Powerscourt, in the county of Wicklow, Feb. 4, 1743, 17 Geo. II.

E 2 *Arms.*]

Arms.] Pearl, on a bend, ruby, cottifed, diamond, three pair of wings conjoined of the firſt.

Creſt.] On a wreath, an eagle riſing with wings expanded, pearl, beholding the ſun in its glory.

Supporters.] Two pegafufes pearl, with wings, manes, and hoofs, topaz.

Motto.] Fidelité eſt de Dieu.

Chief Seat.] Powerſcourt, in the county of Wicklow.

VISCOUNT ASHBROOK.

WILLIAM FLOWER, Viſcount ASHBROOK, and Baron of Caſtle-Durrow, was born June 25, 1744, and ſucceeded his father, Henry, the firſt Viſcount, June 27, 1752.

Henry, the late Viſcount, ſucceeded his father William, firſt Lord of Caſtle-Durrow, in May 1746, and was created Viſcount Aſhbrook, by King George II. He married, in March 1740, Elizabeth, daughter of Lieutenant-general Tatton, by which Lady, who died Feb. 10, 1759, he had iſſue one ſon, the preſent Viſcount; and two daughters, Elizabeth, born Jan. 26, 1741, and Mary, born Feb. 12, 1747-8.

William Flower, of Oakham, in the county of Rutland, Eſq; was Sheriff of that county in the ſixth and tenth of King Richard II. and its Repreſentative in Parliament in the ſixth and eighth of that King, as was his ſon Roger, in the 20th of that King; and in the reigns of Henry IV. and V. in the latter of which reigns he was Speaker; as alſo in the firſt of Henry VI. His son Thomas was Sheriff of the county of Rutland in 1430, as he was five other years. From him defcended Sir Richard, who, in 1501, was Sheriff of Berks, as he was of Rutland in 1507. From him defcended Sir George, who was an active and brave Officer, and acted againſt the rebels in Ireland in the reign of Queen Elizabeth. He was fucceeded by his fon Sir William, who, during the Rebellion in 1641, was an Officer in the army; at the Reſtoration was elected Member of Parliament for Irish Town, afterwards was made Lieutenant-colonel of his Majeſty's Regiment of Guards in Ireland, and one of his Majeſty's Council. His fon Thomas was attainted by King James's Parliament, and his eſtate fequeſtred, to which he was reſtored by King William. He married, firſt, Mary, fourth daughter of Sir John Temple, and ſiſter of Henry, Viſcount Palmerſton, by whom he had a fon, William, his heir, and a daughter, Mary, who died unmarried. He married, fecondly, a daughter of —— Jefferys, of Brecknockſhire, Efq; to whom he left his eſtate, and had a fon, and a daughter, Catharine, who both died young.

William, who fucceeded at Durrow, was created Baron of Caſtle-Durrow, in the county of Kilkenny, by King George II. He married Edith, daughter of Toby Caulfield, of Clone, in the county of Kilkenny, Efq; by whom he had two fons, Jefferys, who died young, Henry, the late Viſcount, and two daughters, the eldeſt of whom died young; and Rebecca, married, in 1741, to James Agar, Efq; Member of Parliament for Gowran.

* E 3   *Crea-*

Creations.] Baron of Castle-Durrow, in the county of Kilkenny, Oct. 27, 1733, 7 Geo. II. Viscount Ashbrook, Sept. 30, 1751, 25 Geo. II.

Arms.] Quarterly, first and fourth, pearl, on a chevron, voided, diamond, three pellets between as many ravens, each having in his beak an ermine spot, proper, by the name of Flower. Second and third, ruby, three towers, pearl, by the name also of Flower.

Crest.] On a wreath, a raven, as in the coat.

Supporters.] Two tigers, reguardant, proper, each gorged with a ducal coronet, and chain, topaz.

Motto.] *Mens conscia recti.*

Chief Seat.] Castle-Durrow, in the county of Kilkenny.

VISCOUNT JOCELYN.

ROBERT JOCELYN, Viscount JOCELYN, and Baron of Newport, Auditor of the Exchequer, a Lord of the Privy-council, &c. succeeded his father, Robert, the first Viscount, in 1758, and, Dec. 11, 1752, married Anne, elder daughter of James, Viscount Limerick, afterwards Earl of Clanbrassil.

Robert, the late Viscount, in 1726, was appointed a Serjeant at Law to K. George I. in 1727, his Sollicitor-general, as also to Geo. II. at his accession. In 1730 he was appointed Attorney-general, and in 1739, Lord High Chancellor of Ireland. He was constantly one of the Lords Justices in the absence of the Lords Lieutenants, and was created a Baron and Viscount. He married, first, Charlotte, daughter and co-heir of —— Anderson, Esq; and

and by her (who died in Feb. 1747-8,) had iſſue the preſent Viſcount. On Nov. 15, 1754, he married, ſecondly, Elizabeth, Lady dowager Roſs, ſiſter of the Marquis of Lothian. This noble family is of great antiquity: for, after the Romans had been maſters of Britain five hundred years, wearied with the wars, they took their final farewel of it, and carried away with them a great many of their brave old Britiſh ſoldiers, who had ſerved them faithfully both at home and abroad, to whom they gave Armorica in France, for their former ſervices, which country was from them afterwards called Little Britain. It is ſuppoſed that there were ſome of this family amongſt them; and that they gave the name Jocelyn to a town in that country, which ſtill preſerves that name; and it is thought probable that they returned with William the Conqueror; for we find in 1066, mention made of Sir Gilbert Jocelyn, who is ſuppoſed to be the father of Gilbert, who founded the Abbey of Sempringham, in Lincolnſhire, about the reign of King Stephen, and became founder of a religious order called the Gilbertines. From him deſcended Thomas, who is mentioned in a charter, wherein he grants to the church of St. Mary and St. Laurence de Blackmore, his lands of Capell, in the village of Selges. This Thomas married, thirty-third of Hen. III. Maud daughter and co-heir of Sir Thomas Hide, of Hide-hall, in Sabridgeworth, in the county of Hertford, Knt. by whom he got the Lordſhip of Sudeley, in the county of Glouceſter, which for more than five hundred years has continued in the poſſeſſion of the family, and is to this day their chief Seat.

* E 4 Sir

Sir Ralph Jocelyn, citizen and Draper of London, was made a Knight in the field, and created a Knight of the Bath at the Coronation of Queen Elizabeth, wife of King Edward IV. in 1465; he was Sheriff of London in 1458, and twice Lord Mayor of that city, in 1464 and in 1476, and Member of Parliament for the city, the seventh of Edward IV. He corrected several abuses practised both by the Bakers and Victuallers of the city of London, and by his diligence the walls of the said city were repaired. He died, Oct. 25, 1478, and lies buried at Sabridgeworth, as appears from this inscription: *Orate pro anima Radulphi Joslyne, quondam militis, et bis majoratus civitatis London. qui obiit*, &c.

Sir Thomas Jocelyn was created a Knight of the Bath at the Coronation of King Edward VI. he had several children, of whom John was a great antiquarian, and collected and penned the *Antiquitates Britannicæ*, by the appointment of Archbishop Parker, to whom he was Secretary. He died Dec. 28, 1603, and lies buried in High-Roothing church in Essex, as appears by an inscription on the wall of that church. The eldest son was Richard, whose son and heir, Robert, was father of Sir Robert Jocelyn, Knight of the county in 1645; his son, Sir Robert, was advanced to the dignity of Baronet, the eighteenth of Charles II. He was succeeded by Sir Strange Jocelyn, the eldest of ten sons; who was succeeded by his son Sir John, who dying unmarried in 1741, the Title and Estate descended to his only brother Sir Conyers Jocelyn, M. D. the present Baronet.

Thomas,

Thomas, the third surviving son of Sir Robert Jocelyn, who was created a Baronet, married Anne, daughter of Thomas Bray, of Westminster; and had one son, Robert, late Viscount Jocelyn, and four daughters, Elizabeth, Jane, Sarah, and Anne.

Creations.] Baron Newport, of Newport, in the county of Tipperary, Nov. 29, 1743, 17 Geo. II. Viscount Jocelyn, Nov. 18, 1755, 29 Geo. II.

Arms.] Sapphire, a circular wreath, pearl and diamond, with four hawk's bells joined thereto in quadrature, or towards the corners of the escutcheon, topaz.

Crest] On a wreath, a falcon's leg, erased, ruby, belled, topaz.

Supporters.] Two falcons, proper, belled, as the crest.

Motto.] *Faire mon devoir.*

Chief Seat.]

VISCOUNT CONYNGHAM.

HENRY CONYNGHAM, Viscount Conyngham, and Baron of Mount-Charles, a Lord of the Privy-council, Member in the British Parliament for Sandwich, in Kent, was created a Baron and Viscount, and married Ellen, only daughter of Solomon Merret, of London, Esq.

This noble Lord is descended from the family of the Earl of Glencairn (see my Scots Peerage,) which family branched out, in Edward VIth's time, by a younger son William, who was Bishop of Argyll, in Scotland, whose grandson, Dean Conyngham, came over into Ireland, about the latter end of James the first's reign,

reign, to sue for a considerable estate, which he recovered. He left issue Halbert Conyngham, who was knighted in King Charles IId's reign; and at the head of a regiment, which he raised at his own expence, joined King William at the battle of the Boyne, which regiment the King established the day after the battle, for their gallant behaviour, and gave him the command thereof: but he was soon after killed near Killoony, in the county of Sligoe. His son Henry was Major in Lord Mountjoy's regiment of Foot at the battle of the Boyne, and for his gallant behaviour King William soon after ordered him to raise a regiment of Dragoons, with a power to nominate his own Officers; and gave him the command thereof. At the battle of St. Stephen's in Spain, in 1705, he was killed, where he commanded in chief, as Major-general in the English service, and Lieutenant-general in the Portuguese service. He married a daughter of Sir John Williams, of the county of Carmarthen, Bart. widow of the Right honourable the Earl of Shelburne, with whom he had a very large estate in Wales, and in the isle of Thanet and county of Kent. He left two sons, Williams and Henry, and a daughter Mary, married to the Right honourable Francis Buxton, of the county of Clare, Esq; Williams married Constance, one of the co-heiresses of Thomas Middleton, of Stanstead-Mountfitchet, in the county of Essex, Esq by whom he had a son and a daughter, and both dying in their minority, all these estates in the counties of Donegall, Derry, and Meath, and also the estates in the isle of Thanet, and county of Kent, and elsewhere in England, and Wales,

devolved

devolved to Henry, now Viscount Conyngham.

Creations.] Baron of Mount-Charles, in the county of Donegall, Sept. 8, 1753, and Viscount Conyngham, July 3, 1756, 27 and 30 Geo. II.

Arms.] Quarterly, first and fourth, pearl, an hay-fork between three mullets, diamond. Second and third quarters, quarterly. First and fourth, emerald, three eagles displayed, topaz. Second and third ruby, three lions pasiant, pearl.

Crest.] On a wreath, an unicorn's head erased, pearl, armed and maned, topaz.

Supporters.] On the dexter side, an horse, pearl, armed and maned; and on his breast an eagle displayed, topaz. On the sinister, a buck, proper, armed and hoofed, and on his breast a griffin's head, erased, topaz.

Motto.] *Over fork over.*

Chief Seats.] At Mount-Charles, in the county of Donegall; at Newtown, in the county of Derry; at Slane, in the county of Meath; and at Mynster-court, in the Isle of Thanet, in Kent.

VISCOUNT LIGONIER.

For an account of this illustrious and noble Peer, see my Peerage of England.

VISCOUNT MOUNT-MORRES.

Redmond-Harvey Morres, Viscount and Baron Mount-Morres, of Castle-Morres, in the county of Kilkenny.

Creations.] Baron, *ut supra,* April 27, 1756, 29 Geo. II. Viscount, Jan. 7, 1763, 4 Geo. III.

Arms.] Quarterly, first and fourth, topaz, a fess dancette, diamond, in base a lion rampant of the second. Second and third, pearl, three boars heads couped, diamond.

Crest.] On a wreath, a demi lion rampant.

Supporters.] Two angels.

Motto.] *Deus nobiscum, quis contra nos.*

Chief Seat.] Castle-Morres, in the county of Kilkenny.

VISCOUNT MOUNT-CASHELL.

Stephen Moore, Viscount Mount-Cashell, and Baron of Kilworth, succeeded his father, Stephen, the late and first Viscount, Feb. 22, 1767.

Stephen, the late Viscount, was created a Baron and Viscount, and married Alicia, only daughter and heir of Hugh Colvil, Esq; (descended from Roger de Colvil, who came from Normandy with William the Conqueror, 1066, was at the battle of Hastings, and went into Scotland with David I. about the year 1120. See my Peerage of Scotland, p. 149.) son and heir of the Right hon. Sir Robert Colvil, of Newtown, in the county of Down (by Sarah, his wife, daughter of James Margetson, Esq; only son of Dr. James Margetson, Archbishop
of

of Armagh, who afterwards married Brabazon, Earl of Besborough,) and by her (who died Aug. 10, 1761, aged sixty) had issue four sons, and four daughters, viz.
1. Stephen, the present Viscount.
2. Colvil, Representative in Parliament for the borough of Clonmell.
3. William, Representative in Parliament for the city of Clogher.
4. Robert.
5. Sarah, married, in 1760, to Henry Sandford, Esq; eldest son of Robert Sandford, of Castlerea, in the county of Roscommon, Esq; and died in October, 1764.
6. Mary, married, in 1660, to the Right Hon. William, Earl of Inchiquin, Knight of the Bath.
7. Elizabeth.
8. Catharine, married, in 1765, to Maurice Mahon, Esq; eldest son of Thomas Mahon, of Stroakstown, Esq; Knight of the shire for the county of Roscommon.

The name of this antient and illustrious family has been variously written; for in the Catalogue of John Brompton, Abbot of Jorville, 1599, they are called St. Mor; Guillym stiles them de la Mores; and Philpot, Somerset-Herald, De More, Atte More, &c. It is descended from Thomas de Moore, who came from Normandy with William the Conqueror, in the year 1066, and whose name is inrolled in the antient List, taken at their embarkation at St. Valery, and also in the List of those who survived the memorable battle of Hastings, fought on Saturday, Oct. 14, in the said year, in which he had a considerable command.

After

After the decease of William I. the family settled in the West of England, and in the year 1355, Henry de Moore accompanied Edward the Black Prince, the Earls of Warwick, Oxford, &c. to France, and was wounded at the battle of Poictiers, in 1356.

In the beginning of the reign of Queen Elizabeth, this family purchased an estate in Shropshire, the mansion-house being near Larden, in the said county, where they were well known by the appellation of the Moores of Salop, for near a century.

In the year 1558, when the King of Spain fitted out the Invincible Armada, against Queen Elizabeth, John de Moore, of Shropshire, had the command of a regiment, in the army encamped at Tilbury, under the command of the Earl of Leicester.

In the reign of King Charles I. Richard Moore came over, (being the first of his family that did so,) and settled at Clonmell, in the county of Tipperary, who had two sons, Stephen; and Thomas, ancestor of the Moores of Barn, in that county.

Stephen, the eldest son, married the granddaughter of Sir George Crooke, Knt. and Bart. Lord Chief Justice of the King's-bench in England in the said reign. (Which great Lawyer, and Hutton, in the year 1636, were the only two, of all the Judges, who disapproved of a prosecution being commenced against Hampden, for refusing to pay Ship-money, and he died in October, 1641.) He had the honour of being personally acquainted with King William III. on whose landing in England, he lent him the sum of three thousand pounds, at Taunton,

Taunton, in Somersetshire. He had one son, Richard, who, in the year 1690, married the hon. Elizabeth Ponsonby, eldest daughter of William, Viscount Duncannon, (who afterwards married Colonel Thomas Newcomen, of Dove-hill, in the county of Tipperary,) by whom he had one son,

Stephen, the first Viscount, above treated of.

Creation.] Baron Kilworth, of Moore-park, in the county of Cork, and Viscount Mount-Cashell, of the city of Cashell, in the county of Tipperary, June 16, 1766, 6 Geo. III.

Arms.] Quarterly, first and fourth, a swan, pearl, membered and beaked, topaz; second and third, ruby, a fess checque, pearl and sapphire. (See the Arms of Lord Colvil, in my Peerage of Scotland.)

Crest.] A goss-hawk, seizing a coney, diamond.

Supporters.] A leopard, proper, on the swan, a rhinoceros, proper, on the Colvil arms, both chained.

Motto.] *Vis unita fortior.*

Chief Seats.] Kilworth, in the county of Cork, (which is also the burial-place of the family;) and Galgorm, in the county of Antrim.

VISCOUNT DUNGANNON.

ARTHUR TREVOR, Viscount DUNGANNON, in the county of Tyrone, and Baron Hill, of Olderfleet, in the county of Antrim, was so created, on Dec. 27, 1765. His Lordship is a Privy-counsellor, and a Commissioner of the Revenue.

Creation.] *Ut supra.*

Arms.]

[112]

Arms.] Quarterly, firſt and fourth party per bend finiſter, ermin and erminois, a lion rampant, topaz, for Trevor. Second and third, diamond, on a feſs pearl, between three leopards paſſant guardant, topaz, three eſcallops, ruby, for Hill.

Creſt.] On a chapeau ruby, turned up ermine, a wyvern riſing, diamond.

Supporters.] Two lions, each gorged with a ducal coronet.

Motto.] *Quid verum atque decens.*

Chief Seats.]

VISCOUNTESS LANGFORD.

ELIZABETH-ORMSBY-ROWLEY, wife of the Right hon. Hercules Langford Rowley, was created Baroneſs Summerhill, and Viſcounteſs Langford, on Dec. 27, 1765, with remainder to her iſſue male, lawfully begotten by the ſaid Mr. Rowley.

[For her Ladyſhip's Arms, &c. ſee the Plate.]

VISCOUNT GLERAWLEY.

WILLIAM ANNESLEY, Viſcount GLERAWLEY, and Baron Anneſley, of Caſtle-Willan, in the county of Downe, was created a Baron, Aug. 22, 1758, and Viſcount Octob. 28, 1766. His Lordſhip married, Aug. 16, 1738, Lady Anne, eldeſt daughter of Marcus, Earl of Tyrone, by whom he has iſſue, 1. Francis-Charles, born in Nov. 1740, Member for the borough of Downe-patrick; 2. Catharine, wife of Arthur, Lord Sudeley; 3. Marcus, born April 17,

17, 1743; 4. Richard, born April 14, 1745; 5. William, born March 3, 1747.

This noble Lord is defcended from Francis Annefley, of Clogh, in the county of Downe, eldeſt ſon of Francis, the firſt Viſcount Valentia (by his ſecond Lady, Jane, ſiſter of Philip, firſt Earl of Cheſterfield, and relict of Sir Peter Courtene, of Aldington, in Worceſterſhire, Bart. who died March 12, 1683,) and half brother of Sir Arthur Annefley, the firſt Earl of Angleſea. Which Francis Annefley, Eſq; oppoſing the arbitrary meaſures of K. James II. was attainted by his Parliament, and marrying Deborah, daughter of Dr. Henry Jones, Biſhop of Meath, and relict of John Boudler, of Dublin, Eſq; by her, (who died Sept. 4, 1672) had iſſue three ſons and five daughters, viz. Francis, his heir; Arthur and Henry, who both died without iſſue; Jane, wife of James Baillie, of Iniſhargie, in the county of Downe, Eſq; and died Jan. 25, 1748; Deborah, of the Rev. Charles Warde; Mary, who died in her infancy; Anne, wife of Henry, only ſon of Sir Edward Wood; and Catharine, who died young.

Francis Annefley, of the Inner Temple, Eſq; the eldeſt and only ſurviving ſon, born in 1663, was appointed one of the Truſtees for the ſale of the forfeited eſtates in Ireland, by K. William; and by Queen Anne, one of the Commiſſioners for ſtating the publick Accompts. He ſerved in ſeveral Parliaments of England and Ireland, for the boroughs of Weſtbury and Downe-patrick; and was the firſt promoter in the Houſe of Commons, of the building fifty new churches, in the city and ſuburbs of London,

don, was Chairman of the Committee, and one of the Commiſſioners for that purpoſe. On July 5, 1695, he married, firſt, Elizabeth, daughter of Sir Joſeph Martin, of London, Knt. by whom he had iſſue ſeven ſons and two daughters; he married, ſecondly, in July, 1732, Elizabeth, daughter of John Cropley, of Rocheſter, Eſq; relict of William Gomeldon, of Somerfield-hall, in Kent, Eſq; who dying May 20, 1736, he married, thirdly, on Aug. 31, 1737, Sarah, only daughter of William Sloan, of Portſmouth, Eſq; relict of Sir Richard Fowler, of Harnage-grange, in Shropſhire, Bart. but by the two laſt had no iſſue. His iſſue by the firſt venter, were,

1. Francis, LL. D. Rector of Winwick, in Lancaſhire, who married Anne, daughter of Robert Gayer, Eſq; by his wife, Lady Elizabeth Anneſley, by whom he had three ſons, Arthur, Francis, and James, and died May 1, 1740.

2. Henry, Captain of the Diamond ſhip of war, who died in the Weſt-Indies, in 1728.

3. Martin, D. D. Rector of Friſham, and Vicar of Buckleburg, Berks, who married Mary, daughter of William Hanbury, of Little-Martle, in Herefordſhire, Eſq; and died in June, 1749.

4. John; 5. James, who both died unmarried.

6. William, the preſent Viſcount, who was a Barriſter at Law; in 1741 he ſerved in Parliament for the borough of Midleton, and, in 1750, was appointed High Sheriff of the county of Downe.

7. Arthur.

8. Eli-

8. Elizabeth, wife of William Maguire, of Dublin, Esq; who has issue.

9. Deborah, who died unmarried.

Creations.] *Ut supra.*

Arms.] Paly of six, pearl and sapphire; over all, a bend, ruby.

Crest.] On a wreath, a Moor's head, side-faced, couped, proper, wreathed about the temples, pearl and diamond.

Supporters.] On the dexter side a Roman Knight, on the sinister a Moorish Prince, both habited and furnished, proper.

Motto.] *Virtutis amore.*

Chief Seat.]

VISCOUNT KINGSTON.

EDWARD KING, Viscount KINGSTON, of Kingsborough, and Lord Kingston, succeeded his father James, the late Lord, and was created Viscount Kingston.

James, the late Lord, succeeded his father, John, the third Lord Kingston, Feb. 15, 1727-8, and married Elizabeth, daughter of Sir John Meade of Ballintobber, widow of Sir Ralph Freke, of Rathbarry, in the county of Cork, Baronet; and by her, who died Oct. 6, 1750, had issue one son, the present Viscount, and two daughters, Elizabeth, who died in Sept. 1750; and Margaret. His Lordship married, 2dly, in July 1751, the Lady Ogle, relict of Sir Chaloner Ogle, Knt. Admiral of his Majesty's Fleet.

John, the third Lord, succeeded his brother Robert, and being Gentleman of the Privy-chamber to James II. and following his Master's fortunes, was outlawed by King William and Queen

Queen Mary, who afterwards restored him in blood. He married Margaret, daughter of Florence O'Cahan, whose ancestor, in the reign of James I. was proprietor of the county of Londonderry; and by her, who died in 1721, had two sons,

1. Robert, who died before his father.
2. James, the late Lord.
3. Catharine, married to George Butler, of Ballyragget, in the county of Kilkenny, Esq; grandson of Edmund, Viscount Mountgarret.
4. Sophia, married to Bretridge Badham, of Rockfield, in the county of Cork, Esq;

Of this noble family, which was antiently seated at Feathercock-hall, near Northallerton, in the county of York, was Sir John King, Knt. who, in the reign of Queen Elizabeth, went into Ireland, where he was Muster-master-general, and one of the Privy-council. He was succeeded by his son, Sir Robert, who also enjoyed the same employment of Muster-master-general. He married to his first wife Frances, daughter of Henry, Lord Folliot, by whom he had four sons, and four daughters. The sons were,

1. Sir John, who was a Major-general in the Army, and a person both active and zealous for the Restoration of King Charles II. by whom he was created Baron Kingston, and made President of the province of Connaught, and one of his Majesty's Privy-council. He married Catharine, daughter of Sir William Fenton, of Mitchelstown, in the county of Cork, Knt. by whom he had two sons, Robert, who succeeded him, and John, the third Lord.

2. Henry,

2. Henry, Fellow of All-Souls College in Oxford.
3. Sir Robert, anceſtor of Lord Kingſborough.
4. William, who was made a Captain of foot by King Charles II.

The ſaid Sir John King married to his ſecond wife, Sophia, daughter of Sir William Zouch, of Woking, in Surry, Knt. and widow of Edward Cecil, Viſcount Wimbledon, by whom he had two daughters.

Creations.] Baron, as above, Sept. 4, 1660, 1 Charles II. Viſcount Oct. 28, 1766, 6 George III.

Arms.] Ruby, two lions rampant, ſupporting a dexter-hand, couped at the wriſt, and erect, pearl.

Creſt.] In a ducal coronet, topaz, a hand erect, as in the coat, the fourth and fifth fingers turning down.

Supporters.] Two lions, party per feſs, pearl, and ruby, each having a ducal crown of the latter.

Motto.] *Spes tutiſſima Cœlis.*

Chief Seats.] At Mitchelſtown, in the county of Cork, and at Upton-Court, in Berkſhire.

VISCOUNT CLAN-WILLIAM.

John Meade, Viſcount Clan-William, Baron Gillford, and Baronet, was created a Peer, Oct. 28, 1766.

This noble Lord is deſcended from Sir John Meade, a very eminent Lawyer, who was Judge of the Palatinate Court of the county of Tipperary, and Attorney-general to James, Duke of York; in whoſe Parliament (when King) 1689, he he was Member for the University of Dublin, and, with Mr. Coghlan, the only Protestants in the House of Commons, of which he was also a Member in the reigns of King William and Queen Anne, by the latter of whom, he was created a Baronet, May 29, 1703. He died Jan. 12, 1706, having had issue,

1. William, who died at the age of 13 years.
2. James, who died in his infancy.
3. Sir Pierce, the second Baronet, who died in his 17th year.
4. Sir Richard, of whom presently.
5. Helen, wife of Richard Ponsonby, of Crotto, in the county of Kerry, Esq; and died March 28, 1743.
6. Catharine, wife, first, of Thomas Jones, of Osberstown, in the county of Kildare, Esq; and secondly, of Nehemiah Donnellan, of Nenaugh, Esq; Member for the county of Tipperary, who had issue three sons and two daughters.
7. Mary, wife of Dennis M'Carthy, of Clogrhoe, in the county of Cork, Esq; and had issue four sons and one daughter.
8. Jane, who died unmarried.

Sir Richard, the fourth son, and third Baronet, served for Kingsale in Parliament, and married, in April, 1736, Catharine, daughter of Henry Pretty, of Kilboy, in Tipperary, Esq; by whom he had issue one son, Sir John, the fourth Baronet, and present Viscount, born April 21, 1744, and one daughter, Elizabeth. He died April 27, 1744, and his Lady afterwards remarried with Henry Cavendish, Esq; Commissioner of the Revenue.

Creations.] *Ut supra.*

Arms.]

Arms.] Sapphire, a chevron ermine, between three trefoils flipt, pearl.
Crest.] On a wreath, an eagle difplayed, with two heads.
Supporters.] On the dexter fide an eagle, collared with a plain collar. On the finifter, a falcon, collared with a plain collar, having a chain affixed thereto.
Motto.] *Toujours preft.*
Chief Seat.] Ballintobber, in the county of Cork.

VISCOUNT FORTROSE.

KENNETH MACKENZIE, Vifcount FORT-ROSE, and Baron of Ardeloe, was fo created Oct. 28, 1766. His Lordfhip's defcent will be feen in my Peerage of Scotland, under the title Earl of SEAFORTH. He married, on Oct. 7, 1765, Lady Caroline, eldeft daughter of William, Earl of Harrington, who died March 24, 1767.

Creation] *Ut fupra.*
Arms.] Sapphire, a ftag's head cabofhed, topaz.
Crest.] On a wreath, a mountain inflamed, proper.
Supporters.] Two favages, wreathed about their temples and middles with laurel, each holding in his exterior hand, a batoon erect, with fire iffuing out of the top of it, all proper.
Motto.] *Luceo, non uro.*
Chief Seats.] Brahan-caftle, and Fortrofe, in the fhire of Rofs, in Scotland.

VISCOUNT CLARE.

Robert Nugent, Viscount Clare, and Baron Nugent of Carlanstown, a Lord of the Privy-council in Great-Britain, and first Lord of Trade and Plantations; Member in Parliament for the city of Bristol, was created a Viscount and Baron, Dec. 20, 1766. His Lordship married, first, Lady Emilia Plunket, second daughter of Peter, the fourth Earl of Fingal, and by her (who died Aug. 16, 1731) had issue a son, the hon. Edmund Nugent, Esq; Member in the present Parliament for St. Maw's, in Cornwall, Groom of the Bed-chamber, and Captain of a company (with the rank of Lieutenant-colonel) in the Foot-guards. He married, secondly, March 23, 1736-7, Anne, daughter of James Craggs, Esq; Secretary of State, relict of John Knight, of Gosfield-hall, in Essex, Esq; Secretary to the Leeward Islands, &c. And thirdly, the Countess Dowager of Berkeley, mother of the present Earl.

His Lordship, in 1741, 1747, and 1754 was elected Representative in Parliament for the borough of St. Maw's, in Cornwall. In November 1747, he was made Comptroller of the Houshold to the Prince of Wales, Ap. 6, 1754, a Lord of the Treasury, was for many years one of the Vice-treasurers for Ireland, and in 1766 was constituted first Lord of Trade and Plantations.

His Lordship's descent is from Sir Richard Nugent, the eighth Lord Delvin, ancestor of the Earl of Westmeath, who sat in the Parliament held at Trim, temp. Ric. III. and had summons

summons to Parliament 1486, 2 Henry VII. also in 1490, and 1493; and being eminently remarkable for his strict loyalty and great resolution, was constituted, by the Lords Justices and Council, June 25, 1496, Commander and Leader in chief of all the forces destined for the defence of the counties of Dublin, Meath, Kildare, and Lowth. He was summoned to a Parliament which met at Castledermot, Aug. 28, 1498, but neglecting to appear, was fined 40s. In 1504 he accompanied the Earl of Kildare to the famous battle of Knocklough, in Connaught, where his behaviour was very remarkable; for when the Lord Deputy was advanced within twenty miles east of Knocklough, and called a council of war, the Lord Delvin declared, " his " learning was not much; that with a glori- " ous tale he could utter his stomach; but I " promise to God, and to the Prince, that I " shall be the first that shall throw the first " spear among the Irish in this battle; let " him speak now that will, for I have done." Accordingly, a little before the joining battle, in which he commanded, and led the horse, he spurred his horse, and threw a small spear amongst the Irish, with which he chanced to kill one of the Bourkes, and retired; whereupon the Lord Deputy told him, " he kept " his promise well, and well did and valiantly, " seeing after his throw he retired back." In 1505 he was intrusted with the manors of Belgard and Foure, married the Lady Elizabeth Fitzgerald, daughter of the Earl of Kildare, and had issue, Sir Christopher Nu-

* F gent,

[122]

gent, his heir; and Sir Thomas, of Carlanstown.

Sir Thomas, of Carlanstown, married Elizabeth, daughter of George Fleming, second son of James, Lord Slane, by whom he had issue seven sons and one daughter, viz.

1. Robert, his heir.
2. Richard, who left no issue.
3. Edward, of Portlomon, in Westmeath, who married Elizabeth, daughter of Thomas Hope, of Mullingar, Esq; and was father of Walter Nugent, who married Elizabeth, daughter of Richard Nugent, of Dunore, and had James, his heir, (the father of Walter, the father of Ridgely Nugent, of Portlomon,) William, Jasper, Elizabeth, and Mary.
4. Lavalin.
5. Christopher, settled by his father at Aghanagaran, in the county of Longford, where he was succeeded by his son Richard, who married the widow of the famous Lord Maguire, and left Robert his heir, who married Bridget, daughter of Miles Reilly, Esq; and dying in 1676, had issue by her (who afterwards married Laurence Nugent, of Drumerg, Esq;) one son, Richard, and two daughters; Mary, wife of Thomas Downing, Esq; and Elizabeth, of Charles Reilly, Esq; Richard, the son, married Bridget, daughter of Lavalin Nugent, of Dysert, Esq; and dying in June, 1701, without issue, the estate centered in the family of Carlanstown.
6. James.
7. Oliver, of Kilmore, in Westmeath, which two last left no issue male: But Oliver had a daughter,

daughter, Joan, wife of Oliver Nugent, of Enegh, Esq;

8. Eleanor, wife of Edmund D'arcie, of Clondaly, in Westmeath, Esq; died without issue.

Robert, the eldest son, was father of Edmund Nugent, Esq; who married the daughter of Christopher, the ninth Lord Killeen; and, secondly, Mary, daughter of —— Cusack, and died in 1599, leaving issue by his last wife, (who remarried with David Spencefield, of Carlanstown, Esq;) three sons; Richard, his heir, who died in his minority; Robert, heir to his brother; Thomas, of Dalystown; and Mary, wife of Theobald Nugent, of New-Haggard, Esq;

Robert, who succeeded, was, at the breaking out of the rebellion, made Governor of Westmeath, and in 1642, chosen Commander of the Irish in those parts, and was very active in those times of confusion. However, on the reduction of the kingdom, by Cromwell, making a submission, he was received into the protection of the Parliament. He married ————, daughter of Kedagh Geoghegan, of Syanon, in Westmeath, Esq; and had two sons, 1. Edmund, his heir; and 2. Matthias, of Cluntiduffy, in the county of Cavan, Captain in King James's army, who married Catharine, daughter of Robert Nugent, of Clonigerah, second brother of James Nugent, of Ballyma, and had Robert, his successor, who married Elizabeth, daughter of Capt. George Barnewall, of Creve, in the county of Longford, and had two sons, and several daughters.

ters. The sons were, John, a Captain in the 32d regiment of Infantry, and Michael, who was a Lieutenant in the 103d regiment of Foot.

Edmund, who succeeded at Carlanstown, and was Member in King James's Parliament for Mullingar, married Clara, daughter of Robert Cusack, of Rathgare, Esq; and died Nov. 1, 1703, leaving issue three sons, Robert, Michael, and Christopher, and eight daughters; Margaret, wife of John Chevers, of Macetown; Anne, of James Reynolds, of Loughscurr, in the county of Leitrim, Esq; Martha, of Ignatius Palles, of Clonbakuk, in the county of Cavan, Esq; Frances, of Edward Nugent, of Dungomine, in the same county, Esq; Mary-Anne, who died unmarried, in 1744; Mary, wife of Edward Nugent, of Dunore, Esq; Elizabeth, of Garret Darditz, of Gigginstown, in Westmeath, Esq; and ———, of Mr. Morpother, of the county of Roscommon.

Robert, the eldest son, succeeded, and married, in July, 1699, Mary, daughter of Sir John Fleming, of Stoholmuch, in the county of Meath, Knt. but dying without issue, in February 1728-9, was succeeded by his brother,

Michael, who married Mary, fifth daughter of Robert, Lord Trimleston, and dying May 13, 1739, had issue by her, (who died at Bath, in September, 1740,) two sons and three daughters, viz.

1. Robert, the present Lord Viscount Clare.

2. Ed-

[125]

2. Edmund, who died at Buda, in the Emperor's service, in 1736.

3. Mary, married, in 1748, to Henry, third son of Geoffrey Brown, of Castle-Margaret, in the county of Mayo, Esq;

4. Clare, in 1740, to George Byrne, of Cappanteely, in the county of Dublin, Esq;

5. Margaret.

Creation.] As above.
Arms.] Ermine, two bars, ruby.
Crest.] On a wreath, a wyvern, emerald.
Supporters.]
Motto.] Decrevi.
Chief Seat.] Gofsfield-hall, in Effex.

ARCHBISHOPS and BISHOPS.

ARMAGH.

THE moſt Reverend Dr. RICHARD ROBINSON, Archbiſhop of ARMAGH, Primate and Almoner of all Ireland, and a Lord of the Privy-council, was promoted to the ſee of Killala in 1751, in the room of Dr. Cary, deceaſed; tranſlated to the ſee of Ferns in 1759, in the room of Dr. Salmon, deceaſed; to that of Kildare in 1761, in the room of Dr. Fletcher, deceaſed; and to the Archiepiſcopal ſee of Armagh in 1765, in the room of Dr. Stone, deceaſed.

Arms.] Sapphire, a paſtoral ſtaff, in pale, enſigned with a croſs pattée, topaz, ſurmounted by a pall, pearl, edged and fringed of the ſecond, charged with four croſſes pattée fitchy, diamond.

DUBLIN.

Dr. ARTHUR SMITH, Archbiſhop of DUBLIN, Primate of Ireland, and a Lord of the Privy-council, was promoted to the ſee of Clonfert, in the room of Dr. Whetcombe, tranſlated, in 1752; tranſlated to that of Down in 1753, in the room of Dr. Downes, tranſlated; to that of Meath in 1765, in the room of Dr. Pococke, deceaſed; and to the Archiepiſcopal ſee of Dublin in 1766, in the room of Dr. Carmichael, deceaſed.

ceased. To the Archbishoprick of Dublin the diocese of Glandelagh is united, and his Grace holds in commendam, the Rectory of Gallowne, in the county of Monaghan, the Prebend of Defart-more, in St. Finburge's church, Cork, and the Treasurership of St. Patrick's, Dublin.

Arms.] Sapphire, a pastoral staff in pale, ensigned with a cross pattée, topaz, surmounted by a pall, pearl, edged and fringed of the second, charged with five crosses pattée, fitchy, diamond.

CASHEL.

Dr. MICHAEL COX, Archbishop of CASHEL, a Lord of the Privy-council, and F. R. S. was promoted to the see of Ossory in 1743, in the room of Dr. Este, translated; and in 1754, translated to the Archiepiscopal see of Cashel, in the room of Dr. Whetcombe, deceased.

Arms.] Ruby, two keys in saltire, topaz.

TUAM.

Dr. JOHN RYDER, Archbishop of TUAM, Primate of Connaught, and a Lord of the Privy-council, was promoted to the see of Killaloe in 1741-2, in the room of Dr. Story, translated; translated to that of Downe in 1743, in the room of Dr. Reynell, translated; and to the Archiepiscopal see of Tuam in 1752, in the room of Dr. Hort, deceased. To this Archbishoprick the see of Enaghdoen is united; and that of Ardagh held in commendam with it.

Arms.] Sapphire, three persons erect, under as many canopies of stalls, their faces, arms, and legs, proper: The first represents an Archbishop, habited in his pontificals, holding a crosier in his left hand; the second the Virgin Mary,

Mary, crowned, with our Saviour on her lft arm; and the third an Angel having his right hand elevated, and a lamb on his left arm, all topaz.

MEATH*.

The Right Rev. and Hon. Dr. HENRY MAXWELL, Bishop of MEATH, and a Lord of the Privy-council, was promoted to the fee of Dromore in 1765, in the room of Dr. Young, translated; and translated to that of Meath in 1766, in the room of Dr. Smith, translated to the Archbishoprick of Dublin.

Arms.] Diamond, three mitres with labels, topaz.

KILDARE.

Dr. CHARLES JACKSON, Bishop of KILDARE, and Dean of Christ-church, Dublin, (which is annexed to this fee,) was promoted to the fee of Leighlin and Ferns in 1761, in the room of Dr. Robinson, translated; and in 1765 translated to the fee of Kildare, in the room of Dr. Robinson, translated to the Archbishoprick of Armagh.

Arms.] Pearl, a saltire, ingrailed, diamond, on a chief, sapphire, a bible expanded and clasped, proper.

CORKE.

Dr. JEMMET BROWN, Bishop of CORKE, was promoted to the fee of Killaloe in 1743, upon

---

* The Bishops of Meath and Kildare take place next to the Archbishops, and the rest according to priority of consecration.

the

the tranflation of Dr. Ryder; in 1745 tranflated to that of Dromore, in the room of Dr. Fletcher, tranflated; and to the fee of Corke in the fame year, in the room of Dr. Clayton, tranflated. The fee of Rofs is united to that of Corke.

Arms.] Pearl, a crofs pattée, ruby, charged in the centre with a mitre, labelled, through which is a crofier, pale-ways, all proper.

DERRY.

Dr. WILLIAM BARNARD, Bifhop of DERRY, was promoted to the fee of Raphoe in 1744, in the room of Dr. Forfter, deceafed; and tranflated to the fee of Derry in 1746-7, in the room of Dr. Stone, tranflated.

Arms.] Ruby, two fwords in faltire, pearl, their pomels and hilts, topaz; on a chief, fapphire, an harp, topaz, ftringed, pearl.

WATERFORD and LISMORE.

Dr. RICHARD CHENEVIX, Bifhop of WATERFORD, to which the Bifhoprick of LISMORE is united, was promoted to the fee of Killaloe in 1745, upon the tranflation of Dr. Brown; and thence tranflated to the fee of Waterford, in 1745-6, in the room of Dr. Efte, tranflated.

Arms.] Sapphire, a Bifhop habited in his pontificals, holding before him, in a pall, a crucifix, or the crofs of Calvary, with the body on it, proper.

* F 5   KIL-

KILLALOE and KILFENORA.

Dr. Nicholas Synge was promoted to the Bishoprick of Killaloe in 1745-6, in the room of Dr. Chenevix, translated.

Arms.] Sapphire, a crozier in pale, topaz, suppress'd in the fess-point by a bible expanded, with clasps, proper.

CLOGHER.

Dr. John Garnet, Bishop of Clogher, in 1752 was promoted to the see of Ferns, in the room of Dr. Downs, translated; and in 1758 translated to the see of Clogher, in the room of Dr. Clayton, deceased.

Arms.] Sapphire, a Bishop habited in his pontificals, sitting in a chair of state, and leaning on the sinister side thereof, holding in his left hand a crosier, his right being extended towards the dexter chief of the escutcheon, all topaz, and resting his feet on a cushion, ruby, tasseled of the second.

LIMERICK, ARDFERT, and AGHADOE.

Dr. James Leslie was promoted to these sees in 1755, in the room of Dr. Burscough, deceased.

Arms.] Sapphire, in the dexter chief, a crosier, erect, in the sinister a mitre, with labels, and in base two keys in saltire, all topaz.

KILMORE.

Dr. JOHN CRADOCK, Bishop of KILMORE, was promoted to that see in 1757, on the decease of Dr. Story.

Arms.] Topaz, on a cross, sapphire, a crosier thrust through a mitre, topaz.

ELPHIN.

Dr. WILLIAM GORE, Bishop of ELPHIN, was promoted to the see of Clonfert in 1758, *vice* Dr. Carmichael, translated; and translated to the see of Elphin in 1762, in the room of Dr. Synge, deceased.

Arms.] Diamond, two crosiers, in saltire, topaz; in base a lamb couchant, pearl.

KILLALA and ACHONRY.

Dr. SAMUEL HUTCHINSON was promoted to this see, in 1759, upon the translation of Dr. Robinson.

Arms.] Sapphire, a crosier in pale, topaz; suppress'd in the fess point by a bible expanded, with clasps, proper.

RAPHOE.

Dr. JOHN OSWALD, Bishop of RAPHOE, was promoted to the see of Clonfert in 1762, in the room of Dr. Gore translated; translated to that of Dromore in 1763, in the room of Dr. Marlay, deceased; and to the see of Raphoe in the same year, in the room of Dr. Downes, deceased.

Arms.]

Arms.] Ermine, a chief, party per pale, sapphire and topaz; on the first, the sun in its splendor, on the second a cross patée, ruby.

CLONFERT and KILMACDUAGH.

Dr. DENISON CUMBERLAND was promoted to this see in 1763, in the room of Dr. Oswald, translated.

Arms.] Sapphire, two crosiers, in saltire, topaz.

LEIGHLIN and FERNS.

Dr. EDWARD YOUNG, Bishop of LEIGHLIN and FERNS, was promoted to the see of Dromore in 1763, on the translation of Dr. Oswald; to those of Leighlin and Ferns in 1765, on the translation of Dr. Jackson.

Arms.] Diamond, two crosiers saltirewise, suppress'd by a mitre, labelled in fess, topaz.

OSSORY.

Dr. CHARLES DODGSON was promoted to this see in 1765, on the translation of Dr. Pococke.

Arms.] ———, a Bishop in his pontificals, standing between two pillars ———, holding in his right hand a bible, close, proper, and in his left a crosier, topaz.

DOWN and CONNOR.

Dr. JAMES TRAIL was promoted to this see in 1765, in the room of Dr. Smyth, translated.

Arms.] Sapphire, two keys in saltire, topaz, suppress'd by a lamb passant in fess, pearl.

DROMORE.

Dr. WILLIAM NEWCOME was promoted to this fee in 1766, on the tranflation of Dr. Maxwell.

Arms.] ———, two keys in faltire ———, fupprefs'd by a bible expanded in fefs, between two croffes pattée fitchy in pale, diamond.

CLOYNE.

The Right Rev. and Hon. HENRY FREDERICK HERVEY, M. A. was promoted to this fee in 1767, upon the deceafe of Dr. Johnfon. To this fee the Rectory of Agheda is united.

Arms.] Sapphire, a mitre with labels, between three croffes pattée fitchy, topaz.

BARONS.

LORD KINGSALE.

THE Right hon. John de Courcy, Lord Kingsale, Baron Courcy, of Courcy, and Baron of Ringrone, succeeded Gerald the late, and twenty-fourth Lord Kingsale, being third son of Miles, son of Anthony, son of David, fourth and youngest son of John, the eighteenth Lord. He is married, and has many children.

Gerald, the late Lord, was one of his Majesty's Privy-council, succeeded his cousin Almericus, Feb. 9, 1719-20, and married, May 13, 1725, Margaret, sole daughter and heir of John Effington, of Ashlyns in the county of Hertford, and of Grossington-hall, in the county of Gloucester, Esq; by which Lady, who died in Oct. 1750, he had issue one son, who died young, and four daughters, viz.

1. Mary-Elizabeth, born April 1, 1726, married, March 28, 1751, to John Grady, of Killballyoen, in the county of Limerick, Esq;

2. Margaret, born March 31, 1727, died an infant.

3. Elizabeth-Geraldina, born Nov. 12, 1729, married, in 1751, to Daniel Macarthy, of Carrignevar, in the county of Cork, Esq;

4. Eleanor, born Dec. 8, 1732.

Patrick,

Patrick, the twentieth Lord of Kingſale, at the age of forty-eight, married Mary, daughter of John Fitz-Gerald, of Dromanagh, Lord of Decyes, of the age of fourteen; and by her lived to have twenty-three children without any twins, of which four ſons and three daughters lived to maturity, viz. John; Edmund, who died without iſſue; Miles, father of the late Lord; and Gerald, who alſo died without iſſue. Of the daughters, Ellena was married to Dermoid-Mac-Teige Mac-Carthy, of Agliſh, in the county of Cork, Eſq; at that time heir apparent to the Earl of Clancarty. Elizabeth, the ſecond wife of David, Viſcount Killmalock; and Margaret, married to Philip-Barry Oge, Eſq;

John, the eldeſt, ſucceeded his father in 1663, and was the twenty-firſt Baron of Kingſale; he married Ellena, daughter of Charles Mac-Carty Reigh, Eſq; by whom he had two ſons, Patrick and Almericus, and a daughter Ellena, married to Sir John Magrath, of Allevollan, in the county of Tipperary, Bart. and dying in 1667, was ſucceeded by his ſon Patrick, who, dying a minor in 1669, was ſucceeded by his brother,

Almericus de Courcy, the twenty-third Baron of Kingſale, who was a very handſome man in his perſon, and was much in favour with King Charles II. as alſo with James II. Under the latter, in 1690, he commanded a troop of horſe, and was Lieutenant-colonel to the Earl of Lucan, for which he was outlawed in 1691, but the outlawry was ſoon reverſed, and he took his ſeat in the Houſe of Peers in 1692 and 1710; but died without iſſue.

Miles

Miles de Courcy, third son of Patrick, the twentieth Lord, marrying Elizabeth, daughter and heir of Anthony Sadlier, of Arley-hall, in the county of Warwick, Esq; left two sons, Gerald, his heir, the late Lord Kingsale; John, who died unmarried in 1750; and a daughter, Mary-Priscilla, deceased.

This antient and illustrious family is allied to most of the Princes in Europe, deriving its descent, in the male line, from the house of Lorraine, of the race of the Emperor Charlemagne; and in the female line, from Rollo, William Longue-Espée, and Richard his son, the three first Dukes of Normandy. Lewis IV. called Transmarine, or d'Outremer, King of France, having married Gerberga, daughter of Henry, the first of the name, called the Fowler, Emperor of Germany, had by her Lotharius, King of France, and Charles, Duke of Lorraine, which dutchy was conferred on him by the Emperor Otho II. his cousin german. Charles, Duke of Lorraine, after the death of his nephew Lewis V. King of France without issue, was excluded from the crown, as next heir of the Carlovingian race, by Hugh Capet, who was chosen King of France. This Duke, by his first wife, left a son Otho, Duke of Lorraine, besides other children; and by his second wife, Agnes of Vermandois, daughter of Herbert, the third of that name, Count Vermandois, Troyes, and Meaux, by Edgitha, or Ogina of England, his wife, daughter of Edward the elder, King of England, and widow of King Charles IV. of France, called the Simple, had issue two sons, Lewis of Lorraine, Count, or Landgrave of Thuringia, now called Hesse, who continued

the

the male line in Germany; and Charles, by some called Hugh, who also lived in Germany; which Charles was father of Wigerius, or Wigman, who was father of two sons, Baldricus and Wigerius, who came from Germany into Normandy in the reign of Richard the second of that name, Duke of Normandy. Baldricus, or Baldrick, the eldest of the two, is called Teutonicus, or the German, in Norman authors, by reason of his coming from Germany; and is by several of them stiled *strenuus et bellicosus Dux*. He married the niece of Gilbert, Earl of Brion, in Normandy, and daughter of Richard Clare, Earl of Clare, by whom he had six sons and as many daughters, of which sons Richard the fourth was father of Gilbert de Nova-Villa, (Neville) who attended the Norman Duke into England in quality of his Admiral, and is ancestor of the noble family of Neville.

Robert de Courcy, the third son, in the year 1020, was Lord of Courcy, in Normandy, in which he was succeeded by his son Richard, who accompanied William, Duke of Normandy, in his expedition into England; was present at the battle of Hastings in 1066; and was rewarded by the Conqueror for his services with a great number of Lordships in England, particularly the Lordship of Stoke in the county of Somerset, called from him Stoke-Courcy, which he held with several others *per Baroniam*; and the Lordships of Newnham, Seccenden, and Foxcote, in Oxfordshire: he died in the year 1098, and was succeeded by his son Robert de Courcy, Lord of Courcy, in Normandy; and Baron of Stoke-Courcy, in England: he was Steward of the houshold to King Henry I. and to his daughter Maud,

Maud, the Emprefs, and was by the faid King created one of the great Barons at Weftminfter, in 1133: he was founder of the nunnery of Cannington in Somerfetſhire, and left five fons, whereof Robert de Courcy, Baron of Stoke-Courcy, in the reign of King Stephen, was principal Commander at the battle of Northampton, againſt the Scots.

William his fon, who fucceeded him, was Dapifer to King Henry II. and as fuch was one of the witneffes to that King's charter of the lands and privileges he gave to the church of St. Peter's Weftminfter; and was one of thofe Englifh Noblemen who teftified to the firm league and pacification made between that King, and William, King of Scots. In the eighteenth of Henry II. he was Lord of Iflip, in the county of Oxford, and Juftice of Ireland.

He was fucceeded by his fon Sir John de Courcy, who ferved Henry II. in all his wars; and in Ireland, at his own charge, fought five remarkable battles, whereby he conquered the province of Ulfter, and great part of Connaught; and was founder of feveral churches and abbies, which he plentifully endowed. In the year 1181, he was created, by K. Henry II. Earl of Ulfter, and Lord of Connaught; and had a patent from the faid King, for him, his heirs and affigns, to enjoy all the lands in that kingdom he could conquer with his fword, together with the donation of bifhopricks and abbies, referving from him only homage and fealty. From the year 1175 to 1179 he was joint Governor of Ireland; and from 1185 to 1190 fole Governor: but being that year accufed, by Hugh de Lacy, of difrefpect to the

King,

King, he was sent prisoner to London, and was confined in the Tower for the space of one year; when a dispute arising between John, King of England, and Philip-Augustus, King of France, about the title to the Duchy of Normandy, they agreed to refer the dispute to the decision of two champions. The French champion being ready, the King of England could find none of his subjects to undertake the combat: but being informed, that the Earl of Ulster was the only man in his dominions who could undertake it, he sent twice to the Earl in the Tower for that purpose; but was refused, by reason of the ungrateful returns the said King had made to the Earl's services, by imprisoning him unheard, at the suit of his rival and enemy, Hugh de Lacy: but the King sending the third time, the Earl replied, "That " though he would not fight for the King, yet " he would hazard his life for the crown and " dignity of the realm." The day of combat being appointed in Normandy, the Earl's own sword was sent for out of Ireland: but when the day came, and every thing was ready for the fight, and the champions were entered the lists, in the presence of the Kings of England, France, and Scotland, the French champion, not liking the strong proportion of the Earl's body, nor the terrible weapon he bore in his hand, when the trumpets sounded the last charge, set spurs to his horse, broke through the lists, and fled into Spain, from whence he never returned. The French champion being thus fled, the victory was adjudged to the Earl of Ulster. But the Kings hearing of his great strength, and being willing to see some trial of
it,

it, they ordered an helmet of excellent proof, full faced with mail, to be laid on a block of wood, which the Earl with one blow cut afunder, and ftruck his fword fo deep into the wood, that none there prefent but himfelf could draw it out again; which fword, together with his armour, are to this day preferved in the Tower of London.

After this noble performance, the King reftored him to his titles and eftate, which was valued at that time at twenty-five thoufand marks fterling per annum, a vaft income in thofe days; and likewife bad him afk for any thing elfe in his gift he had a mind to, and it fhould be granted. Upon which the Earl replied, "That he had titles and eftate enough, "but defired that he and his fucceffors, the "heirs male of his family after him, might "have the privilege, after their firft obeifance, "of being covered in the royal prefence of "him and his fucceffors, Kings of England;" which the King granted; and the faid privilege is preferved in the family to this day. For Almericus, the twenty-third Lord, in 1692, being one day at King William's court, and admitted into the Prefence-chamber, walked to and fro with his hat on, which the King obferving, fent one of his Nobles to enquire the reafon of his appearing before the King with his head covered. To whom he replied, "He very well knew in whofe prefence he "ftood; and the reafon why he wore his hat "that day was, becaufe he ftood before the "King of England." This anfwer being told the King, his Lordfhip approached near the Throne, and being required by his Majefty to
explain

explain himfelf, he fpoke as follows: "May it pleafe your Majefty; My name is Courcy, and I am Lord of Kingfale, in the kingdom of Ireland; the reafon of my appearing covered in your Majefty's prefence is, to affert the antient privilege of my family, granted to Sir John de Courcy, Earl of Ulfter, and his heirs, by John, King of England, for him and his fucceffors for ever." The King replied, "That he remembered he had fuch a Nobleman, and he believed the privilege he afferted to be right;" and giving him his hand to kifs, his Lordfhip made his obeifance, and remained uncovered. And Gerald, the late Baron of Kingfale, being prefented to King George I. by the Duke of Grafton, Lord Lieutenant, on June 13, 1720, had the honour to kifs the King's hand, and affert the antient privilege of his family, of being covered in his prefence; and, on June 22, 1727, he was prefented by the Lord Carteret, Lord Lieutenant of Ireland, to King George II. by whom he was gracioufly received, and had the honour of kiffing his Majefty's hand, and being covered in his prefence.

The faid Sir John Courcy, Earl of Ulfter, afterwards arriving in England, is faid to have attempted fifteen feveral times to crofs the feas from thence into Ireland, but was every time put back by contrary winds; whereupon he altered his courfe, and went to France, where he died, about the year 1210, leaving iffue by Africa his wife, daughter of Godred, King of the Ifle of Man, and of the Weftern Ifles of Scotland, Miles, his heir, who fucceeded him, and was one of the bail for his father's fidelity on his being

ing released out of the Tower, in order to fight the French champion, as appears in the records of the fourth year of King John, kept in the said Tower. He was kept out of the Earldom of Ulster by Hugh de Lacy, who had a grant of it from King John, on taking Earl John and sending him prisoner to London: for Miles claiming the Earldom after his father's death, the said Lacy replied, That he would maintain the King's last grant of it to himself, since Earl John never returned to Ireland to reverse the outlawry. Miles being forced to quit his pretensions, was, however, created Baron of Kingsale; and afterwards living altogether in Ireland, never claimed the Barony of Stoke-Courcy; and was succeeded by his son Patrick de Courcy, who, in the fifth of King Henry III. was named in a commission with Thomas Fitz Anthony, the King of Connaught, the King of Leinster, and Obryen, the King of Munster, directing them to remove Sir Geofry de Marisco from being Lord Justice of Ireland; and in his room to substitute Henry de Laundres, Archbishop of Dublin. This Lord of Kingsale, in right of his wife, enjoyed one half of the kingdom of Cork; and in the twentieth of King Henry III. we find him stiled *Dominus Medietatis Regni Corcagiæ*.

Edmund, the fourth Lord of Kingsale, was named by King Edward I. with Richard de Bourke, Earl of Ulster, Thomas Fitz-Maurice, Earl of Desmond, and ten others, as Peers of Ireland, to accompany that King in his wars to Scotland. Miles, the seventh Lord, overthrew Florence Mac-Carty More, with a great army of his followers, in a battle at Ringrone, and

drove

drove them into the river Bandon, near Kingfale, where Mac-Carty and a great number of them were drowned. William, the ninth Baron of Kingfale, had, in the year 1397, a fpecial licence from King Richard II. by patent, to buy a fhip, to pafs and repafs whenever he pleafed, between England and France. Patrick, the eleventh Baron, founded the Convent of Auftin-Friers, in the city of Cork.

King Henry VII. having fent for moft of the Temporal Lords out of Ireland, and admitted them to his prefence at Greenwich, they attended the King in a folemn proceffion to Church, but James, the thirteenth Baron of Kingfale, not being there that day, loft his precedency of the firft Baron of Ireland, which the King gave to the Lord Athenry, who was a Lancaftrian, whereas the Lord Kingfale was a Yorkift; but that Lord's defcendant being lately created Earl of Lowth, the Lord Kingfale is now premier Baron of Ireland.

Gerald de Courcy, the feventeenth Baron of Kingfale, commanded an Irifh regiment at the fiege of Boulogne, in France, under Henry VIII. and having been a great inftrument in the taking of that town, was, for his fignal fervices and bravery, knighted in the field, under the royal ftandard, which was efteemed a great honour in thofe days. John, the eighteenth Lord of Kingfale, behaved himfelf gallantly againft the Spaniards, at the fiege of Kingfale, and was in great favour with King James I. to whom he was a Lord of the Bed-chamber.

Creation.] Baron of Kingfale, &c. in the county of Cork, originally by tenure; afterwards

wards by writs of summons to Parliament; and by patent in 1397, 20 Richard II.

Arms.] Pearl, three eaglets displayed, ruby, and crowned with ducal coronets, topaz.

Crest.] In a ducal coronet, proper, an eagle displayed, pearl.

Supporters.] Two unicorns, sapphire, their horns, manes, collars of crosses pattée, and fleurs de lis, chains, and hoofs, topaz.

Motto.] *Vincit omnia veritas.*

Chief Seat.] At the Castle of the Old Head of Kingsale, in the county of Cork.

LORD CAHIER.

James Butler, Baron of Cahier, in the county of Tipperary, born Aug. 1, 1711, succeeded his father, Thomas, the late and eighth Baron, in May 1744, and in Jan. 1739, married Christian, fourth daughter and coheir of Michael Moore, of Drogheda, Esq; but has no issue. His Lordship being a Roman Catholick, is disqualified from sitting in the House of Peers.

Thomas, the late and eighth Lord Cahier, succeeded his father Theobald in 1700, and married Frances, daughter of Sir Theobald Butler, Knt. Sollicitor-general to K. James II. by whom he had six sons and two daughters, viz. 1. James, the present Lord; 2. Theobald, who died young; 3. Thomas; 4. Jordan; 5. Pierce; and, 6. John: 7. Margaret, married, in 1752, to Andrew Kennedy, of Dublin, Esq; and, 8. Mary.

James

James Butler, the third Earl of Ormond, befides his lawful children, had two illegitimate fons, Thomas, Prior of Kilmainham, and Lord Deputy of Ireland, in the reigns of Henry IV. and V. and (by Catharine, daughter of Gerald, Earl of Defmond) James de Botiller, anceftor of the Lord Cahier, whofe defcendants, by the fettlements of Thomas, the tenth Earl of Ormond, were made the next in remainder to the houfe of Ormond, after the family of Dunboyne. The faid James married the daughter of ―― Mac-Walter, and died in 1485, leaving a fon Pierce, whofe fon and heir Thomas, by Alice, daughter of the Earl of Defmond, had Edmund his heir, who was father of Thomas, created Baron of Cahier, by Queen Elizabeth: he was father of

Edmund, the fecond Lord, who dying without iffue, the honour was conferred anew upon

Theobald Butler, fon of Pierce, younger brother of Thomas, the firft Lord Cahier.

Creation.] Baron, *ut fupra*, May 6, 1583, 25 Eliz.

Arms.] Quarterly of fix coats, three in chief, and two in bafe. Firft, Pearl, on a crofs of Calvary, ruby, our Saviour crucified, topaz, borne in memory of one of the family's fighting againft the Turks. Second, Topaz, a chief indented, fapphire. Third, Ruby, three covered cups, topaz, both for the name and office of Butler, and both differenced with a crefcent. Fourth, Ermine, a faltire, ruby, in memory of his anceftrix, Catharine of Defmond, by whom a great part of the eftate accrued to the family. Fifth, Party per pale, indented,

indented, topaz and ruby, for Bermingham. Sixth, Pearl, an eagle, diamond, displayed, between three crosses patonce, diamond, ruby, for Morrys.

Crest.] In a ducal coronet, topaz, a plume of five feathers, and thence a falcon rising, all pearl.

Supporters.] Two tigers, party per fess, sapphire and topaz, each beaked, ducally gorged, and chained, of the latter.

Motto.] God be my guide*.

Chief Seats.] Cahier-castle, in the county of Tipperary; Burton, near St. Edmundsbury, in Suffolk.

LORD MAYNARD.

See an account of this noble family, in my Peerage of England, under the same title.

LORD DIGBY.

The descent, and other particulars of this noble Lord, see in my Peerage of England, under the same title.

---

* This Coat was granted to Theobald, Lord Cahier, Nov. 30, 1583, by Nicholas Narbonne, Ulster King at Arms.

LORD BLAYNEY.

CADWALLADER BLAYNEY, Lord BLAYNEY, Baron of Monaghan, a Major-general, and Colonel of the twenty-eighth regiment of Foot, succeeded his brother, Charles-Talbot, the late and eighth Lord, in 1765.

Charles-Talbot, the late Lord, was Dean of Killaloe, succeeded his father Cadwallader, March 19, 1732-3, and, in Nov 1734, married Elizabeth, daughter of Nicholas Mahone, Esq; by his wife Eleanor, daughter of Henry-Vincent, the fifth Lord Blayney, by whom he had an only son, Henry-Vincent, born Dec. 28, 1737, who died before his father.

Cadwallader, the seventh Lord, was born in April 1693, succeeded his father William, Jan. 3, 1705; and married, April 22, 1714, Mary, daughter of James Touchet, Esq; second son of the Earl of Castlehaven, and niece of Charles, Duke of Shrewsbury; and by her, who died in 1721, had two sons, Charles-Talbot, the late Lord; and Cadwallader, the present Lord; and a daughter, Mary, married, first, to Nicholas Mahone, Esq; and, secondly, to John Campbell, of Dublin, Esq; and in 1724, his Lordship married to his second wife Mary, only daughter and heir to Sir Alexander Cairnes, of Monaghan, Bart.

This noble family is descended, in a direct line, from Cadwallader, a younger son of the Prince of Wales; and the first Peer was

Sir Edward Blayney, Knt. who was Knight for the county of Monaghan, and one of the Privy-council to King James I. by whom he was created a Baron, July 29, 1621: he was succeeded by

Sir Henry, his eldeſt ſon, who was the ſecond Lord, and loſt his life at the battle of Benburb, in the county of Tyrone, June 5, 1646: he was ſucceeded by

Edward, his eldeſt ſon, who dying unmarried, in 1669, was ſucceeded by

Richard, his brother, the fourth Lord, who, in 1656, was, by Oliver Cromwell, appointed Keeper of the Rolls of the Peace within the county of Monaghan; as he was, by his ſon, Richard Cromwell, Eſcheator of the province of Ulſter, and was returned to Parliament for the county of Monaghan at the Reſtoration: he was ſucceeded by his ſon,

Henry-Vincent, the fifth Lord, to whom K. James II. in 1689, before he left Ireland, ſent an invitation for him to enter into his ſervice, promiſing him a pardon for what had paſſed: to which his Lordſhip anſwered, "That he had "now a King upon whoſe word he could de- "pend and truſt; but never would to his, "without his ſword in his hand:" and heading a body of Proteſtants in the province of Ulſter, he took the paſs of Louth-Bricklan, ſeized Armagh, and cauſed King William and Queen Mary to be proclaimed there; as alſo at Hillsborough, and ſeveral other places, with great ſolemnity. Having died without iſſue male, he was ſucceeded by his only ſurviving brother,

William, the ſixth Baron of Blayney.

Creation.] *Ut ſupra.*

Arms.] Diamond, three horſes heads, eraſed, pearl.

Creſt.]

Crest.] On a wreath, a horse's head, couped, pearl, bridled, ruby; and on his forehead a piece of armour, in the midst whereof is a spike, like that of a target, all proper.

Supporters.] Two horses, diamond, their bridles, saddles, and hoofs, topaz.

Motto.] *Integra mens augustissima possessio.*

Chief Seat.] Castle-Blayney, in the county of Monaghan.

LORD BALTIMORE.

FREDERICK CALVERT, Baron BALTIMORE, of Baltimore, in the county of Longford, Lord Proprietor and Governor of Maryland, F. R. S. was born Feb. 6, 1731, and succeeded his father, Charles, the late and sixth Lord, April 24, 1751. On March 9, 1753, he married Lady Diana, youngest daughter of Scrope, Duke of Bridgwater (by his second wife, the Lady Rachel, sister of John, Duke of Bedford) which Lady died July 18, 1758.

Charles, the late and sixth Lord Baltimore, married, July 20, 1730, Mary, youngest daughter of Sir Theodore Janssen, of Wimbledon, in Surry, Bart. by whom he had two sons, Frederick, the present Lord, and another, born Jan. 21, 1737, who died young; and three daughters, of whom Frances-Dorothy died March 5, 1736. His Lordship, in 1731, was appointed a Gentleman of the Bed-chamber to the Prince of Wales; in 1734, he was elected Member in Parliament for St. Germain's, in Cornwall; and, in 1741, and 1747, for the county of Surry. In 1741 he was appointed a

G 3   Lord

Lord of the Admiralty, which he resigned in 1745; and, in 1747, was made Cofferer to the Prince of Wales, and Surveyor-general of the Duchy lands in Cornwall.

Benedict-Leonard, the fifth Lord, succeeded his father Charles in Feb. 1714; and, Jan. 2, 1698-9, married the Lady Charlotte Lee, eldest daughter of Edward-Henry, Earl of Litchfield, by which Lady, who died July 20, 1731, he had four sons and three daughters, viz.

1. Charles, the late Lord, born Sept. 29, 1699.
2. Benedict Leonard, born Sept. 20, 1700, was, in 1726, appointed Governor of Maryland, and died on his return from thence in 1732.
3. Edward-Henry, born Aug. 31, 1701, was Commissary-general, and President of the council in Maryland, and is deceased.
4. Cecil, a twin with his sister Charlotte, born in Nov. 1702.
5. Charlotte, married to Thomas Breerwood, Esq; died in Dec. 1744.
6. Jane, born in Nov. 1703.
7. Barbara, born in Oct. 1704, but died young.

The original of this family is from an ancient and noble house of that surname in the Earldom of Flanders, whereof

Sir George Calvert, Knt. among other honourable employmen's, was Secretary of State to King James I. by whom he was created a Baron, Feb. 16, 1624, and from whom he had a grant, to him and his heirs, of the Province of Maryland and Avalon.

Creation.]

Creation.] *Ut supra.*

Arms.] Pally of six, topaz and diamond, a bend counterchanged.

Crest.] In a ducal coronet, proper, two pennons, the first topaz, the other diamond, with staves, ruby.

Supporters.] Two leopards, guardant-coward, proper.

Motto.] *Fatti maschii parole femine* *.

Chief Seat.] At Woodcote, near Epsom, in the county of Surry.

LORD LEITRIM.

An account of this noble family is given in my Peerage of England, under the title of Earl of HARBOROUGH.

LORD HAWLEY.

FRANCIS HAWLEY, Lord HAWLEY, Baron of Donamore, and Baronet, Lieutenant-governor of Antigua, succeeded his father, Francis, the late and second Lord, on May 30, 1743, and married Margaret, daughter of Thomas Tyrrel, of the city of London, Esq; by whom he has issue one daughter, ———, married in May, 1755, to John Brettle, Esq;

In 1377, Walter Hauleigh, or Hawley, Esq; was Member of Parliament for Shaftsbury, in

---

* This Coat-armour was given and confirmed, Nov. 30, 1622, by Sir Richard St. George, Norroy King of Arms; the bearing of the family before being, Or, three martlets, sable.

the county of Dorset, as he was the six succeeding years; and in the 2d, 7th, 28th, and 30th of Queen Elizabeth, Francis Hawley, Esq; was Member for Corfe-castle, in the same county.

Sir Francis Hawley, of Buckland, in the county of Somerset, Knt. was created a Baronet; and a Baron, as above, by Charles I. He had a son, Francis, who died before him, and left issue, by Gertrude, daughter of Richard Gethins, of the county of Cork, Esq; two sons, Francis and Richard; and a daughter, Catharine, married to Robert Napier, of Pucknoll, in the county of Dorset, Esq. Francis, the eldest son, succeeded his grandfather, Dec. 28, 1684, was the second Baron Hawley; and marrying the Lady Elizabeth, daughter of William Ramsay, Earl of Dalhousie, in Scotland, had by her, who died in Feb. 1712, two sons, Francis, the present Lord, and William, who died January 31, 1755; and three daughters, Rachel, Elizabeth, and Gertrude.

Creations.] Baronet, March 14, 1643, 19 Charles I. Lord Hawley, Baron of Donamore, in the county of Meath, July 8, 1646, 22 Charles I.

Arms.] Emerald, a saltire ingrailed, pearl.

Crest:] An Indian goat's head, holding a three leaved sprig of holly, proper.

Supporters.]

Motto.] *Suivez moi.*

Chief Seat.] Buckland-house, in Somersetshire.

LORD BELLEW.

John Bellew, Lord Bellew, of Duleek, in the county of Meath, was born in 1702, succeeded his father, Richard, the third and late Lord, March 22, 1714, and on December 31, 1731, married, at Rome, Lady Anne Maxwell, daughter of William, Earl of Nithsdale, and by her (who died May 3, 1735,) had issue one son, Edward, who died in his infancy, and one daughter, Mary-Frances, born in 1733. In 1737 his Lordship married, secondly, Mary, only daughter of Maurice Fitzgerald, of Castle-Ishin, in the county of Cork, Esq; relict of Justin, Earl of Fingal, and of Valentine, Viscount Kenmare, and by her (who died March 19, 1741) had two daughters; Emilia, who died in the sixth year of her age; and Anne, born June 24, 1739. In May, 1749, he married to his third wife, Lady Henrietta Lee, fourth daughter of George-Henry, Earl of Litchfield, and by her, (who died April 30, 1752) had a son and daughter, who both died in their infancy.

Of this antient family, which came into England with William, Duke of Normandy, and were Marshals in his army, were eighteen Knights Bannerets, in a direct line of succession; and in 1479, the Order of the Garter being established in Ireland, Richard Bellew was elected into that most noble Order. From this Richard descended three brothers, who were, Sir John Bellew, of Duleek, Matthew Bellew, of Rogerstown, and Thomas Bellew, of Gaffney.

* G 5   John,

John, the eldest, was created a Baron by King James II. He had two sons, Walter and Richard, and being shot in the belly, in Aughrim fight, July 12, 1691, he died Jan. 12, following, and was succeeded by Walter, the second Lord, who dying without issue male, in 1694, Richard his brother succeeded him, who, with John his father, was outlawed for their service to King James II. but his outlawry was reversed in 1697; and in 1713 he had a pension settled on him of three hundred pounds a year, which was continued to him by King George I. He married Frances, sister of George Brudenel, Earl of Cardigan, in England, and widow of Charles Livingston, the second Earl of Newburgh in Scotland, with a portion of seventeen thousand pounds, and had issue by her,

1. John, the present Lord.
2. Walter-Bermingham, born May 21, 1707, who died young.
3. Dorothea, married to Captain Gustavus Hamilton, father of the present Viscount Boyne; secondly, to William Cockburn, of Redford, in King's county, Esq; and, thirdly, to Joseph Dixon, Esq; Captain in the army.

Creation.] Baron Bellew, of Duleek, Oct. 29, 1686, 2 James II.

Arms.] Diamond, frettée-topaz.

Crest. On a wreath, a dexter arm in armour, embowed, brandishing a sword, proper.

Supporters.] On the dexter side a leopard, topaz, gorged with a collar embattled on the upper side, sapphire; on the sinister, a wolf of the latter, gorged with a ducal coronet, topaz.

Motto.]

Motto.] *Tout d'en haut.*
Chief Seat.] Bellewstown, in the county of Meath *.

LORD CONWAY.

An account of this noble family will be seen in my Peerage of England, under the title, Earl of HERTFORD.

LORD TYRAWLEY.

JAMES O HARA, Lord TYRAWLEY and KILMAIN, a Lord of his Majesty's most hon. Privy-council in Great Britain and in Ireland, Field-Marshal of his Majesty's forces, Governor of Portsmouth, Colonel of the second regiment of Foot-guards, F. R. S. was born in 1690, succeeded his father, Charles, the first Lord Tyrawley, on June 9, 1724, and married Mary, only surviving daughter of William, Viscount Mountjoy, by whom his Lordship has no issue. In 1721 he was created Baron of Kilmain, in the life-time of his father. On Jan. 20, 1727, he was appointed Envoy extraordinary to the court of Portugal; and, in Nov. 1743, to that of Russia. In 1752 he was sent Minister Plenipotentiary to the King of Portugal, as he has been several times since.

This noble Lord is descended from Milesius, King of Spain, by his eldest son Hiberius, who,

---

* The family of Bellew, of Bermeath and Castle-Bellew, Baronets, are probably of this family: however, the first Baronet of the family was so created, Ap. 25, 1687, by the interest, and at the recommendation, of John, Lord Bellew.

with

with his brother Heremon, established a Colony in Ireland.- Sir Charles O'Hara, Lieutenant-colonel of a regiment of foot guards, was knighted at Whitehall in 1689, by King William; and, in 1706, created Baron of Tyrawley by Queen Anne; at which time he was a Lieutenant-general, and Colonel of the royal regiment of Fuzileers; and the next year he was made General in Spain, where his son, the present Lord, was wounded, at the battle of Almanza. In Sept. 1714, he was appointed one of the Privy-council to King George I. and on Nov. 9 following, General and Commander in Chief of all his Majesty's land forces in Ireland. He married Frances, daughter of Gervaise Rous, of Rouselench, in the county of Worcester, Esq; and by her, who died Nov. 10, 1733, left a son, James, the present Lord, and a daughter Mary, who died in March 1759, unmarried.

Creations.] Baron of Tyrawley, in the county of Mayo, Jan. 10, 1706, 5 Anne. Baron Kilmaine, of Kilmaine, in the same county, Feb. 8, 1721, 8 George I.

Arms.] Emerald, on a pale radiant, topaz, a lion rampant, diamond.

Crest.] On a wreath, a demi-lion, ermine, holding between its paws a chaplet of laurel, proper, fructed, ruby.

Supporters.] On the dexter side, a lion pean, (viz. black, spotted with yellow) gorged with a collar, radiant, topaz. On the sinister, a lion ermine, gorged with a chaplet, as that in the paws of the crest.

Motto.] *Try.*

Chief Seat.] At Blackheath, in Kent.

LORD CARBERY.

GEORGE EVANS, Lord CARBERY, succeeded his father, George, the late and second Lord, on Feb. 8, 1759.

George, the late Lord, succeeded his father, George, the first Lord, Aug. 28, 1749, was elected to Parliament for Westbury, in 1734, and 1741, and May 23, 1732, married Frances, youngest daughter of Richard, Viscount Fitz-William, by whom he had issue two sons and one daughter; George, the present Lord; John, and Frances-Anne, wife of —— Wilson, Esq;

Of this antient family, which has been long seated in the Principality of Wales, was George Evans, who had a command in the army sent to Ireland for the suppressing the Rebellion in 1641; and after that, settled at Ballygrenane, in the county of Limerick, where, and in other counties, he acquired a plentiful estate; and dying in 1707, left two sons and one daughter. The youngest son, John, was bred to the Law, but quitted that profession at the Revolution for a military life; and at last took to the sea, where he commanded several of the King's ships, and died in 1723, without issue.

George the eldest brother was also bred to the Law, and was very active in promoting the Revolution of 1688; he served in many Parliaments for Charleville, in the county of Cork; was Custos Rotulorum of the county of Limerick; one of the Privy-council in Ireland; and died in the year 1720, leaving three sons and seven daughters. Of the sons, George, the elder, being many years Knight of the Shire
for

for the county of Limerick, where he moft ftrenuoufly exerted himfelf for the good of the public, his Majefty King George I. was pleafed to create him a Peer, appointed him one of the Privy-council, and Conftable of the Caftle of Limerick. He was chofen in the two Parliaments of K. George I. for Weftbury in Wilts; his Lordfhip married Anne, daughter of William Stafford, of Blatherwick, in the county of Northampton, Efq; and coheir of William Stafford, her brother, by whom he had iffue four fons and one daughter, viz.

1. Stafford, born in 1704, died young.
2. George, the late Lord Carbery.
3. William, deceafed.
4. John Evans, of Bulgaden-hall, Efq; Sheriff of the county of Limerick, for the year 1743, who, in June, 1741, married Grace, fifter of Sir John Redmond Freke, Bart. and had five fons and two daughters.
5. Anne, married in 1734, to Major-general Charles du Terme, and is deceafed.

Creation.] Baron Carbery, of Carbery, in the county of Cork, May 9, 1715, 1 George I.

Arms.] Pearl, three boars heads, couped, diamond.

Creft.] On a wreath, a demi-lion, reguardant, topaz, holding between his paws, a boar's head, as thofe in the coat.

Supporters.] Two lions, reguardant, topaz, ducally crowned, fapphire.

Motto.] *Libertas.*

Chief Seats.] Caharas, in the county of Limerick; Laxton, in the county of Northampton; and Woolfton, in the county of Southampton.

LORD

LORD SOUTHWELL.

Thomas-George Southwell, Lord Southwell, of Caſtle-Mattreſs, and Baronet, a Lord of the Privy council, was born in May 1721, ſucceeded his father Thomas, the late and ſecond Lord, on Nov. 19, 1766, and June 18, 1741, married Margaret, eldeſt daughter and co-heir of Arthur-Cecil Hamilton, of Caſtle-Hamilton, in the county of Cavan, Eſq; and by her (who died in July, 1766,) he had iſſue Thomas-Arthur, born in 1742; Henry, born in Oct. 1745; and a daughter, Frances-Lucia.

Thomas, the late Lord, was born Jan. 7, 1698, ſucceeded his father Thomas, Aug. 4, 1720, and, in March 1719, married Mary, eldeſt daughter of Thomas Coke, of Melburne, in the county of Derby, Eſq; (grandſon of Sir John Coke, Secretary of State to Charles II) by the Lady Mary Stanhope, eldeſt daughter of Philip, the ſecond Earl of Cheſterfield, and by her, who was a Lady of the Bed-chamber to the late Princeſs of Orange, to whom his Lordſhip was appointed Maſter of the horſe, in Oct. 1733, he had three ſons, viz.

1. Thomas, born Jan. 9, 1719-20, died an infant.
2. Thomas-George, the preſent Lord.
3. Coningsby, born Feb. 15, 1724, died an infant.

Of this antient family, who took their ſurname from the town of Southwell, in the county of Nottingham, was Sir Simon de Southwell, Knt. who lived in the reign of Henry III. and from him the chief branch continued at Southwell

well till the time of Henry VI. In the reign of Edward II. John de Southwell was in such great repute for his wisdom and fidelity, that, in the 20th thereof, being in Gascoigne in France, he had power to confederate with any Princes, who desired the King's friendship; and in the 13th of Edward III. 1338, being then a Knight, at the King's desire putting himself an hostage for freeing Charles, King of Sicily, who was prisoner in Arragon, he was thereupon by the said King Edward III. made Seneschal, or Steward of Gascoigne, and had the castle of Bourdeaux given him, and all the emoluments thereunto belonging, for his life. In 1449, John Southwell, of Felix-hall, in the county of Essex, Esq; served in Parliament for the borough of Lewes, in Sussex. From him descended John, who removed into Ireland in the time of James I. whose youngest son, Edmund, was seated at Castle-Mattress, and had five sons, of whom, Thomas, the youngest, being the only son that had issue, was created a Baronet by King Charles II. His only son, Richard, dying in his life-time, and having married Elizabeth, daughter of Murrough Obryen, Earl of Inchiquin, by her had five sons and two daughters, viz.

 1. Sir Thomas, successor to his grandfather.
 2. John, killed at the siege of Namure.
 3. William, who became an Officer in the army; and, in Sept. 1705, at the head of four hundred Grenadiers, supported by a detachment of six hundred foot, took the fort of Monjuic, sword in hand, and made the garrison, of three hundred men, prisoners of war, for which service he was rewarded with the government
of

of that caftle; in Feb. 1706, had a regiment of foot; and, during Queen Anne's reign, ferved in Parliament for the borough of Caftle Mattrefs; in 1714 he was appointed Captain of the company of Foot-guards, armed with battle-axes; and in 1717, was Member of Parliament for the borough of Baltimore. He married Lucy, youngeft daughter and coheir of William Bowen, of Ballyadams, in Queen's county, Efq; by whom he had fix fons, and nine daughters; of the fons, Bowen is now in poffeffion of his father's eftate, who died Jan. 23, 1719; and in 1753, married the Lady Elizabeth Cornwallis, eldeft daughter of Charles, Earl of Cornwallis.

4. Courtnay, died unmarried.

5. Richard, was Collector for the county of Limerick; and married Agnes, fifter to Henry Rofe, Efq; and had an only daughter, Agnes-Elizabeth, married, Aug. 11, 1750, to John, now Earl of Wandesford.

6. Elizabeth, married to —— Morris, of the county of Kerry, Efq;

7. Catharine, married to General David Creighton, Governor of the Royal Hofpital near Dublin.

Sir Thomas, who was the eldeft, having in the reign of James II. joined others againft the rebels in the Province of Connaught, he, with his party, was taken prifoner, and condemned to be hanged and quartered at Galway: but upon the victory of King William at the Boyne, they were all releafed. In 1704, he was Member for the county of Limerick, and one of the Commiffioners of the revenues in Ireland. In 1714, he was appointed one of the Privy-council,

cil; and 1715, one of the Commiffioners of the Excife; and one of the Commiffioners and Governors of all other his Majefty's Revenues in the Kingdom of Ireland; and, was created a Baron. He married Meliora, eldeft daughter of Thomas Earl of Coningfby, by whom he had fix fons and five daughters, viz.

1. Thomas, the late Lord.
2. Henry, an Officer in the army, and Reprefentative for the county of Limerick, who married Dulcinea, daughter of the Rev. Henry Royfe, of Nantinan, in that county, and had iffue a fon Henry, and two daughters.
3. Robert, killed in a duel, May 30, 1724, by Mr. Luttrel.
4. Edmund, born March 16, 1705.
5. Richard, Rector of Dungurney, &c. &c. in the diocefe of Cloyne.
6. William, born March 13, 1715.

The daughters all died young except Frances and Lucia.

Creations.] Baronet, Aug. 4, 1562, 14 Charles II. Baron Southwell of Caftle Mattrefs, in the county of Limerick, Sept. 4, 1717, 4 Geo. I.

Arms.] Pearl, three cinquefoils, ruby, each charged with fix annulets, topaz.

Creft.] On a wreath a demi-Indian goat, pearl, charged on the body with three annulets, ruby.

Supporters.] Two Indian goats, pearl, each charged with three annulets, as the creft, ducally gorged, and chained, ruby.

Motto.] *Nec male notus Eques*; and, *Dulce eft pro patria mori.*

Chief Seats.] Rathkeal, in the county of Limerick; Clantarfe, in the county of Dublin.

LORD

LORD AYLMER.

Henry Aylmer, Lord Aylmer, succeeded his father Henry, the late and third Lord, in 1766, and is a minor.

Henry, the late Lord, was a Captain in the Royal Navy, and succeeded his father, Henry, the second Lord, on June 26, 1754, and had issue Henry, the present Lord.

Henry, the second Lord Aylmer, succeeded his father Matthew, Aug. 18, 1720; in 1722, was chosen one of the Barons for the Port of Rye, in Sussex; and was made Comptroller of the Mint in 1727. He married Elizabeth, daughter of Henry Priestman, Esq; and by her, who died Jan. 12, 1749-50, had four sons, viz.

1. Matthew, made an Ensign in the first regiment of foot guards in 1737, died Sept. 2, 1748.
2. Henry, the late Lord.
3. Philip, deceased.
4. John.

Of this ancient family, which has been long settled in Ireland, and said to be originally descended from Aylmer, a Saxon Duke of Cornwall, was Sir Gerald Aylmer, who, 1533, was Baron of the Exchequer in Ireland; in 1536, appointed one of the Commissioners to treat with O'Neal on the borders of Ulster; and, in 1541, the said Sir Gerald, being very active in assisting the Lord Grey, then Lord-lieutenant of Ireland, when he defeated O'Neal, was for his good services knighted by the said Lord Grey; and on the accession of Edw. VI. made one of the Privy-council, joined with Sir Thomas Cusack in the Government of Ireland; and, in 1553, was

was made Chief Juſtice of the Queen's Bench. From him deſcended Sir Chriſtopher Aylmer, who was created a Baronet; whoſe grandſon, Sir Matthew Aylmer, is the preſent Baronet.

Matthew, the ſecond ſon of the ſaid Sir Chriſtopher, in the reign of King William, was Rear-admiral of the Red, and choſen one of the Barons for the Port of Dover in Kent; in 1701, was made Governor of Deal-Caſtle; and, in 1709, appointed Admiral, and Commander in chief of his Majeſty's Fleet; as he was alſo by George I. He was made Governor of Greenwich Hoſpital, Houſekeeper of his Majeſty's palace there, and Keeper of Greenwich park. In 1717, he was made one of the Commiſſioners of the Admiralty, next year Maſter of Greenwich Hoſpital, by patent for life; and created a Baron. He married Sarah, daughter of Edward Ellis, of the city of London, Eſq; by whom he had iſſue, Henry, the ſecond Lord; and two daughters, Elizabeth, and Lucy, married to Hugh Forteſcue, of Filley, in the county of Devon, Eſq;

Creation.] Lord Aylmer, Baron of Balrath, in the county of Meath May 1, 1718, 4 George I.

Arms.] Pearl, a croſs diamond between four corniſh choughs, proper.

Creſt.] In a ducal coronet, topaz, a chough, as thoſe in the coat, its wings diſplay'd.

Supporters.] Two mariners, habited, the dexter holding in his exterior hand, a foreſtaff; and the ſiniſter, a lead-line, all proper.

Motto.] *Steady.*

Chief Seat.] At Greenwich, in the county of Kent.

LORD

LORD DESART.

John Cuffe, Lord Desart, was born Nov. 16, 1730, succeeded his father John, the late and first Lord, June 26, 1749, and Sept. 2, 1752, married Sophia, daughter and heir of Brettridge Badham, of Rockfield, in the county of Cork, Esq; relict of Richard Thornhill, of the same county, Esq;

This noble family derives its origin from the counties of Somerset and Northampton; and had its first settlement in Ireland in the reign of Queen Elizabeth, when Hugh Cuffe became seated at Cuffe's-wood, in Kilmore. Maurice Cuffe, of Ennis, in the county of Clare, had seven sons, of whom Joseph, the sixth, took up arms in 1649, under Oliver Cromwell, and commanded a troop of horse. He died in 1679, and was succeeded by his eldest son, Agmondesham, who was attainted by King James's Parliament in 1689, with his brother Thomas, and had his estate sequestred, but was restored to it by King William, to whom he did great service in the reduction of the kingdom. In 1679 he married Anne, daughter of Sir John Otway, of London, and died in 1727, having had many children, of whom five survived their infancy, viz.

1. John, created Lord Desart.
2. Denny Cuffe, of Sandhill, in the county of Carlow, Esq; Captain of a company of foot, and in 1723 Sheriff of Kilkenny, who left issue.
3. Maurice Cuffe, of Killaghy, in the county of Kilkenny, Esq; Member of Parliament for the city of Kilkenny, in the reign of King George I.

George I. and one of his Majesty's Council at law, married first, Martha, daughter of John Fitz-gerald, of Ballymaloe, in the county of Cork, Esq; by whom he had five daughters; and secondly, Hannah, sister of John, the first Earl of Darnley.

4. William.

5. Martha, married to John Blunden, of Clanmolan, Esq; Member of Parliament for the city of Kilkenny, who died in 1726.

John Cuffe, of Desart, the eldest son, in the reign of King George I. was Member of Parliament for Thomastown, and created a Peer by King George II. He married, first, Margaret, daughter and heir of James Hamilton, of Carnesure, in the county of Downe, Esq; by whom he had no surviving issue. He married, secondly, Feb. 12, 1726-7, Dorothea, eldest daughter of General Richard Gorges, of Kilbrew, in the county of Meath, by whom he had seven sons and four daughters, viz.

1. Joseph; and
2. Agmondesham, who both died infants.
3. John, the present Lord.
4. Otway, educated at Christ-church, Oxford.
5. Gorges, who died young.
6. Hamilton; 7. William.
8. Nichola-Sophia; 9. Lucy-Susanna;
10. Martha;
11. Margaret, who died in Nov. 1742.

Creation.] Baron of Desart, in the county of Kilkenny, Nov. 10, 1733, 7 Geo. II.

Arms.] Pearl, on a bend, indented, diamond, three fleurs de lis, of the field, between two cottizes, sapphire, each charged with three bezants.

Crest]

Crest.] An arm in pale, couped below the elbow, crested, topaz, charged with two bends undée, sapphire, and turned up, ermine; the hand proper, holding a pole-axe, topaz, the staff thereof sapphire.

Supporters.] Two leopards reguardant, proper, both collared, as in the bend, charged as in the arms, and chained, diamond.

Motto.] *Virtus repulsæ nescia sordidæ.*

Chief Seat.] Desart, in the county of Kilkenny.

LORD FORTESCUE.

HUGH FORTESCUE ALAND, Lord FORTESCUE, succeeded his father, John, the first Lord, Dec. 19, 1746, is married, and has issue.

The family of Fortescue is descended from Sir Richard Le Forte, a person of extraordinary strength and courage, who accompanied William Duke of Normandy in his conquest of England, and bearing a strong shield before the Duke, at the battle of Hastings, had three horses killed under him, and from that signal event the name and motto of the family were assumed; for the Latin word *Scutum*, or the French word *Escue*, a *Shield*, being added to *Forte*, *Strong*, composes their name, and the motto is, *Forte Scutum Salus Ducum.*

Sir Adam his son was also a principal Commander, and behaved so well, that for the good service he and his father had done, the Conqueror gave him lands in Devonshire, where he established a noble family at Winston. His son Adam was father of another Adam, who had three sons, of whom Sir Richard and Sir

Sir Nicholas, both Knights of St. John of Jerusalem, attended King Richard I. to the Holy Land, to fight againſt Saladin the Soldan of Egypt. Sir John, the eldeſt, was a Commander in the army raiſed in aid of King John againſt the rebellious Barons. He was father of Richard, the father of William, who married Elizabeth, daughter of Richard Beauchamp, Earl of Warwick and Albemarle; and had two ſons, William, his heir, from whom deſcended the families of Winſton, Pruteſton, and Spridleſton; and Sir John, the ſecond ſon, ſignalized himſelf at the battle of Agincourt, and was made Governor and Captain of Meaux. His eldeſt ſon Sir Henry was Chief Juſtice of the Common Pleas in Ireland, and anceſtor of Sir Peter Forteſcue, of Wood, in Devonſhire, created a Baronet in 1666; and of Sir Edmund Forteſcue, of Fallow-pit, created a Baronet in 1664, both which families are extinct.

Richard, the third ſon of Sir John, was anceſtor of the family of Punſburn in Hertfordſhire, of which was Sir John Forteſcue, who was made Porter of the town of Calais by King Edward IV. and accompanied the Earl of Richmond to England againſt King Richard III. Sir Adrian, his brother, alſo attended in the ſame expedition, was knighted under the Earl's banner; and had ſeveral honours conferred on him by King Henry VII. He likewiſe ſerved under King Henry VIII. at the battle of the Spurs; but was condemned and executed for high treaſon, July 10, 1539. He left three ſons, Sir John, Thomas, and Sir Anthony, who was knighted by Queen Mary, and made Marſhal of Ireland, but was convicted

victed for high treason in the reign of Queen Elizabeth for his attachment to Mary, Queen of Scots, and discharged in 1566. Sir John, elder son of Sir Adrian, was Master of the Wardrobe to King Henry VIII. and Knight of the Shire for the county of Bucks; in 1590 he was Chancellor of the Exchequer, and a Privycounsellor to Queen Elizabeth; and, in 1603, was made Chancellor of the Duchy of Lancaster. His eldest son, Sir Francis, was made Knight of the Bath at the Coronation of King James I. Sir John, the second son, died in 1656, and his posterity continued at SaldenHouse, Bucks, till the death of Sir Francis Fortescue in 1729, when this branch became extinct.

Sir John, second son of Sir John, Governor of Meaux, in the year 1442 was made Lord Chief Justice of England. He is stiled by authors, *that great and famous Lawyer; that learned and upright Judge;* by Sir Walter Ralegh, *that notable Bulwark of our Laws;* and is celebrated by Lord Lyttelton in his History of Henry II. He was succeeded by his son Martin, who had two sons; John, his heir, and William, ancestor of the family of Dromisken, in the county of Louth. John, the eldest, had Bartholomew, whose eldest son Richard, was father of John, whose son and heir, Hugh, had five sons: 1. Colonel Robert Fortescue, who left no issue; 2. Arthur, who had four sons, of whom Hugh was father of the late Earl Clinton; 3. Edmund; 4. Joseph; and 5. Samuel, who left a son John, the father of Samuel Fortescue, of Ware.

* H Edmund,

Edmund, the third son, married Sarah, eldest daughter of Henry Aland, of Waterford, Esq; by whom he had three sons, of which Edmund the eldest, and Henry the youngest, died unmarried; and the second son, Sir John Fortescue-Aland, Knt. born March 7, 1670, was one of the Judges of the Common Pleas in England, which he resigned in June 1746; was created a Peer in 1746, and died Dec. 19, the same year. He had issue a daughter, who died Oct. 5, 1731; and two sons, John Fortescue, Esq; Counsellor at Law, who died in Jan. 1743; and Hugh, the present Lord.

Creation.] Baron Fortescue, of Credan, in the county of Waterford, August 15, 1746, 20 George II.

Arms.] Sapphire, a bend ingrailed, pearl, cottized, topaz, a crescent, for difference.

Crest.] On a wreath, a leopard passant, guardant, proper.

Supporters.] Two leopards, proper, gorged with mural coronets, topaz.

Motto.] Forte Scutum Salus Ducum.

Chief Seat.] Specot, in the county of Devon.

LORD KNAPTON.

THOMAS VESEY, Lord KNAPTON, and Baronet, Captain in the 18th regiment of Dragoons, succeeded his father John-Denny, the late and first Lord.

John Denny, the late Lord, was created a Peer in 1750, and married, May 15, 1732, Elizabeth, eldest daughter of William Brownlow, of Lurgan, Esq; Member of Parliament for the county

county of Armagh, by the Lady Elizabeth Hamilton, daughter of James, Earl of Abercorn, by whom he had one son, and three daughters, viz.

1. Thomas, the present Lord.
2. Elizabeth, married, July 4, 1751, to Robert Handcock, of Waterstowne, in the county of Westmeath, Esq;
3. Anne, married, Aug. 25, 1753, to Thomas Knox, of Dungannon, Esq; Member of Parliament for that borough.
4. Jane.

The truly noble family of Vesci, Vescey, or Vesey, derives its origin from Charles the Great, King of France and Emperor of the West, who died at Aix la Chapelle, in Germany, Jan. 28, 814, whose fifth son, Charles, Duke of Ingelheim, had Rowland, father of Godfrey, defender of the Christians in Palestine, in the Holy War against the Infidels; to which his Lordship's coat armour bears an allusion. His son Baldwin had another Baldwin, who was founder of the house of Blois, in France, and was father of John, Earl of Comyn, and Baron Tonsburgh, in Normandy; and the founder of the noble families of Clanrickard and Knapton, in Ireland. His son Eustace, Lord of Knaresborough, had a son William, who assumed the name and arms of Vesey, which he transmitted to his posterity, as descended from Beatrice, daughter and sole heir to Ivo de Vesey, a Norman; he also received from King Henry II. a confirmation of the Castle and Barony of Alnwick, being a principal commander in the battle fought near

* H 2 Alnwick,

Alnwick, where the Scots army was totally routed. He married Burga, daughter of Robert Stutevil, Lord of Knaresborough; and dying in 1185, had two sons, Eustace his heir, and Guarin, Lord of Knapton. Eustace, the eldest son, married Margaret, daughter of William, King of Scotland, and left a son, William, who was father of four sons, John, William, Thomas, ancestor of the Lord Knapton, and Richard, of Chimley, in the county of Oxford, from whom the Veseys of that place are descended. The said William was first married to Isabel, daughter of William Longue-Espée, Earl of Salisbury, natural son of King Henry II. by Rosamond, daughter of Walter, Lord Clifford; and, secondly, to Agnes, daughter of William Ferrers, Earl of Derby. Of the said sons, John, Baron Vesey, of Knapton, in Yorkshire, was chief Commander in the wars of Gascoigne; and by King Edward I. was appointed Governor of Scarborough castle. He was succeeded by his brother, William, Lord Vesey, who was Chief-Justice in Eyre north of Trent, Governor of Scarborough-castle, and Lord-Justice of Ireland: He left an only daughter, Isabel, married to Gilbert de Aton, Lord Aton, in Yorkshire, to whom the estate in that county devolved, with the title of Lord Vesey. Thomas de Vesey, third son of William, Lord Vesey, settled at Newland, in Cumberland, where the family continued till William Vesey, having the misfortune to kill a man in a duel, fled to Scotland, where he married a daughter of the family of Ker, of Cesford; after which, in the reign of Queen
Eli-

Elizabeth, he settled in Ireland, and had an only son, Thomas, Archdeacon of Armagh, whose son John was advanced to the Archbishoprick of Tuam, and died May 28, 1716. His eldest son, Thomas, was created a Baronet by King William; and entering afterwards into Holy Orders, was promoted to the see of Killaloe, from whence he was translated to that of Ossory, and died Aug. 6, 1730. He married Mary, only daughter and heir of Denny Mu champ, of Horsley, in Surry, Esq; Muster-master-general of Ireland, and left Sir John Denny, the late Baron Knapton, and two daughters; the eldest of whom married Cesar Colclough, of Duffrey-hall, Esq; and the youngest married, first, to William Handcock, of Willbrook, in Westmeath, Esq; and, secondly, to Agmondesham Vesey, of Lucan, in the county of Dublin, Esq; Comptroller and Accomptant-general of Ireland.

Creations.] Baronet, Sept. 28, 1698, 10 Will. III. Baron of Knapton, in the Queen's county, April 10, 1750, 23 Geo. II.

Arms.] Topaz, on a cross, diamond, a patriarchal cross of the field.

Crest.] On a wreath, a hand in armour, holding a laurel branch, both proper.

Supporters.] Two Hercules's, with clubs over their shoulders, proper, crined and habited about the middle, topaz.

Motto.] *Sub hoc signo vinces.*

Chief Seat.] Abbyleix, in Queen's county.

LORD CARYSFORT.

John Proby, Lord Carysfort, a Lord of the Privy-council, Knight of the Bath, and Knight of the Shire for the county of Huntingdon, was created a Peer, Dec. 14, 1751. His Lordship was born Nov. 25, 1720, and Aug. 27, 1750, married Elizabeth, daughter of Joshua, the second Viscount Allen, and coheir to her brother John, the third Viscount, by whom he has issue Joshua-John, born Aug. 29, 1751; and Elizabeth, born Nov. 14, 1752. This family hath been long seated at Elton-hall, in the county of Huntingdon. Sir Heneage Proby, Knt. Member of Parliament for Amersham, in Bucks, in 1661, left two sons; Thomas, his heir, who represented Amersham in 1660, and the county of Huntingdon in 1681; and was created a Baronet, March 7, 1661-2. He left three daughters, by his wife, Frances, the daughter of Sir Thomas Cotton; two whereof, Frances and Elizabeth, died unmarried; and the third, Alice, born in 1673, became sole heir to her father, and married Thomas Watson Wentworth, by whom she was mother of the late Marquis of Rockingham. John Proby, the second son of Sir Heneage, succeeded to the estate at Elton, was Knight of the Shire for the county of Huntingdon in the reigns of King William and Queen Mary, and died in 1710. He married Jane, daughter of Sir Richard Cust, Bart. and having an only daughter, who died young, the estate descended to William Proby, Esq; Governor of Fort St. George, son of Sir Heneage's younger brother,

ther. He married a Lady of the family of Cornewall, in the county of Hereford, and had iffue. Charles, who died young; Editha, married to Sir John Osborne, of Newton, near Clonmel, in Ireland; and John Proby, Efq; chofen Knight of the Shire for Huntingdon in 1722, and Reprefentative for Stamford in 1734 and 1741. He married Jane, fifter of the late Earl Gower; and by her, who died June 10, 1726, had iffue five fons and one daughter:
1. John, now Lord Carysfort.
2. William, who died at fea.
3. Thomas, an Officer in the Army.
4. Charles, a Captain in the Royal Navy.
5. Baptift, Rector of Dodington, in the ifle of Ely.
6. Carolina, who died in her infancy.

Creation.] Baron of Carysfort, in the county of Wicklow, *ut fupra.*

Arms.] Ermine, on a fefs, ruby, a lion paffant, topaz.

Creft.] On a wreath, an oftrich's head, erafed, fapphire, gorged with a ducal coronet, holding on its bill a key, topaz.

Supporters.] On the dexter, a lion, gorged with a collar, dove-tail. On the finifter, an oftrich, fapphire, gorged with a ducal coronet, holding in its bill a key, topaz.

Motto.] *Manus hæc inimica tyrannis.*

Chief Seats.] Elton-hall, in the county of Huntingdon; and Stillorgan, in the county of Dublin, in reverfion.

* H 4   LORD

LORD MILTON.

An account of this Family may be seen in my English Peerage, under the same title.

LORD LONGFORD.

Edward-Michael Pakenham, Lord Longford, a Captain in the Royal Navy, was born April 12, 1743, and in 1765 was elected Knight of the Shire for the county of Longford. On April 30, 1766, he succeeded his father, Thomas, the late and first Lord.

Thomas, the late Lord Longford, was chosen to represent the town of Longford in 1746, and in 1756 was created a Peer. In 1740 his Lordship married Elizabeth, only daughter and heir of Michael Cuffe, of Ballynrobe, in the county of Mayo, Esq; by whom he had issue,

1. Edward-Michael, the present Lord.
2. Elizabeth-Frances, wife of John Ormsby Vandeleur, of Maddens-town, in the county of Kildare, Esq;
3. Helena.
4. Robert, an Ensign in the 64th regiment of foot.
5. Mary; 6. William; 7. Thomas.

This ancient and noble family is of Saxon original. Sir Lawrence Pakenham, Knt. in 35 Edward III, married Elizabeth, second sister, and coheir of Thomas Engaine, Baron of Blatherwick, who died without issue male, in the 41st of that reign. From him descended Sir John Pakenham, and Sir Hugh Pakenham, brothers,

brothers, who lived in the reign of Henry VIII. Sir John was poffeffed of the manor of Lordington, in Suffex, which went with his only daughter and heir, Conftance, in marriage to Sir Geoffry de la Pole, Knt. fecond fon of Sir Richard de la Pole, by Margaret Plantagenet, Countefs of Salisbury, only daughter of George, Duke of Clarence, brother of King Edward IV. His brother, Sir Hugh, was poffeffed of the manor of Northwitham, in Lincolnfhire, and left iffue John, who fucceeded to his eftate, and Anne, married, in the reign of Henry VIII. to Sir William Sidney, firft Tutor, then Chamberlain and Steward of the Houfhold, to King Edward VI. and fhe dying in the year 1544, left iffue one fon, afterwards Sir Henry Sidney, and four daughters.

John Pakenham, Efq; her brother, had iffue one fon, Robert, whofe wardfhip and marriage was granted by Queen Mary, in the firft year of her reign, to Sir Henry Sidney. He left one fon, Hugh, who having eighteen fons, three of them, Henry, Robert, and Philip, went over to Ireland in the year 1642, and were Officers in the Army fent over to fupprefs the Rebellion raging at that time there. The iffue of the other brothers remaining in England, probably failed, as there are none of the name now to be found there.

Henry, the eldeft of the three brothers, had, for his fervices, a grant of the lands of Tullinally, now called Pakenham-hall, in the county of Weftmeath, ftill the feat of the family, with other lands. At the Reftoration of Charles II. he was chofen one of the Reprefentatives in

* H 5 Parlia-

Parliament for the borough of Navan, in the county of Meath, and was succeeded by his eldest son,

Sir Thomas Pakenham, Knt. his Majesty's Prime Serjeant in Ireland, who dying in 1709, was succeeded by his son Edward, who in 1713, was chosen Knight of the Shire for the county of Westmeath, and again at the Accession of King George I. and dying in the year 1719, was succeeded by his eldest son,

Thomas, the late Lord Longford.

Creation.] Baron of Longford, in the county of Longford, April 27, 1756, 29 George II.

Arms.]
Crest.]
Supporters.]
Motto.] *Vis unita fortior.*
Chief Seats.] Pakenham-hall, in the county of Westmeath, and Longford-castle, in the county of Longford.

LORD BRANDEN.

Maurice Crosbie, Lord Branden, Baron of Branden, in the county of Kerry, a Lord of the Privy-council, was created a Peer on Aug. 22, 1758.

Arms.]
Crest.]
Supporters.]
Motto.] *Indignante invidia florebit justus.*
Chief Seat.]

LORD LISLE.

John Lysaght, Lord Lisle, Baron Lisle, of Mount-North, in the county of Cork, was so created in the year 1758, and in 1725 his Lordship married Catharine, third daughter and co-heir of Joseph Dean, of Crumlin, Chief Baron of his Majesty's Court of Exchequer in Ireland (by his wife Margaret, sister of Henry, late Earl of Shannon) by whom he had issue;

1. John, Member in the present Parliament for the borough of Castle-Martyr.
2. Joseph; 3. James, both of the Inner Temple.
4. Margaret; 5. Mary, wife of Kingsmill, son of Colonel Richard Pennefeather, both Members for the city of Cashell, by whom she has three sons, Richard, John, and Kingsmill, and one daughter.

His Lordship married, secondly, in 1746, Elizabeth, only daughter of Edward Moore, of Mooresfort, in the county of Tipperary, Esq; (by his wife, Mary, eldest sister of Colonel Richard Pennefeather, abovementioned) by whom he has issue one son, Edward; and two daughters, Elizabeth and Grace. On the happy Accession of his present Majesty, he was elected Member to Parliament for the borough of Charleville.

This noble Lord is descended from the ancient and illustrious house of Obryen, in the county of Clare, some of which being auxiliaries in the provincial wars of Ireland, so distinguished themselves as to receive the appellation of *Güil-Ysaght*, in the native language *Lent-men*, which has been contracted into the name Lyfaght.

From this family defcended John Lyfaght, the elder, of Mount-North, in the county of Cork, a Cornet of Horfe under Lord Inchiquin, and very active in the fuppreffion of the Rebellion in 1641. He particularly behaved with great gallantry at the battle of Knocknenofs, in that county.

He had two fons, Nicholas and James, who entered into the fervice of King William, of glorious memory; James, the younger, was killed at the battle of Steenkirk, in Flanders, being then a Captain in the royal regiment of Foot; and Nicholas, the elder, commanded a troop of Dragoons, in the King's own regiment, in Flanders, England, Scotland, and Ireland, particularly at the ever memorable battle of the Boyne, and in feveral garrifons in Munfter, the regiment being difmounted to fupply the place of infantry, then greatly diminifhed by ficknefs. He married Grace, youngeft daughter of Colonel Thomas Holmes, of Killmalock, by whom he had iffue,

1. John, the prefent Lord Lifle.
2. Anne, wife of Lieutenant-general Holmes, of the Ifle of Wight.
3. Mary, wife of Beverley Ufher, Efq; Knight of the fhire for the county of Waterford.
4. Nicholas; 5. Henry; 6. James.
7. Arthur, who left iffue three fons; Nicholas, Lieutenant in Gen. Kennedy's regiment, in Canada; Arthur, Lieutenant in General Holmes's regiment, in Scotland; and Henry; and two daughters, Jane and Grace, both unmarried.

Creation.]

Creation.] Baron Lifle, as above, Aug. 22, 1758, 31 George II.

Arms.] Sapphire, a lion paffant, guardant, topaz, over three fpears, ruby, in a field, pearl.

Creſt.] An hand and fword, proper.

Supporters.] Two lions, topaz.

Motto.] *Bella! horrida bella!*

Chief Seats.] Mount-North, and Curriglafs, in the county of Cork; Lifle, or the Little Ifland, in the harbour of Cork; Brickfield, in the county of Limerick; Crumlin, near Dublin; and a manfion-houfe in Dawfon-ftreet, in that city *.

LORD MOUNT-FLORENCE.

JOHN COLE, Lord MOUNT-FLORENCE, of Mount-Florence, in the county of Fermanagh, was fo created Aug. 26, 1760, 33 George II. His Lordfhip was born Oct. 13, 1709, in 1732 was Member in Parliament for Ennifkillen, and High Sheriff for the county of Fermanagh. In October 1728 he married Elizabeth, eldeft daughter of Hugh Willoughby, of Carrow, in the faid county, Efq; by whom he had iffue two fons and five daughters; William-Willoughby, Member in the prefent Parliament for Ennifkillen; Arthur; Mary-Anne, Flora-Carolina, Catharine, Mary, and Elizabeth.

Sir William Cole fettled in the county of Fermanagh, in the reign of James I. and was

---

* The foregoing account is an extract from an entry in the Heralds Office, which his Lordfhip was fo condefcending as to confirm, Aug. 4, 1767.

a per-a person of great eminence in that and the following reign. He was knighted in 1617, and was greatly serviceable against the Irish, in the rebellion of 1641. He married Catharine, eldest daughter of Sir Laurence Parsons, of Birr, in the King's county, second Baron of the Exchequer, and had issue by her, Michael, his heir; and Sir John Cole, father of the late Sir Arthur Cole, Lord Ranelagh, upon whose death that title became extinct.

Michael, the elder son, was Member for Enniskillen in 1661, knighted, and married Alice, daughter of Chidley Coote, of Killester, Esq; brother of Charles, the first Earl of Mountrath, and by her, who died in 1671, had seven children, who all died young, or unmarried, except his successor,

Sir Michael Cole, who, in 1671, married Elizabeth, daughter of Sir John Cole, Bart. and by her, who died Aug. 19, 1733, had issue sixteen children, of whom survived John, Michael, and Fenton; and dying Feb. 11, 1710, was succeeded by his eldest son,

John Cole, of Florence-court, Esq; born in 1660, who enjoyed all the estate of the family of Cole, in the county of Fermanagh, and greatly improved both his own seat, and the town of Enniskillen, with new buildings. In 1723 he was Sheriff of the county of Fermanagh, and served in Parliament for the before-mentioned town. In 1707 he married Florence, only daughter of Sir Bourchier Wrey, of Taviftock, in Devonshire, Bart. and Knight of the Bath, (by his wife Florence, daughter of Sir John Rolle, of Stevenstone, in Devonshire, Knight of the Bath, ancestor of the Lord Rolle,) and by her,

her, who died in August, 1718, had issue five sons and two daughters: 1. John, now Lord Mount-Florence; 2. Bourchier; 3. Michael; 4. William; 5. Henry; 6. Elizabeth, wife, first, of Edward Archdall, of Castle-Archdall, in the county of Fermanagh, Esq; and, secondly, of Bysse Molesworth, Esq; brother of Richard, Viscount Molesworth; 7. Florence. He married, secondly, ———, daughter of Robert Saunderson, of Castle-Saunderson, in the county of Cavan, Esq; and died in 1726. He was succeeded by his said eldest son, the present Lord.

Creation.] *Ut supra.*

Arms.] Pearl, a bull passant, diamond, armed and unguled, topaz, within a bordure of the second, besantée; in a dexter canton, sapphire, a golden harp, with silver strings.

Crest.] On a wreath, a demi-dragon, emerald, armed and langued, ruby, holding in his dexter paw, a dart, topaz, headed pearl; and on the sinister, a shield sapphire, charged as the canton, (not expressed in the plate.)

Supporters.] Two dragons reguardant, emerald, armed and langued, as the crest.

Motto.] *Deum Cole, Regem serva.*

Chief Seat.] Florence-court, in the county of Fermanagh.

LORD MOUNT-EAGLE.

John Browne, Lord Mount-Eagle, of Mount-Eagle, in the county of Mayo, was so created, Aug. 26, 1760, 33 Geo. II.

Arms.]
Crest.]

Sup-

Supporters.]
Motto.] *Suivez Raison.*
Chief Seat.]

LORD COLERAINE.

GABRIEL HANGER, Lord COLERAINE, Member in the British Parliament for Bridgwater, in Somersetshire, was created a Peer, Dec. 1, 1761, 1 Geo. III. His Lordship served in two Parliaments for the borough of Maidstone, in Kent, and married Elizabeth, daughter and heir of Richard Bond, of Cowbury, in the county of Hereford, Esq; by whom he has issue, now living, three sons; John, William, and George; and one daughter, Anne.

This illustrious family was originally seated in the counties of Essex and Hertford, particularly in the latter, at Blakesware, a fair seat in the parish of Ware. At different times, they have written their names variously, as Annger, Ainger, Anger, and Aungre, which was plainly taken from *Aunzpe*, the ancient Saxon name for the town of Ongar, in Essex, signifying (we are told*) *the place*, by way of eminence. A family of that name flourished in the last named county in the 14th century; for Philip de Aungre, and Alice his wife, in the year 1348, gave lands in Chelmsford, and Bromfield, to the Chantry of the Church of St. Mary de Thele, in Hertfordshire: however, the name was also well known in many other parts of the kingdom. The more modern name Hanger, is derived from the Saxon word *Hanze*, or *Hanzpe*, an hill.

---

* History of Essex.

Towards the latter end of the sixteenth century, this family (for what reason is not clearly known) disposed of their estates in Essex and Hertfordshire, and dispersing themselves, Francis Aungier, one of the younger sons, went over into Ireland, the stage for preferment in Queen Elizabeth's reign, and becoming Master of the Rolls, was created Lord Longford, June 29, 1628, and his son, afterwards, an Earl; another son, John, going abroad as a Turkey-merchant *, brought home a very plentiful fortune, out of which he purchased the estate and seat at Dryffield, in the county of Gloucester, where his posterity have been ever since seated.

George Hanger, Esq; descended from this John, had two sons, George, and John, who was for many years, a Director of the Bank of England, and his eldest daughter Anne, was married to Henry Hare, late Lord Coleraine.

George, the eldest son, was knighted by K. William, for his steady attachment to the religion and laws of his country. He married Anne, daughter and coheir of Sir John Beale, of Farmingham, in the county of Kent, Bart. by whom had four sons; George; John; Gabriel, now Lord Coleraine; William: and four daughters, Anne; Delicia; Jane, and Mary.

Creations.] *Ut supra.*
Arms.]
Crest.]
Supporters.]
Motto.] *Artes honorabit.*
Chief Seats.] Driffield, in Gloucestershire; Farmingham, in Kent.

---

* Hist. Essex. prædict.

LORD CLIVE.

Robert Clive, Lord Clive, Baron Clive, of Plaſſey, in the county of Clare, Governor of Bengal, in the Eaſt-Indies, a Major-general of his Majeſty's forces, Member in Parliament for Shrewſbury, in Shropſhire, Knight of the moſt honourable Order of the Bath, and LL. D. was born on Michaelmas-day, 1726, and married Margaret, daughter of Edmund Maſkelyne, of Weſtminſter, Eſq; by whom he has iſſue, now ſurviving, one ſon, and three daughters; the hon. Edward Clive, aged thirteen; Rebecca, aged ſix; Charlotte, to whom her preſent Majeſty ſtood godmother, aged five; and Margaret, aged four.

This ancient family has been ſeated, from the reign of Henry VII. at Styche, in the county of Salop. Walfricus de Croxton, in that county, was father of Lidulph de Twemloe, father of Sir Richard de Croxton, Knt. father of Warin de Clyve, father of Stephen Clyve, of Croxton and Clyve, father of Henry Clyve, of Clyve, living in the reign of Henry III. It appears, by a deed without date, that Walter Greenfield deviſed one meſſuage in the villa of Clyve, to Henry, the ſon of Henry de Weever, paying the aforeſaid Henry Clyve, ſon of Stephen, chief Lord of Clyve, ſix pence a year, and reſerving to himſelf a pair of white gloves. Witneſs Roger de Gray, Juſtice of Cheſter, William de Venablis, Rudolph de Vernon, William de Pieres, Viſcount Cheſter, John de Hoult, Thomas de Weever,

Henry

Henry de Clyve, and others. To this Henry, succeeded his son, Henry, Lord of Clyve, who married Agnes, third daughter and co-heir of Robert Huxleigh, of Huxley, in Cheshire, Esq; by whom he had another Henry de Clyve, who married Eva, second daughter and co-heir of Hugh Tew, Esq; in 5 Edw. III. By her he had Thomas Clyve, of Huxley, Esq; father of Hugh, of the same place, who marrying Matilda, daughter of John Manwaring, of Whitmore, in Shropshire, Esq; had a son, Richard Clyve, of the same place, Esq; which Richard made his will, Feb. 22, 1448, in which he recites, in the first place, that he gives " his soul " to God, the blessed Virgin Mary, and all " Saints; and my body to be buried in the " church of St. Werburg, Chester. Item, I " give five wax candles to burn round my " body." He was not, however, buried according to his will, till twenty years after. He married Catharine Handford, by whom he had Peter Clyve, of Huxley, Esq; who leaving issue only a daughter, Helena, who died unmarried, was succeeded by his brother,

James Clyve, Esq; who married Catharine, daughter and heir of Thomas Styche, of Styche, in the county of Salop, Esq; in 22 Henry VII. He was succeeded by his son, Richard Clyve, of Huxley and Styche, Esq; who married Alice, daughter of Hugh Calveley, Esq; This Richard had a pardon granted him, in the said 22 Henry VII. in the following terms: " Henry, " by the grace of God, King of England, " France, and Lord of Ireland, to all our " faithful subjects, to whom these presents " shall come, greeting: Know that we of our
" special

"special grace, have pardoned, remitted, and released, and by these presents do pardon, remit and release Richard Clyve, late of Huxley, in the county of Chester, Esq; otherwise called Richard Clyve, late of Styche, in the county of Salop, Esq; otherwise called Richard Clyve, late of Clyve, in the county of Chester, Esq; son and heir of James Clyve, Esq; and Richard Brydd, of Huxlegh, in the county of Chester, Yeoman." He was succeeded by his son Richard, who married Margaret, daughter of Sir Richard Corbet, of Longner, in the county of Salop, Esq; by whom he had his successor, Richard, who married Jane, sister of Sir William Brereton, Knt. and died in the year 1573. He had issue, beside Sir George Clive, Knt. who succeeded him, several other children, of whom Robert, the second son, was Clerk of the Checque to King Edward VI. His eldest daughter was of the Bedchamber to Queen Elizabeth, and made her will, dated July 16, 1 Eliz. wherein she appoints Lady Elizabeth Clinton, and John Baptist Castillion, of the Queen's Chamber, Trustees; and died unmarried, at Ottford, in Kent, where the Court then resided, and was, by the Queen's command, and at her expence, honourably interred in Ottford Church, a crowd of Nobles and Courtiers attending the funeral. Their father was Treasurer to Sir Richard Cotton, Knt. Keeper of the Records of the King's expences about the towns of Bononia and Newport, from July 8, 8 Hen. VIII. to Aug. 15, 4 Edw. VI. He was also the first of the name that bore three wolves heads in his coat, by the assignment of Gilbert Dethick, in 4 Edw. VI.

whereas

whereas the coat belonging to the family was formerly borne without that charge, as appears by the arms of Clyve, long before set up, in two windows of their parish church of Montonsay, in Shropshire, and by an escutcheon of their arms, carved on a window, at the time of building their manor house of Huxlegh, near two hundred years before.

Sir George, his eldest son, was knighted in the field, in Ireland, by William Fitz-Williams, Lord Deputy, Aug. 4, 1588, 30 Eliz. and died Sept. 1, in the 33d of that reign. He was Chancellor of the Exchequer in Ireland, of the Queen's Privy-council, and made Supervisor of the River Shannon, on the resignation of Sir Edward Waterhouse, Knt. He married Susan, daughter of Henry Copinger, Esq; by whom he had Ambrose Clive, of Styche, Esq; who marrying Alice, eldest daughter of Thomas Townsend, of Brakenash, in the county of Norfolk, Esq; was father of Colonel Robert Clive, of the same place, who by Mary, daughter of Sir Edward Aleyn, Knt. had George Clive, of Wormbridge, in the county of Hereford, Esq; which estate he acquired by marriage with Mary, daughter and heir of Martin Husbands, of that place, Esq; and dying in the life time of his father, left issue three sons and four daughters. Robert Clive, of Styche, Esq; his eldest son sold the Lordship of Wormbridge to his younger brother, Edward Clive, of Wormbridge, Esq; who left issue five sons and one daughter: the eldest of the sons is the present Sir Edward Clive, of Wormbridge, Knt. one of the Justices of the Court of Common Pleas. George, the second son of George Clive

Clive abovementioned, was Curſitor Baron of the Exchequer, died unmarried, and lies buried in Lincoln's-inn, London; all his ſiſters died unmarried.

Robert Clive, of Styche, Eſq; abovementioned, eldeſt ſon of George, of Wormbridge, Eſq; married Elizabeth, daughter of —— Amphlett, of the Four Aſhes, in the county of Worceſter, Eſq; and had iſſue by her, four ſons, Robert, George, Richard, and Benjamin, and four daughters. He was ſucceeded by his third ſon,

Richard Clive, of Styche, Eſq; who married Rebecca, daughter and coheir of —— Gaſcoyne, of Mancheſter, Eſq; by whom he had iſſue, Robert, now Lord Clive; Richard, an Enſign in the Guards, who was killed in the late war, in Flanders; and William, now a Cornet in the Earl of Pembroke's regiment of Dragoons; alſo five daughters, who are all married. Their father is Member in the preſent Parliament for the town of Montgomery.

Robert Clive, Eſq; his eldeſt ſon, went young to the Eaſt-Indies in the ſervice of the Company, where he acquired a conſiderable fortune, was twice Governor of Bengal, and Commander in Chief of the King's and Company's forces in that province. For the eminent ſervices he performed in thoſe ſtations, to the kingdom and the Company, particularly in the battle of Plaſſey, againſt the Nabob, Suraja Dowlah, his Majeſty was pleaſed to raiſe him to the dignity of a Baron of Ireland, and to that of Knight of the Bath: the Company likewiſe preſented to his Lordſhip a ſword ſet with diamonds, and ordered his ſtatue to be erected in the India-houſe. His Lordſhip is

certainly

certainly one of the greateſt military geniuſes of the preſent age, and by his intrepidity, courage, and ſkill, has raiſed the reputation and commerce of his native country, in that part of the world, from the moſt melancholy and diſtreſsful ſituation, to a pitch of glory never known before.

Creation.] Baron, *ut ſupra*, Dec. 1, 1761, 2 Geo. III.

Arms.] Pearl, a feſs, diamond, charged with three mullets, topaz.

Creſt.] On a wreath, a griffon, with wings expanded, pearl, ducally gorged, ruby.

Supporters.] On the dexter, an elephant, pearl; on the ſiniſter a griffon, with wings expanded, pearl, powdered with mullets, diamond, and ducally gorged, ruby.

Motto.] *Audacter & ſincere*; Sir George Clive's Motto.

Chief Seats.] Styche, and Walcot, in the county of Salop *.

---

* This account of the eldeſt branch of the Clives, is taken from a pedigree of the family, continued down to the year 1623, by Robert Treſwell, Somerſet, and Aug. Vincent, Rouge-Croix, generouſly communicated by Henry Clive, of Mortlake, Eſq. The brevity of this work will not admit of my entering into the collateral branches, and marriages of the daughters, which otherwiſe I ſhould gladly have done.

LORD ORWELL.

Francis Vernon, Baron Orwell, of Newry, in the county of Downe, was so created on March 27, 1762, 3 George III. is Colonel of the second battalion of the Suffolk militia, Member in Parliament for Ipswich, in Suffolk, and President of the Free British Fishery.

His Lordship's family is a branch of the noble family of the Vernons, the chief of which is the Lord Vernon, of Great Britain, and he was nephew and heir of the late brave Admiral Edward Vernon, Esq; whose great actions will be celebrated in the history of this kingdom, and needs no further mention here.

Creation.] *Ut supra.*
Arms.]
Crest.]
Supporters.]
Motto.] *Semper ut te digna sequare.*
Chief Seat.] Nacton, in the county of Suffolk.

LORD WALTHAM.

Drigue-Billers Olmius, Lord Waltham, Baron Waltham, of Philipstown, succeeded his father, John, the late and first Lord, in September, 1762, who was created a Peer on May 8, in that year, and marrying a daughter of the late Sir William Billers, Knt. Alderman, and some time Lord Mayor of the City of London, had issue the present Lord, and other children.

His Lordship is descended of an antient and worthy family, seated at Newhall, in the county of

ty of Essex. John the late Lord, represented the boroughs of Weymouth and Melcombe Regis in the eighth Parliament of Great Britain.
Creation.] *Ut supra.*
Arms.]
Supporters.]
Crest.]
Motto.] Meritez.
Chief Seat.] Newhall, in the county of Essex.

LORD BALTINGLASS.

JOHN STRATFORD, Lord BALTINGLASS, was so created on May 10, 1763.
Arms.]
Crest.]
Supporters.]
Motto.] *Virtuti nihil obstat & armis.*
Chief Seat.]

LORD St. GEORGE.

USSHER ST. GEORGE, Lord ST. GEORGE, Baron of Hatley-St.-George, was so created on April 19, 1763, 3 George III. and married Elizabeth, only daughter of Christopher Dominick, Esq;

This antient and noble family were of great antiquity in Cambridgeshire, and in possession of Hatley St. George, for more than five hundred years; when Sir George St. George, second son of Sir Richard St. George, came to Ireland, in the reign of Queen Elizabeth. A Knight-Adventurer, Sir Oliver St. George, his eldest son, for his good services in the restoration of King Charles II. was the first Baronet,

ronet, created by that Monarch, in Ireland: And Sir George St. George, Bart. his eldeſt ſon, was, on Mar. 15, 1714-15, 1 Geo. I. created Baron St. George, of Hatley St. George *. He married Margaret, daughter of the Lord Viſcount Maſſareene, by whom he had iſſue one daughter, married to the Hon. John Uſher, who, for his ſervices in Flanders, in the

---

* The Preamble to his Lordſhip's Patent, is as follows:

"It being our will and pleaſure to raiſe to the Peerage ſuch perſons as have, in an eminent manner, deſerved well of us and our kingdoms; no one comes more powerfully recommended to us, than our truſty and well-beloved Sir George St. George, Bart. eldeſt ſon of Sir Oliver St. George, who, for his good ſervices, in the reſtoration of King Charles the ſecond, was the firſt Baronet created in Ireland, by that Monarch, and is the twenty-firſt heir, in a direct line, deſcended from Baldwin St. George, a fellow-ſoldier of William the Conqueror. Juſtly have we beſtowed additional honours, upon a Gentleman of ſo diſtinguiſhed a character, who, upon the account of his ancient family is already illuſtrious: Inaſmuch among his anceſtors (dignified with Knighthood in the reign of Henry the third) he may reckon thoſe, who by Intermarriages in the houſes of the Argentines, Barons of England, became allied to the noble family of De Vere and St. John, and to Margaret Beauchamp, grand-mother of King Henry the ſeventh, our famous progenitor; nor yet muſt we paſs by in ſilence (leſt we ſhould ſeem to pay to the glory of his forefathers what is due to his own ſingular merit) that we now think fit to enoble him, for his ſteady adherence to us, and the ſucceſſion in our line, and by that means, to the Proteſtant Religion and the Laws of his Country. Know ye, &c."

reign

reign of King William and Queen Anne, was made Governor of Galway, and Vice-Admiral of Conaught, and was father of the prefent Lord.

Creation.] *Ut fupra.*
Arms.
Creft.]
Supporters.]
Motto.] *Firmitas in cœlo.*
Chief Seat.] Hatley-St.-George, Cambridgeshire.

LORD GORE.

Sir RALPH GORE, Bart. Lord GORE, Baron Gore, of Manor-Gore, in the county of Donegal, was fo created June 16, 1764.
Arms.]
Creft.]
Supporters.]
Motto.] *Sola falus fervire Deo.*
Chief Seat.] Manor-Gore, in the county of Donegal.

LORD PIGOT.

Sir GEORGE PIGOT, Bart. Lord PIGOT, Baron Pigot, of Patfhul, in the county of Dublin, was fo created on Dec. 27, 1765, and was Governor of Fort St. George, in the Eaft Indies, where his bravery and conduct, during the late war, is recorded in the annals of thofe times, and will be the fubject of hiftory. His Lordfhip is Member in the Britifh Parliament for the borough of Wallingford, in Berkfhire.
Arms.]
Creft.]

Supporters.]
Motto.]
Chief Seats.] Frogmore, near Windsor; Uske-Castle, in Monmouthshire; and Pattishul, in Staffordshire.

LORD ANNALY.

John Gore, Lord Annaly, Baron Annaly, of Tennelick, in the county of Longford, Lord Chief-Justice of the Court of King's-Bench, and a Lord of the Privy-council, was created a Baron, as above, Dec. 27, 1765.
Arms.]
Crest.]
Supporters.]
Motto.] *In hoc signo vinces.*
Chief Seat.]

LORD MULGRAVE.

Constantine Phipps, Esq; was created Baron Mulgrave, of New Ross, in the county of Wexford, on Aug. 15, 1767. On Feb. 26, 1742-3, his Lordship married Lady Le Pell, eldest daughter of John, Lord Hervey, of Ickworth, and sister of George-William, the present Earl of Bristol, by whom he has issue. His Majesty was pleased to grant, by his warrant, dated June 6, 1753, to her Ladyship and her sisters, the same place and precedency in all assemblies, as daughters of Earls of Great-Britain. (See Earl of Bristol, in my Peerage of England.)

William Phipps, Esq; by his wife Catharine, daughter of James, the fourth Viscount Valentia,

tia, (by his wife, the Lady Catharine Darnley, natural daughter of King James II. afterwards married to John Sheffield, Duke of Buckingham, by whom she was mother of the last Duke of that family; and which Catharine afterwards married John Sheldon, of Croydon, in Surry, and died Jan. 18, 1735,) had issue two sons, and one daughter; viz. Constantine, Lord Mulgrave; ———; and Catharine, born Feb. 9, 1723. He died Feb. 1, 1735, and was succeeded by his eldest son, Constantine, as above.

The said William Phipps, Esq; was son and heir of Sir Constantine Phipps, Lord Chancellor of Ireland, who resigned the Seals on Oct. 19, 1714.

Arms.]
Crest.]
Supporters.]
Motto.] *Virtute quies.*
Chief Seat.]

LORD LIFFORD.

JAMES HEWITT, Lord LIFFORD, Baron Lifford, of Lifford, in the county of Donegal, Lord High Chancellor of the kingdom of Ireland, and a Lord of his Majesty's most honourable Privy-council, was created a Baron of that kingdom, on Nov. 24, 1767. His Lordship was a Serjeant at Law, and King's Serjeant, when in Nov. 1766, he was constituted one of the Justices of the Court of King's-Bench, till which time he represented the city of Coventry in the present Parliament. On the decease of John, Lord Bowes, late Lord

* I 3 Chancellor

Chancellor of Ireland, he was appointed, on Nov. 24, 1767, to succeed him in that high Office.

His Lordship married, first, the sole daughter and heir of Mr. Archdeacon Weld, by whom he had issue four sons, the eldest of which, the Hon. John Hewitt, was born in 1750. He married, 2dly, Ambrosia, daughter of the Rev. Mr. Bayley, by whom his Lordship has no surviving issue.

Arms.] Ruby, a chevron ingrailed, pearl, between three owls of the same.

Crest] On a wreath, an owl, crested, winged, and tailed, ruby.

Supporters.] On the dexter a vultur, on the sinister a gryphon, both topaz, with wings expanded, pearl, collared, sapphire; the collars charged with bezants.

Motto.] *Be just, and fear not.*

Chief Seat.] Awson, in Warwickshire.

SECOND TITLES

Of the DUKE, and EARLS, by which their eldest Sons are, in Courtesy, distinguished.

ANTRIM, Earl,	Visc. Dunluce.
Arran, Earl,	Visc. Sudley.
Barrymore, Earl,	Visc. Buttevant.
Bective, Earl,	Visc. Headfort.
Bellamont, Earl,	Lord Colloony.
Belvedere, Earl,	Visc. Bellfield.
Besborough, Earl,	Visc. Ducannon.
Blessinton, Earl,	Visc. Montjoy.
Brandon, Countess,	
Carrick, Earl,	Visc. Ikerrin.
Castlehaven, Earl,	Lord Audley.
Catherlough, Earl,	Visc. Barrels.
Cavan, Earl,	Lord Lambart.
Charlemont, Earl,	Lord Caulfield.
Clanbrassil, Earl,	Visc. Limerick.
Clanricarde, Earl,	Lord Dunkellyn.
Corke and Orrery, Earl,	Visc. Dungarvan.
Courtown, Earl,	Visc. Stopford.
Darnley, Earl,	Lord Clifton.
Desmond, Earl,	Visc. Callan.
Donegal, Earl,	Visc. Chichester.
Drogheda, Earl,	Visc. Moore.
Egmont, Earl,	Visc. Perceval.
Ely, Earl,	Visc. Loftus.
Farnham, Earl,	Visc. Maxwell.
Fife, Earl,	Visc. Macduff.
Fitz-William, Earl,	Visc. Millton.
Granard, Earl,	Lord Forbes

SECOND TITLES.

Grandison, Countess,	Visc. Villiers.
Hillsborough, Earl,	Visc. Kilwarlin.
Howth, Earl,	Visc. St. Lawrence.
Inchiquin, Earl,	Lord Obryen.
Kerry, Earl,	Visc. Clan-Maurice.
Lanesborough, Earl,	Lord Newton-Butler.
Leinster, Duke,	Marquis of Kildare.
Louth, Earl,	Lord Athenry.
Ludlow, Earl,	Visc. Preston.
Malton, Earl,	Lord Malton.
Massareene, Earl,	Lord Loughneagh.
Meath, Earl,	Lord Brabazon.
Mexborough, Earl,	Visc. Pollington.
Milltown, Earl,	Visc. Russborough.
Moira, Earl,	Lord Rawdon.
Montrath, Earl,	Visc. Coote.
Mornington, Earl,	Visc. Wesley.
Panmure, Earl,	Visc. Maule.
Shannon, Earl,	Visc. Boyle.
Shelburne, Earl,	Visc. Fitz-Maurice.
Thomond, Earl,	Lord Ibrackan.
Tilney, Earl,	Visc. Castlemain.
Tyrconnel, Earl,	Visc. Carlingford.
Tyrone, Earl,	Lord Beresford.
Verney, Earl,	Visc. Fermanagh.
Upper Ossory, Earl,	Lord Gowran.
Wandesford, Earl,	Visc. Castlecomer.
Waterford and Wexford, Earl,	Lord Talbot.
Westmeath, Earl,	Lord Delvin.
Winterton, Earl,	Visc. Turnour.

INDEX.

INDEX.

☞ Note, With the Viſcounts the Pages are repeated, 1, 2, &c.

A.

	Page.	Arms.
ALLEN, Viſc.	69	12
Annaly, L.	196	22
Antrim, E.	11	2
Armagh, Archbiſhop,	126	16
Arran, E.	95	7
Aſhbrook, V.	100	13
Aylmer, L.	163	20

B.

	Page.	Arms.
Baltimore, L.	149	19
Baltinglaſs, L.	193	22
Barrington, V.	77	12
Barrymore, E.	20	2
Bateman, V.	93	13
Bective, E.	109	8
Bellamont, E.	118	8, 20
Bellew, L.	153	20
Belvedere, E.	69	6

Beſbo-

INDEX.

	Page.	Arms.
Besborough, E.	46	4
Blayney, L.	147	19
Blesington, E.	49	4
Boyne, V.	66	12
Branden, L.	178	21
Brandon, Countess	75	6
Bulkeley, V.	35	10

C.

	Page.	Arms.
Cahier, L.	144	19
Carbery, L.	157	20
Carrick, E.	55	5
Carysfort, L.	174	21
Cashel, Archbishop,	127	15
Castlehaven, E.	10	
Catherlough, E.	97	7
Cavan, E.	26	3
Charlemont, E.	99	8
Chetwynd, V.	60	12
Clanbrassil, E.	67	6
Clanricarde, E.	7	2
Clanwilliam, V.	117	14
Clare, V.	120	15
Clive, L.	186	22
Clogher, Bishop,	130	17
Clonfert, Bishop,	132	18
Cloyne, Bishop,	133	18
Coleraine, L.	184	22
Conway, L.	155	20
Conyngham, V.	105	13
Corke, E.	10	2
Corke and Ross, Bishop,	128	17
Courtown, E.	95	7
Cullen, V.	28	10

D. Darn-

INDEX.

D.

	Page.	Arms.
Darnley, E. ---	43	4
Derry, Bishop, ---	129	17
Desmond, E. ---	17	2
Desart, L. ---	165	21
Digby, L. ---	146	19
Donegal, E. ---	23	2
Downe and Connor, Bishop,	132	18
Downe, V. ---	43	11
Drogheda, E. ---	35	3
Dromore, Bishop, ---	133	18
Dublin, Archbishop,	126	16
Dungannon, V. ---	111	14

E.

Egmont, E. ---	46	4
Elphin, Bishop, ---	131	18
Ely, E. ---	106	8

F.

Fairfax, V. ---	22	10
Farnham, E. ---	97	7
Fife, E. ---	78	6
Fitz-William, E. ---	40	3
Fitz-William, V. ---	24	10
Fortescue, L. ---	167	21
Fortrose, V. ---	119	14

G.

Gage, V. ---	85	12
Gallway, V. ---	95	13
George, St. L. ---	193	23
Glerawly, V. ---	112	14

Gore,

	Arms.	Page.
Gore, L. ---	195	22
Granard, E. ---	38	3
Grandison, Countess,	114	8
Grimstone, V. ---	71	12

H.

	Arms.	Page.
Hawley, L. ---	151	20
Hillsborough, E. ---	56	5
Howe, V. ---	49	11
Howth, E. ---	115	8

I, J.

	Arms.	Page.
Inchiquin, E. ---	28	3
Jocelyn, V. ---	102	13

K.

	Arms.	Page.
Kerry, E. ---	41	3
Kells, V. ---	42	11
Kildare, Bishop, ---	128	17
Killala, Bishop, ---	131	18
Kilaloe, Bishop, ---	130	17
Kilmore, Bishop, ---	131	17
Kilmorey, V. ---	4	9
Kingsland, V. ---	38	11
Kingston, V. ---	115	14
Kinsale, L. ---	134	19
Knapton, L. ---	170	21

L.

	Arms.	Page.
Lanesborough, E.	64	5
Langford, Viscountess,	112	14
Leighlin, Bishop,	132	18
Leinster, Duke,	1	1

Leitrim,

INDEX.

	Page.	Arms.
Leitrim, L. ---	151	19
Lifford, L. ---	197	23
Ligonier, V. ---	107	13
Limerick, Bishop,	130	17
Lisburne, V. ---	44	11
Lisle, L. ---	179	22
Longford, L. ---	176	21
Louth, E. ---	75	6
Ludlow, E. ---	88	7
Lumley, V. ---	8	9

M.

	Page.	Arms.
Malton, E. ---	56	5
Massareene, V. ---	62	5
Maynard, L. ---	146	19
Mayo, V. ---	6	9
Meath, E. ---	18	2
Meath, Bishop, ---	128	17
Mexborough, E.	102	8
Midleton, V. ---	63	12
Milltown, E. ---	96	7
Milton, L. ---	176	21
Moira, E. ---	91	7
Molesworth, V. ---	54	11
Molyneux, V. ---	19	10
Montrath, E. ---	33	3
Mornington, E.	86	6
Mountgarret, V.	1	9
Mount-Cashel, V.	108	14
Mount-Eagle, L.	183	22
Mount-Florence, L.	181	22
Mount-Morres, V.	108	14
Mulgrave, L. ---	196	23

N. Net-

N.

	Arms.	Page.
Netterville, V. ---	3	9

O.

	Arms.	Page.
Orwell, L. ---	192	22
Ossory, Bishop, ---	132	18

P.

	Arms.	Page.
Palmerston, V. ---	89	13
Panmure, E. ---	49	4
Pigot, L. ---	195	22
Powerscourt, V. ---	97	13

R.

	Arms.	Page.
Ranelagh, V. ---	16	10
Raphoe, Bishop, ---	131	18

S.

	Arms.	Page.
Shannon, E. ---	59	5
Shelburne, E. ---	59	5
Southwell, L. ---	159	20
Strabane, V. ---	54	11
Strangford, V. ---	8	9
St. George, L. ---	193	23

T.

	Arms.	Page.
Taaffe, V. ---	13	10
Thomond, E. ---	72	6
Tilney, E. ---	43	4
Tracy, V. ---	30	10

Tuam,

INDEX.

	Page.	Arms.
Tuam, Archbishop,	127	16
Tyrawley, L. ---	155	20
Tyrconnel, E. ---	89	7
Tyrone, E. ---	52	4

V, U.

Vane, V. ---	82	12
Valentia, V. ---	3	9
Verney, E. --	47	4
Upper-Ohory, E. ---	57	5

W.

Waltham, L. ---	192	22
Wandesford, E. ---	73	6
Waterford and Wexford, E.	38	3
Waterford, Bishop,	129	17
Wenman, V. ---	10	9
Westmeath, E. ---	13	2
Winterton, E. ---	106	8

ADDITIONS

ADDITIONS *and* CORRECTIONS, *since the foregoing Sheets were worked off at Press.*

PAGE 2. Line 3. *read* 1 George, &c.
Ib. The Marquis of Kildare has been elected a Representative in Parliament for Dublin.
Ib. The Duchess of Leinster was delivered of a son, in Dec. 1767.
14. Sir Gilbert de Nugent, the first Baron of Delvin, was a Norman by descent, and according to Camden, and other Antiquarians, sat as a Baron in Parliament in England.
4. The Viscount Kilmorey died April 12, 1766; and was succeeded by his son Thomas, the present Viscount.
97. Line 22. *for* Richard, *read* Edward. The present Viscount Powerscourt married Amelia, daughter of Lord Baltinglass, and has issue.
100. On Aug. 28, 1767, the Viscountess Ashbrook was delivered of a son and heir. She had before a daughter, born Dec. 24, 1766.
129. Dr. Barnard, Bishop of Derry, died on Jan. 11, 1768.
147. Lord Blayney, on Dec. 26, 1767, married Miss Tipping, daughter of Thomas Tipping, of Beaulieu, Esq; a Lady of a large fortune.
159. The Hon. Thomas Southwell is elected Knight of the Shire for the county of Limerick.

Page
165. Lord Defart deceafed on Dec. 26, 1767.
181. John Lord Mount-Florence, died on Jan. 6, 1768, and was fucceeded by his eldeft fon, William-Willoughby, the prefent Lord.
192. On June 3, 1767, Lord Waltham married Mifs Coe.

His Majefty having been pleafed to refer the petition and claim of Catharine, Countefs Dowager of Tyrone (fee that Title, page 51.) to the ancient Barony of Le Poer, to the Houfe of Lords of Ireland, for their opinion; their Lordfhips, in December 1767, were pleafed to determine in her favour. It is faid to be the firft claim of that kind determined by the Houfe of Lords in that Kingdom.

The arms of the Vifcount Powerfcourt, are, Pearl, on a bend, topaz, cottifed, pearl, three pair of wings of the firft. Creft, On a wreath a griphon's head erect, pearl, with wings expanded, beholding the fun in its glory, topaz. See page 100.

FINIS.

www.ingramcontent.com/pod-product-compliance
Lightning Source LLC
Chambersburg PA
CBHW070227230426
43664CB00014B/2233